A LIFE ALOFT

Thomas Gompf with Elaine K. Howley

Praise for Tom and *A Life Aloft*

Tom Gompf has a unique ability to tell a story and also has a unique story to tell. Not only did he earn an Olympic medal in his sport, he also presided over the sport for many of its glory days. His contribution to diving continued as his suggestions to make the sport more fun to watch also doubled the number of medals available to the athletes competing at the Olympic level. I have learned a great deal from Tom, and now, you can learn from him as well.

– John Naber
Olympic gold medalist, swimming, 1976

The great sport of diving finally has its story told. And Olympic bronze medalist Tom Gompf is the perfect storyteller.
Tom began diving as a youngster and now, decades later, he is still on the front line. *A Life Aloft* is about Tom's passion, which expanded diving from city pools to international venues across the globe. His journey is remarkable and special in so many ways. You will enjoy every minute.

– Micki King
Olympic gold medalist, springboard diving, 1972

Tom Gompf contributed to USA and world diving for over 50 years as an Olympic medalist, coach and administrator. He has been a great leader in worldwide diving development.

– Ron O'Brien
USOPC Hall of Fame, 8-time Olympic diving coach.

Tom was a major force in the diving world for decades. Among his many accomplishments was his leadership in introducing synchronized diving to the Olympic program. That was a game-changer for FINA and for Olympic viewing.

– Peter Diamond
Former executive vice president, Olympic programming at NBC

A Life Aloft

Author: Thomas Gompf

Contributing Author: Elaine K. Howley

Foreword: Steve McFarland

Editor: Marla McKenna

Associate Editors: Holly Neumann, Lyda Rose Haerle

Cover Design: Nicole Wurtele
Graphic Designer with The CG Sports Company

Interior Layout: Michael Nicloy

All images courtesy of Thomas Gompf.

Published by CG Sports Publishing

A Division of The CG Sports Company
Cejih Yung, CEO and Founder
www.cgsportsco.com

ISBN: 978-1-7359193-4-8

Quantity order requests can be emailed to:

publishing@cgsportsmanagement.com

Printed in The United States of America

To my family.

Foreword

by Steve McFarland

Tom Gompf loves to tell stories about himself! Well, to be fair, those stories are not just about himself, and they are, in fact, beautiful tales of American life that we should all recognize. They take us from a childhood of hardship to becoming a voice to which people from all over the world listen. They take us to places like Vietnam, the White House, Monaco, Acapulco, the Olympic Games, and one very intense USOC meeting in 1980. These accounts are filled with courage, hope, and triumph but also, they remind us of who we once were and who we could become again—if we listen.

I should know, because for 50 years I have listened to these anecdotes many times and, in some cases, experienced them firsthand. Some of these stories are my stories, too. I first met Tom when I was an age-group diver at Dick Smith's Swim Gym in Phoenix, Arizona, in 1964, when Tom would make the Olympic team and win his bronze medal on platform. Then in 1971, I entered the University of Miami, where Tom coached me for the rest of my diving career. Little did I know then, but my life would be forever transformed by Tom, his many tales, and his love and encouragement for me to join him on his journey.

When you read *A Life Aloft*, you will be reminded of an unlikely path to success and yet a wonderful adventure that we all want to have in life. Tom's fun-loving spirit, captured in a high school moment where a case of flatulence launched his comedy trampoline/diving career, is evident throughout this book. You can see this spirit come out of these pages and say to us, "Isn't this great! Come along and let's see where it takes us!"

This memoir also reveals struggle and hardship, triumph and success, and ends with a reflection on a life Tom says was filled with luck and good fortune. Maybe it was more than that, because

Tom Gompf has shown us that how you approach life and its circumstances presents a choice. You can see how Tom always chose the path forward with hope and courage and a little humor thrown in for good measure.

Steve McFarland
St. Louis, MO
October 2, 2021

Prologue

High Flight

"Oh, I have slipped the surly bonds of earth,
And danced the skies on laughter-silvered wings;
Sunward I've climbed and joined the tumbling mirth
of sun-split clouds—and done a hundred things
You have not dreamed of—wheeled and soared
and swung high in the sunlit silence.
Hovering there I've chased the shouting wind along
and flung my eager craft through footless halls of air.

"Up, up the long delirious burning blue
I've topped the wind-swept heights with easy grace,
where never lark, or even eagle, flew;
and, while with silent, lifting mind I've trod
the high untrespassed sanctity of space,
put out my hand and touched the face of God."
– John Gillespie Magee, Jr., 1941

"Captain, do you know what the cargo is?" my loadmaster asked.

"I have no idea," I replied. "But it must be important because they're violating all kinds of flight rules to make sure this gets sent over to Thailand."

It had been a long day already, and even as the sun went down, the tropical air pressed close against me. I'd just gotten back from flying 16 hours, transporting cargo around Vietnam, and had finally returned to my BOQ, or bachelor officer quarters, to get some much-needed rest.

But no sooner had I arrived did I receive an emergency order to return to base operations. This was unusual because we were supposed to have a rest period after so many hours of flying.

But my orders were clear—I was being sent on a tactical emergency mission. I would have to fly a load of cargo over to a base in Thailand and then return immediately after dropping off the load. Only after I got back would I get a break, and I'd be off for a glorious 24 hours. I could already feel the pull of sleep and was anxious to get the mission behind me.

Wearily, I roused my crew—who had also just gotten off a long day of flying—to ready themselves for the two- or three-hour flight to Thailand. We'd offload our cargo there and then turn right around and come back to our base in Nha Trang, which is now a beautiful resort area on the east coast of Vietnam.

So, when the loadmaster asked me if I knew what was so urgent that it would require our five-man crew to add another eight hours of work on top of an already very long day, I assumed it must be something mission critical. But the look on his face made clear he knew what we were carrying. And he was not impressed.

"Pretzels, beer, and party supplies," the loadmaster told me. Our load was a bunch of munchies and drinks for a party being thrown at a base in Thailand.

Of course, such items wouldn't normally merit an emergency delivery, but in this case, the load had been bumped three times for more urgent supplies to help fuel American troops' efforts in the nascent conflict. And any cargo that's been bumped that many times automatically gains elevated status.

Apparently, these cases of beer and noisemakers were required to send off a base commander who was retiring, and he sure wasn't getting any younger as the load got bumped from previous flights.

Despite our exhaustion, and the apparent frivolous nature of our cargo, my crew and I took these orders in stride, understanding that the rules were the rules, and we were there to do as ordered. It was late at night and pitch black out—you've never seen darkness like remote, jungle darkness. We were all so very tired as we taxied and took off for Thailand.

We arrived a few hours later and unloaded the cargo. As we prepped the C-130 for our return journey to Vietnam, the evident signs of fatigue forced us to come up with a plan. We made an agreement that one pilot would stay awake and in charge after we got to altitude for a period of time while the other pilot would take a rest. The navigator could take little cat naps, too, and the flight engineer could operate safely as long as there was one person to fly the aircraft, which would be on autopilot anyway.

I let the copilot take the first rest as I ascended into the black night, eager to reach my bunk. We were halfway back to our base when I woke the copilot.

"I'd like to take just a quick nap. We're about 45 minutes to an hour out from the base," I told him. "That way I'll have a little bit of rest before I have to make the landing." It's always best to make a landing well rested, and while 45 minutes wouldn't be enough sleep to be 100 percent functional, it would be better than the fumes of energy I was drawing from by then.

"OK. I've got it, Captain," my copilot replied.

Satisfied he had it under control, I slumped back in my seat and tried to catch a little catnap.

The next thing I knew, a burst of bright, white light shattered my slumber.

I don't know how long I'd been asleep, but the sun's first rays had found me in the cockpit and blasted me awake. We'd flown all night and I had no idea where I was or where I was headed.

In a panic, I looked down at the instruments, and the first thing I saw was a needle tuned to a radio station on our base pointing behind me with a mileage indicator reading "156 miles."

I looked over and saw that the copilot was sound asleep.

The navigator was sound asleep.

The flight engineer was sound asleep.

The whole crew had fallen sound asleep at the wheel as we cruised through the clouds, thousands of feet above Southeast Asia.

I'd woken up just in time, as we'd lost radio navigation contact with our base. Just as the light had dawned to wake me, the realization raced through my brain with a flash of bright, white terror: we'd overflown the base by more than 150 miles.

Now fully wide awake and in a state of high adrenaline, I turned the plane 180 degrees and headed back toward our base. I woke up the rest of the crew, who all felt that same searing embarrassment I had. How foolish we were! How close we'd come to unimaginable disaster! All because we had pulled a double shift and had to forgo that most basic of all needs—sleep.

Our landing was unremarkable, as if the flight had been routine. We laughed uneasily about the close call and chalked the experience up to combat exhaustion. But it was a scary moment. Any pilot who overflies his destination could get into serious trouble for that, and it's not something I ever did again.

But that was in the early days of the Vietnam War. There was no air traffic control to speak of at the time, and no one to really monitor flights. And there, in a combat zone, many of those rules were thrown out the window temporarily. Ours wasn't the only story of such an incident.

Still, that vision of the morning sun creeping above the horizon somewhere over the Philippines piercing the cockpit window and my ill-timed nap has stuck with me ever since. It was as though Lady Luck herself had reached right into the cockpit to wake me with divine force, thereby preventing the disaster my crew and I seemed to be flying blindly toward. Fortune had again intervened and helped guide me along what I would later come to understand was the charmed (flight) path of my life.

Chapter One: In the Beginning

"When once you have tasted flight, you will forever walk the earth with your eyes turned skyward, for there you have been, and there you will always long to return."

– Leonardo DaVinci

My home office in Lakeland, Florida, is littered with mementos from a life in diving, flying, and service to others. In this small space, the plaques, pins, artwork, and awards are arranged as neatly as possible, but sometimes it seems like the room is ever-shrinking. I recently purged some of the items—I stashed some old prizes and other items that were just getting in the way, in cardboard boxes and deposited them on shelves in the garage where they'll likely spend the rest of their lives. Or the rest of my life, at least.

But there's still plenty to look at in my office space. And one souvenir in particular takes center stage on the middle credenza shelf.

Flanked by a portrait of me running with the Olympic flame during the relay for the 1996 Games in Atlanta on one side, and an American flag on the other, sits a print depicting one of the earliest known representations of man's love of diving.

Encased in a simple, brushed gold frame, the image shows a reddish-brown male figure executing a joyful swan dive against an ivory frescoed background. He's just leapt from a tower of stacked bricks into a swirling seascape. The muted palatte of the image does nothing to tone down the delight expressed by the anonymous diver.

The painting, which dates to about 480 BCE, was discovered on the underside of a grave inside the Tomba del Tuffatore, or the Tomb of the Diver, an archaeological monument in Paestum, formerly Greek Poseidonia, an ancient city in southern Italy. The tomb is a remarkably well-preserved example of the way people of that time and place honored their dead. I like to think the tomb was that of a diver of high status being celebrated by his community, but I don't think anyone knows for sure who rests underneath that jubilant fresco.

Painted by an ancient Greek master, the image is important to archaeologists for many reasons. But to me, it represents a different kind of historical import—the long, graceful arc of diving's story.

In the beginning, there were only steep cliffs rimming deep water and man's curiosity about whether he could survive launching himself from that height into the water below. Whether humans first dived in pursuit of dinner or in avoidance of becoming lunch, for recreation or obligation, we'll likely never know for certain. But no matter the goal, it seems to me that first diver—just like me many millennia later—probably enjoyed the ride, and the splash, and the thrill of flight, if only for an instant. Gravity (nearly) always wins in the end.

For much of human history, the concept of diving meant controlled, graceful falling—think long lines and straight angles—from a high ledge. This staid approach eventually gave way to so-called fancy diving, which featured more complex movements—twists, somersaults, and rotations aplenty. That type of diving got its start in Sweden in the 1890s and was soon exported to England where the Amateur Diving Association formed in 1901.

Organized sports as we know them today only began to coalesce in the late 1800s, as the amateur athletic movement gathered steam. The industrial revolution had worked its magic on people's available free time and disposable income, so leisure pursuits like sport began to gain influence and audience. Playtime was no longer the strict domain of very young children—as the 19th century came to a close, adults began having the time and money to have some fun, too.

America's love affair with diving and its evolving understanding of the practice as a competitive sport continued growing in the early 20th century, with the sport formally entering the still-young modern Olympic Games in 1904 in St. Louis. There, George Sheldon, a 30-year-old eye doctor, claimed the gold medal in his hometown. But those Games were tinged with controversy as the judges argued over which aspect of diving was more important—form or complexity. In fact, it took about a week until a protest brought by German divers—who were experts in stunt diving that favored somersaults with unclean entries—was resolved. But Sheldon's elegant approach and splash-less finishes eventually carried the day.

Just three years later, Sheldon would be dead of heart problems that had plagued his whole short life. But in his limited time on earth and in the sport, he pioneered American diving on a world stage and helped establish the still-held philosophy that the total dive, not just the airborne tricks and stunts, should be considered when judging a competition.

That 1904 Games also featured a less controversial but far quirkier offshoot, called long-distance plunging. Competitive plunging looks nothing like what we recognize as diving today, nor like anything we might think of as a real sport. But apparently it was all the rage for a while there.

Plunging for distance is exactly what it sounds like—the competitor starts from a stationary point 18 inches above a body of water, such as a pool wall or fixed pier. The plunger dives off the ledge and enters the water in a streamlined position, which he holds for either a set time (60 seconds became a standard event), or for as long as possible without breaking streamline and without employing any forward propulsion. The competitor who glides the farthest in either scenario wins.

Plunging for distance favors chunky athletes with prodigious breath capacity and an ability to stay tightly streamlined. The world record for the 60-second event was set in 1933 at 86 feet, 8 inches by British swimmer Frank Parrington—who just so happens to be the grandfather of the University of Tennessee's diving coach, Dave Parrington. The elder Parrington was inducted into the International Swimming Hall of Fame in 1986 as a pioneer diver—or should that say plunger—in recognition of his multiple world records and 11

British National Championship wins in the 1920s and 1930s. He was sadly killed on May 8, 1941, at age 42 during a German bombing raid on Liverpool.

Competitive plunging might seem odd to us today. We've grown accustomed to watching divers execute incredibly complex and difficult dives that involve so many twists and turns at dizzying speed that the average person has difficulty keeping count of all the rotations. But at the time, it was an exciting sport that competitors battled fiercely to win. It fit into an overall theme of watching people do unusual things for the entertainment value and to show off an odd talent or skill.

As such, vaudeville shows were also on the rise during the first part of the 20th century, providing a wealth of inexpensive and eccentric entertainment opportunities to a growing leisure class. For a penny or nickel entrance fee, audiences around the country were invited to watch a variety of skits, parodies, and send-ups. But nestled in among the guffawing gigs were some demonstrations of real athletic skill—often of an aquatic persuasion.

One of the best-known vaudeville performers, and, indeed, a woman who earned enduring fame splashing across American cabaret stages was Annette Kellerman. Now, there was a gutsy athlete. Born in Australia in 1886, Kellerman became a champion swimmer and diver in her native land, despite having had rickets as a child. By age 19 she held every women's world record there was to hold in the sport.

A household name in Australia, Kellerman struck out to England in 1905 to make her fortune on London's vaudeville stages. To drum up interest in her act—which featured lots of high diving stunts, fancy diving, and swimming demonstrations—Kellerman staged long distance swims in the Thames, the Seine, and attempted to cross the English Channel solo.

The gambit worked. The media couldn't get enough of the intrepid, liberated woman from Down Under who was multifaceted in her notoriety and influence. She would go on to champion wearable swimsuits for women while earning the title "the perfect woman" for how closely her measurements matched those of the Venus de Milo statue from ancient Greece.

In 1907, Kellerman decamped to the United States, poised to pioneer women's rights and access to swimming in ways she probably didn't even presage at the time—she was more interested in capitalizing on her growing celebrity and had set her sights on Hollywood.

Between 1909 and 1924, Kellerman starred in 14 silent films and eventually became known as the "Million Dollar Mermaid" for her ability to draw audiences and their money. They oohed and ahhed at her swimming and diving skill and her physical beauty.

At the core of this glamorous entertainer's success was a disciplined, daring athlete. In a film called *Neptune's Daughter*, Kellerman set a high-diving world record with a dive from 28 meters—that's nearly 92 feet! In a famous scene in her next film, the three-hour epic *Daughter of the Gods*, Kellerman made an 18-meter dive, just shy of 60 feet high. Not a world record, sure, but still a massive dive, especially considering there were six alligators waiting for her in the pool below.

Kellerman achieved enduring global renown, and in 1952, champion backstroker and artistic swimmer Esther Williams portrayed her in the blockbuster film *Million Dollar Mermaid*, a lavish, aquacade-style production that signified the very height of the celebration of swimming and diving on screen. Fearless barely begins to describe Kellerman's approach to life, a good quality for anyone seeking to dive from great heights, whether for sport or stunt.

Indeed, stunt diving is part of diving's narrative arc, and I and many other divers have enjoyed staging exhibitions that show off athletic skill with a daring or comedic flair. It's a marvelous feeling to fling yourself off a diving board to the collective astonishment of an audience that cannot conceive of doing so themselves, only to land safe and sound exactly where you intended to go.

Larry Griswold is perhaps the best example of this type of entertainment. World-famous for his antics, Griswold came to be known as the "Clown Prince of Diving," and the "World's Greatest Comedy Diver," with over four decades of performing. His flagship routine, dubbed "The Diving Fool," was hilariously entertaining. But it also showcased superlative tumbling and diving talent.

Born Laurens V. Griswold in Des Moines, Iowa, in 1905, Griswold got his start in acrobatics and gymnastics as a child. As a student at the University of Iowa, Griswold displayed a robust athleticism that earned him varsity letters in diving, wrestling, track and field, and gymnastics. As captain of the gymnastics team, Griswold won the 1929 Big Ten Tumbling Championships.

He soon got bitten by the performance bug, a water bug of sorts. The UI Fieldhouse pool was a state-of-the-art facility and had staged an annual amateur aquatic production called the "Dolphin Show" since 1919. Griswold stole the show with a daring series of tricks on a 42-foot-high trapeze above the pool. During another bit called the "Drunken Clown," Griswold honed his comedic skills into a program that would eventually become his life's work.

Soon after graduating in 1932, Griswold ran off to the circus. No, really. He launched the First Annual Iowa Circus that featured a range of performances including tumbling, tap dancing, clowning, bike racing, and roller hockey. That experience set him up for a lifetime of performing and traveling.

In the mid-1930s, Griswold also acted as UI's assistant gymnastics coach, and one of his star athletes was George Nissen, a top tumbler who won the National Intercollegiate Tumbling Championship three years in a row. A natural fit working together, Griswold and Nissen developed an ingenious device that would radically alter the sport of diving. They designed and built the world's first trampoline.

It was a simple device, inspired by the nets used to catch trapeze artists. Nissen worked on fabricating a strong frame while Griswold took charge of rigging the canvas and springs that would eventually come together as the trampoline—a name derived from the Spanish word for diving board.

This "dry" diving system opened a whole new horizon for tumblers, gymnasts, and divers in both training and competition. It became one of my very favorite things and the eventual source of a national championship title.

While this ingenious invention offered Griswold some potential financial prospects, his passion was performing. Thus, when "Water Follies of 1937" came calling, he jumped "into show business with both feet," he said later in life.

Other offers followed, including Billy Rose's Aquacade at the 1939 New York World's Fair where Griswold performed alongside Olympian Eleanor Holm and Tarzan himself, Johnny Weissmuller.

While recovering from an injury in 1941, Griswold penned the first ever textbook describing trampoline technique. He and Nissen also formalized their trampoline venture, creating the Griswold-Nissen Trampoline & Tumbling Company. Trampolines began appearing in every school and YMCA around the country, and they became a wonderful way for kids to burn off energy. I was one of the kids who benefited greatly from the ubiquity of trampolines during this era.

Griswold leveraged his invention to improve the act during the latter half of his career. In 1945, a sinus condition prevented him from going underwater anymore, so, he subbed in a trampoline for the water tank. Rather than having a negative impact on his show, this simple switch only increased the range and number of tricks he could do and made the show much more portable. Now, virtually any stage could host him, and television networks came calling.

Back in the '50s, you hadn't made it as a performer until you were invited onto the late-night television circuit, and this new dry routine was all but purpose-built for the small screen. Griswold performed his signature bit, "The Diving Fool," on several hit shows, including *The Frank Sinatra Show* in 1951 and *The Ed Sullivan Show* in 1956. Performing on *The Ed Sullivan Show* was something the Beatles and Rolling Stones did. These programs beamed into millions of homes every evening, and Griswold's appearance meant that people across the country could see top-quality diving and trampolining from the comfort of their living rooms, just by tuning in.

Griswold's success came from a deep reservoir of talent, sure, but also a lifetime of hard work. I remember watching his routine and admiring his skill when I was young. I was just getting into diving and tumbling myself, and I studied how he entertained his audience.

The fluidity of movement and his ability to tell a convincing story with his body was nothing short of genius. And he only seemed to get better at it over time, honing his routine over many years. But he also put his body and life at risk every time he stepped onto the stage. "The Diving Fool" is deceptively physical, and Griswold suffered many injuries over the four-plus decades he performed it.

The routine starts with his arriving on stage pretending to be a drunk relative filling in for an even drunker Griswold who was "out celebrating," and unable to keep his commitment to come perform, he tells the host. Determined to deliver on the promise nephew-Griswold made, this elder relative insists he's up to the task and climbs the ladder to start the show.

Hilarity ensues as Griswold puts his body through the paces of a highly demanding and complex series of near-disaster spills and trips, climbing up the ladder, falling down the ladder, tumbling off the edge of the board, struggling to remove his shoes, socks, and watch while also donning a diving cap to keep the water out of his delicate ears. His movements are precise, yet clearly describe the kind of drunk uncle you always worry a little about when he's out on the town. Even better when you consider the laughs are guilt-free—you're in on the joke, you're laughing at the slapstick, but at the same time marveling at the sheer skill required to pull it off.

After a build-up of more than four minutes, Griswold finally finds the end of the board and executes a dive into a hidden trampoline that leads to an endless series of cymbal crash–accompanied airborne somersaults. These bounces, twists, turns, and tumbles are so practiced as to seem nearly automatic as he spins and flips, to and fro, up and down, effortlessly.

A man who defied age as well as gravity, Griswold was still performing this acrobatic act well into his 60s when a head injury finally sidelined the consummate performer. But for some 45 years, his unique and brilliant mix of comedic commentary, technical skill, and intuitive sense of timing made his routine a showstopper and made Larry Griswold a household name. His kinesthetic humor was likely an inspiration to many other physical comedians—Steve Martin comes to mind—who followed. And he performed this rigorous routine night after night all over the world, to the delighted squeals and gasps of audiences that couldn't wait to see what he'd do next.

Diving and tumbling allowed Griswold to see the world and helped him make trampolining a major gymnastic event. But even with that trampoline emphasis, Griswold always retained his diving sensibilities. If you do a Google search, you'll find several videos of Griswold diving and performing, and you can see how even when performing his stunt shows on the trampoline, elements of competitive diving remain integral to how he executes these skills. His pedigree as a diver is also a big part of his unique ability to draw the audience in and make them believe he might truly be in danger when performing his stunts and tricks, and yet walk away without a scratch—most of the time.

Griswold and other performers in the aquatic sphere engaged in their craft during a golden era of entertainment that brought together the athleticism of swimming and diving with the grand stage of vaudeville and the glitz of Hollywood.

Building on the legacy of big stage productions, like Billy Rose's Aquacade that had captivated audiences in the late 1930s, and water-heavy films and spectacles such as *The Million Dollar Mermaid* tapped into a sense of exuberance as America moved past the War years. The financial expansion and cultural stability of the era created a rich environment for such shows and aquacades to thrive, elevating swimming and diving to a widely and wildly enjoyed form of entertainment. Alongside all that, trampolining and gymnastics also grew by leaps and bounds, through sheer availability.

Across the board, amateur sports enjoyed a Renaissance period that offered prospects for many of us kids to create a life in sport, whether just for fun or something more serious.

It was against this backdrop of near limitless opportunities and the growing influence of organizations like the YMCA and the Amateur Athletic Union that I came of age as an athlete in Dayton, Ohio.

Chapter Two: Tumbling Up

"Olympic Help May Someday Come From These Daytonians"

– *Headline of December 9, 1956, story in the* Dayton Daily News *about teenage gymnasts Shirley Carroll and Tom Gompf*

Summer is the best time for kids who enjoy the water—the heat, the sunshine, the freedom from school, plenty of others to race around with, and, of course, going to the local pool every day.

Growing up in Dayton, Ohio, in the 1940s and 1950s, I would spend four or five hours every day at the Oakday pool in the summertime, playing tag in the sunshine and swimming with friends. Much like any other outdoor pool, there wasn't a lot to this place. The clubhouse with a front desk and locker rooms opened onto a glittering azure oasis nestled in a concrete deck. A grassy lawn extended beyond, with some trees rimming the edges of the property. Of course, we kids loved the snack bar that offered hotdogs for a quarter apiece. It all worked together to create a welcoming environment for families to bring a picnic or to camp out all day in the open air without a care in the world.

In the midst of this serene scene, something beckoned to me from the far end of the pool. There, a series of diving boards promised a free thrill if only I had the courage to accept the challenge and climb up.

I was probably five or six years old when I first approached the diving boards. I had long watched my older brothers perform cannonballs and other tricks—mostly simple dives, but very stylish in my young, impressionable mind.

Of course, I wanted to be like them.

So, one day, left to my own devices as I often was, I wandered to the deep end of the pool and stood in front of the 1-meter diving board and sized it up. On close inspection, it didn't seem so bad. I figured there'd probably not be too much danger in bouncing off a 1-meter-high springboard, even for a little kid—and especially one motivated by trying to keep up with his big brothers.

For any spectator, my first leap from a diving board was unremarkable. I was just one of hundreds of kids doing exactly the same thing in hundreds of pools all across America that day. Just like any other little body plopping into the water for fun on a sunny, summer day.

But for me, that first jump was earth-shattering—it was my first taste of something that would define the rest of my life and dictate the whole trajectory of whom I would become.

I'd seen the older kids approximate it and loved watching birds' mastery of it. But until that moment, I had never tasted flight. But that first, albeit modest and relatively uncoordinated, trip off the end of the lowest board lit something inside me. I just wanted to launch myself into thin air again, and again, and again.

I was soon trying flips, dives, and cannonballs, whiling away the lazy days of summer. All these tricks came easily to me, which was a pleasant surprise. I remember watching the older kids sometimes struggle to land a dive or flip, but my natural knack created in me this feeling that I was somehow special in my ability to direct and control my body in flight. I reveled in being able to show off and, like all children should, embraced the freedom of play.

But the novelty of the 1-meter board wore off quickly, so I graduated to the 3-meter board. That's about 10 feet high, and there's a little more fear involved. It was easier for me to see how I could have a mishap and land flat on my stomach or flat on my back. I'd seen other kids and even some adults do that, and it sure looked like it hurt, as suggested by the big red blotch that lingered on the skin for a time afterwards.

But still, the challenge beckoned, and I pushed through my trepidation. I figured I hadn't mangled myself thus far, so why not? Once again, I quickly progressed in my ability to execute dives and tricks without injury over a week or two. I got so comfortable with that board, that it, too, eventually became passé.

However, next to the 3-meter board was a 15-foot-high board—about 4.5 meters if we're sticking with metric.[1] And even more daunting, a 20-foot-high board (6 meters) next to that. Now, 15 feet isn't truly a high dive, but it can give you quite a whack if you land wrong. I can remember standing behind the ladder leading up to the board and looking up.

The sun was bright that midday, and oddly, the world seemed to go quiet around me. It was almost like I was suddenly in a Wild West film about to have a standoff in the middle of a Main Street with just a few breathless townspeople looking on and a couple tumbleweeds rolling past. Maybe it was more like the feeling a rock climber feels just before ascending a steep cliff face, with nothing but stark blue sky beyond and the certainty of death with a single misplaced hand or foot waiting below.

In any event, the top of the ladder and the diving board felt so far away. But I was intrigued. I carefully climbed the ladder, straight up into the cloudless blue of a Dayton summer day. There were no guardrails to protect a small slip from turning into a big fall, and it was a proper ladder—hand over foot, straight up, up, up.

After what felt like hours, I made it up the ladder to the board in the sky. That was an achievement in itself, as I'd concentrated hard during the climb to prevent slipping on the wet steps. I arrived at the board almost startled to find there was another greater challenge to overcome just in front of me. I suddenly I realized I'd have to come back down one way or another.

I had gone up, and indeed, now I must come down. Just like that *Boy on the High Dive* painting by Norman Rockwell that appeared on the cover of the *Saturday Evening Post* in 1947, I found myself peering over the edge of the board, the sun-chased water sparkling miles below me. But I'd come too far and couldn't concede just yet. Besides, my brothers were watching.

I started with a simple jump, feet first and with my heart in my throat. That worked out all right. However, the true challenge would

---

1   The 1- and 3-meter boards were regulation height, but the other two were not, hence the discrepancy in units of measurement.

be to go off headfirst. I felt real pressure to quickly complete an actual dive, an early illustration of my budding competitive spirit.

I still remember my first attempt at a head-first dive off the 15-foot board. I was probably six or seven years old at the time, and unsurprisingly, I miscalculated.

Smack!

I'd over-rotated and landed flat on my back.

I got out of the pool with a stinging red rebuke on my back and a healthy dose of respect for what could happen when gravity, water, and poor form collide. As easy as the other boards had seemed, I discovered that this one would take a little more effort to best.

Somehow, the experience didn't dissuade me from trying again. Far from it—that flub only fueled my desire to master this new challenge, after a couple days of licking my wounds first, of course.

I returned to the 3-meter board to practice some dives where I knew I had control. I soon realized that to prevent myself from going over on my back from the higher board, I'd need to dive out a little farther from the end and hold the position almost flat or level until I reached the water. I mulled over that technique insight and practiced some more at the 3-meter level.

A few days later, I finally gathered up the gumption to climb the ladder to the 15-foot board again. With some trepidation, I applied my new, hard-earned knowledge and nailed the dive. It was a piece of cake, it turned out, once I understood the physics—not the textbook science, but the kinetic intuition—of the dive and how gravity would exert its inexorable influence over my body enroute to the water.

My efforts did not go unobserved. The pool was frequented by several hundred people each day, but there probably weren't more than 10 people in a day who could land a successful header off the 15-foot board. Fewer still were children. I got a lot of attention for being able to do that as such a small kid.

That response from the audience further whetted my appetite to scale the ladder to the 20-foot board, which I did about a week later. Again, I started by jumping feet first, but I knew I'd eventually have to do a head-first dive.

The dive followed soon after, but it was the other stunts I did from the highest board that not only gave me a buzz, but also thrilled the pool patrons sitting around sunbathing. They're lounging, but here's this little kid going up to the 20-foot board to knock out a bunch of somersaults with no problem. It was something, and they cheered and applauded every time I landed a difficult dive. I ate up that positive feedback and reveled in the attention. Little did those casual observers realize just how much they were emboldening me to try doing more daring stunts and new dives.

By the time I was around 8 years old, I had honed a particularly rousing trick where I could "fall" off the 20-foot springboard backwards and at the last minute, flip over and go in feet first. It was essentially a back somersault, but I would ham it up a little by walking out to the end of the board and turning around and acting like I stumbled and fell backwards.

While this might seem scary, it's a basic skill most divers have mastered, and not all that difficult to do. But it sure was entertaining, as the sunbathers gasped and clapped when I surfaced with a smile and a wave. I like to think the king of comedy diving himself, Larry Griswold, would have appreciated my little show.

Mastering this series of challenges—and finding that I loved to perform and compete—marked the beginning of my career in diving, gymnastics, and trampoline. Across all three disciplines, it seemed I was always trying to find some higher goal or some more difficult trick or clever stunt. Whether it was taking on progressively taller towers or mastering new maneuvers, climbing the ladder to the next highest board was a strategy I would go on to employ throughout my life and my competitive career. It's an approach that has always served me well.

✷ ✷ ✷

Summers were built for the pool, but in the colder months, tumbling, gymnastics, and trampoline ruled the day. And I could pursue these activities to my heart's content at the YMCA. The YMCA was in large parts my home from about the time I was 12 years old until I went away to college.

The YMCA was different back then. People don't understand today, but the YMCA was another animal when I was a kid. It was a community center in every sense of the word, and a place where young men could lodge and recreate when they were new to town or down on their luck.

Even more importantly, for athletic kids like me, the Y was an invaluable resource and a crucial part of my upbringing. As much as it was my home, it was also an escape.

I don't much think about my childhood as being anything all that unusual or bad. But my wife, Fran, insists that my situation wasn't ideal, and my life could have turned out very differently because I didn't have the kind of parental support and happy home life that many other folks who've excelled in sports and their careers have.

I think in many ways, I just didn't fit with my family. There were five of us kids, and my three brothers and one sister were all significantly older than me. I had different priorities and came from a completely different generation than my siblings—even my closest brother, who's just four years older than me.

I was born in 1939 and don't much remember the War years. But my parents had struggled through the Depression, and my siblings grew up in a very different world than I did. I think it was difficult for them to relate to my motivations and priorities, as seemingly frivolous as they appeared to be to people who were forced to focus on working and keeping body and soul together during so many lean and difficult years.

Our father worked lengthy days for the Frigidaire company and later as an environmental specialist at Wright Field, a military installation in Dayton. In addition, he ran a refrigeration and air-conditioning repair service, and I don't think he ever worked a day shorter than 18 hours. Doing all that while raising five kids in the 1930s and 1940s was both rough and nothing to sniff at.

He was a product of the Depression—it made him tough and resilient, but also took away many opportunities. Though he was a multi-talented musician who nearly went to college on a music scholarship, he married young, and the needs of his family precluded that prospect. His three eldest sons followed in his workman's footsteps.

I, however, was a bit of a mystery. The youngest child, I was a member of a post-War generation and lifestyle that seemed always assured to have plenty, built on the backs of others' sacrifices. I remember a conversation I had with my dad one morning when I was about nine or 10 that really stuck with me all these years. He said, "You know, maybe you ought to quit all this swimming and diving stuff and get a good paper route."

That was the attitude he had.

I sometimes wonder what might have happened if I'd taken that suggestion and gotten that paper route. How different would my life have been?

I'm not complaining about it, but I never got any validation from my dad or brothers. I feel like I spent those years trying to prove myself to them indirectly and maybe trying to make up for the lack of attention at home. That was why I responded so keenly to the adulation I received from the pool patrons, and why that was a driving force behind my will to excel. I always needed to show them that just because it wasn't "work" in the sense that they understood it, that didn't mean my sport and passions weren't still meaningful and important.

Diving had value—just how much, neither I nor my family realized then. But it would define my life, create opportunities, and open doors I didn't even know existed at the time. I worked hard at diving and school. But for my father and brothers, physical labor carried more weight. Looking back now, this philosophical divide would push me down a very different path from theirs.

My dad and older brothers all worked in the trades from the first chance they could. It was just what was expected. No one in my family had ever gone to college. Fooling around with sports and schooling didn't enter the picture for them, and they had little means of understanding or connecting with that part of my life—which was quickly becoming my entire world.

My sister was 11 years older than me and even more alien to me in some ways, despite the fact that I lived with her for several years after my parents split up. By the time I was about 12, my parents had had their fill of each other and raising children, and they exited my life to begin separate lives of their own anew.

As strange as it may sound, when my mom left, I actually stayed in our house. My parents had moved into their own places, but they rented the family home to a young couple. Some rental agreements stipulate that certain items of furniture will stay with the house. Apparently, I was akin to an ottoman. I came with the house.

They were nice people, but I wasn't their kid. Why would they have time for me? I was more like a young roommate. I just went about my business going to school and the Y. After about a year, they moved out, and my sister moved in.

But she'd recently gotten married and was trying to start her own family. I never felt very comfortable in the house after she and her husband moved in. I always felt like I was in the way and unwanted. So, I relied upon high school gymnastics and YMCA swimming and tumbling to provide routine and grounding.

Because I was a child of divorce and left largely to my own devices from such a young and formative age, Fran says that I raised myself. I'm not sure I agree with that completely. I never thought my situation was all that extraordinary. It was just my life.

She's right that from my high school years on, I didn't have a family in the sense that most people think of it. Certainly, my situation was different from a lot of other kids' at the time. Divorce was still relatively rare in the 1950s, and there weren't many kids like me who had so few demands from home and neither parent on the scene anymore. Most kids would head home for dinner. But I scrounged for myself and made my way without much help from my blood relatives.

During high school, I'd leave the house by 7 a.m. with a peanut butter sandwich in hand. When school concluded for the day, I'd hop on a bus to the YMCA where I'd swim, dive, tumble, and do my homework. I also worked in the clothing sales room or the basket room to make enough money so I could buy meals from the café there. When it was time for the gym to close, one of my coaches would bring me home, usually sometime around 10:30 or 11 p.m. I'd slip quietly into the house, so as not to wake my sister or her family, and get to sleep. I'd start the whole process over again first thing in the morning.

So, while I might have been technically "living" with my sister, that house wasn't my home. It was just a place to sleep and do laundry.

None of my kin ever saw me compete or had much interest in my athletic pursuits. They were just happy to not have to be involved. I kept busy and kept my nose clean. That said, when I started getting a lot of attention—articles in the paper and so forth—they were somewhat more enthusiastic about my diving. But I'm not sure they ever really understood why I loved it so much and why it was so important to me.

So, I see why Fran says I was very much on my own in my teens. Because I was.

Except that really, I wasn't.

The YMCA was my real home, and I met so many great mentors and learned about real leadership and real family there. And I'm just so grateful for the opportunities the YMCA offered me.

The people I met through my interest in gymnastics, trampolining, and diving took superlative care of me. I had coaches who were like parents. My high school gymnastics coach, Joe Sullivan, and the swimming coach at the YMCA, George Berger, were both big influences on me. Raymond Zahn, a volunteer coach at the Y, was probably the first person to sit me down and encourage me to focus on diving with the idea of going to the Olympics one day. He really pushed me to reach for more. My teammates were like siblings. We made our own family and our own home. We trained. We worked. We played. We ate together—all at the YMCA.

To me, diving has always been my family. This is why it's never been difficult for me to give back to the sport. As I came to understand, through the example set by the many dedicated coaches and mentors I had along the way, when a family member asks you for help—even when it's arduous or inconvenient—you say yes.

✳ ✳ ✳

As a member of the YMCA's tumbling team, I participated in exhibitions to show off our routines and abilities to a range of audiences. We would perform at Knights of Columbus and Kiwanis Club events and so forth. Similarly, in high school the gymnastics team staged exhibitions for other schools at basketball games and the like.

By the time I reached high school—I attended Stivers High School in Dayton—I was fully immersed in tumbling, gymnastics, and diving. Even when I was as young as 14, I had a reputation for diving, and I was beginning to think that diving was my thing.

In fact, as a high schooler, my diving allowed me to perform before crowds large and small, near and far, casual and highly competitive. I was often called upon to do exhibitions in tumbling and diving, and I sometimes performed with a local synchronized swimming club.

It was the 1950s after all, and water shows were all the rage in Hollywood and around the globe. Megawatt stars like Esther Williams brought beauty and glamour to the screen, and also the attention of adoring audiences to the sports of synchronized swimming and diving with their spectacularly choreographed aquatic sequences.

At a more local level, synchronized swimming clubs around the country would often stage performances to show off their skills and provide entertainment. And so, it was that a synchronized swimming club in Dayton invited me to perform in their swimming shows in the summertime—about one a week at country clubs, public pools, and the Air Force Officers' Club pool. They were an organized synchronized swimming team trying to promote the sport, but they also wanted to include my diving to give them a little break between numbers.

I'd begin after the conclusion of the swimmers' first act by performing a series of basic dives or some of the required dives that were done in all competitions—the sort of graceful dives that would make Greg Louganis famous.

The swimmers would return for their next performance, and when they concluded that, I'd come out and do a series of more difficult dives—multiple twisting dives, a two-and-a-half, and a reverse one-and-a-half—more complex and thrilling dives designed to entertain the crowd while also showing off the beauty and complexity of an emerging sport.

The grand finale was a big water number with all the girls participating. At the completion of that, the other divers and I would come out and do a comedy dive routine. We'd worked diligently on it, and to my mind, it was quite entertaining.

Comedy and diving have a long-standing relationship, thanks to vaudeville and the lengthy history of diving as entertainment. Some clown diving shows like Larry Griswold's might seem silly and corny, but they usually had a good effect on the audience. In fact, they were so popular, I performed in a variety of exhibitions and shows in gymnastics, trampoline, and diving.

It's a contradiction: the simplicity of the physical humor belies the level of skill and body control it takes to spectacularly fail a dive or pull off a complex tumbling stunt in such a way as to make it funny while keeping it safe.

But sometimes, the humor was completely unintentional and originated from a lack of coordination, as I learned during one pre-Christmas tumbling exhibition during a high school assembly.

If you've ever bounced on a trampoline or done gymnastics, you realize that sometimes, the forces involved with such movement can limit your ability to control certain physiological functions. Such was the case on that fateful day in the high school auditorium.

I was executing a complex pairs tumbling sequence when unplanned comedy struck. During this particular move, I was supposed to run up to my partner who would bend down, and I'd plant my foot into his hands. He'd launch me into the air where I'd do a back somersault with a full twist with only the assist of that push from his cupped hands.

Unfortunately, I'd had a pretty good lunch that day, and when we squatted down and I pushed hard to get enough air to make the somersault, I released a little air of my own. But it was more than passing a bit of gas—I released a thunderous, booming, unmistakably flatulent sound. There's no way anyone in the auditorium with functioning ears could have missed it or mistaken what had happened.

When I landed, I fell back on the mat and looked out at the crowd. Every last person was laughing hysterically. I happened to see one of my favorite English teachers and another gentleman bent over almost crying, they were cackling so hard. My partner pointed at me as if I did it. I pointed back at him as if he did it, and we both just kind of shook our heads. Our simple, seemingly pre-scripted "it wasn't me" reactions only seemed to intensify the suddenly slapstick moment and heighten the crowd's laughter. Energized by the guffaws of the audience, we finished our act to shouts and applause.

For a few moments it was very embarrassing, and I wasn't sure whether I could ever go back out into the school. But as soon as I did, my friends said that my not-so-tiny toot was the absolute best part of the whole act. They all thought we had planned it!

Best to go out with a bang.

Or something like that, I guess.

Chapter Three: New Heights

"Citius, Altius, Fortius."

– Olympic motto

Throughout high school, my diving and tumbling took me to various exhibitions and competitions around the country and sometimes across international borders. On one of these trips, I learned in a very visceral way that timing is everything—in diving and in life.

I was doing a show at the Canadian National Exhibition, a multi-day event in Toronto. We had already completed several days of a diving act out on the seawall followed by the Cypress Garden Ski Team demonstrating waterskiing stunts.

The show performed to sellout crowds every day at the exhibition, and the diving element was a key piece of the extravaganza. The grand finale of that show involved an elephant—yes, a real, live elephant—water skiing.

I couldn't make this stuff up if I tried.

Billed as "the world's only water-skiing elephant!" the act featured Queenie, a docile female pachyderm who'd been born in Thailand and learned a lot of tricks during her time in North America. I read she'd been purchased at a pet store in New York City as a baby, and having been trained from a youngster, ended up entertaining folks with her various and unusual skills. This particular stunt saw her with feet strapped to two extra-large, pontoon floats side by side—water skis for beginners, albeit jumbo-sized.

The show took place along the shore of Lake Ontario at an aqua stadium of sorts. Seven of us divers would be out on the breakwall, diving from a 10-meter platform tower erected there. The platform was five meters long, and we'd peel off, running along the platform to the edge, launching ourselves into various somersaults into the water far below.

Some of the divers executed a two-and-a-half, others went all the way up to a three-and-a-half off the tower and into the lake depending on their confidence and position in the choreography. We'd dive off to the left, middle, and right of that platform in a perfectly timed, continuous flow of divers. It was like something you'd see in an Esther Williams production, full of verve and fluid motion, a real spectacle of energy and a great example of both the art and profession of diving.

I was the youngest diver in attendance—the only one still in high school—and as such, I obviously drew the short straw to go last. That's generally considered the most dangerous position because every time we performed the stunt, there were six people already in the water trying to get out of the way. I would also have to run off the end of the platform without being able to see where exactly they were as I was taking off. I expended a lot of mental energy hoping I wouldn't land on anyone.

Meanwhile, the boat with the elephant was idling off to the left a few hundred yards away, waiting for its turn to come across the watery stage. The handlers in the boat would pull Queenie across the diving zone just as we finished our dives for a suitably spectacular finale.

Typically, this potentially dangerous climax went off without a hitch, with the crowd loving the precision timing. But the last day of the exhibition, that careful synchronicity was off just enough to raise the stakes.

The elephant escort began its journey from the dock just a moment too soon and started crossing the water in front of the diving tower. I only realized this after I'd committed to that last dive and was already in mid-air.

Picture it: I'm spinning, spinning, in the middle of a two-and-a-half somersault in pike position and see the elephant trundling beneath me, heading right for the square foot of water where I'm supposed to land in another split second.

I held my breath and braced for impact. A pachyderm face-plant, if you will.

The next thing I knew: Splash!

I felt the cool water slip around my skin. I hadn't landed afoul of poor, tired Queenie, and I realized I was OK. I had somehow, mercifully, missed colliding with the star of the show. In just such an instance, I would have come off worst, of course, but fortunately both our professional modesties were preserved. We'd narrowly avoided a major mishap.

As I surfaced, all I saw was an elephant's rear end less than 15 feet in front of me cruising toward the horizon. It was perhaps the closest call I've ever had in diving, and the nearest I ever came to serious injury. All because a waterskiing elephant jumped the gun.

I didn't think elephants could jump at all.

I had a lot of fun in high school tumbling and diving, and I earned enough accolades to garner scholarship interest from a handful of colleges. I flirted with the idea of attending the University of Michigan where Bruce Harlan was the coach. It was an excellent program, and I knew I could do well there. I really appreciated Bruce's dedication to the sport and his own extraordinary achievements therein.

I'd had a long-standing relationship with Bruce over the years, as he took an active interest in my diving career. In fact, he was the reason I ended up at that Canadian National Exhibition show with Queenie—Bruce often passed along opportunities for me to dive. From time to time when I was still in high school, he'd call to let me know when a show was coming to town that I could join or if there was an exhibition that he couldn't perform in himself.

Bruce often did comedy diving routines with another top-flight coach, Hobie Billingsley. The two often toured doing exhibition and comedy diving routines that inspired me and provided great material to adapt for my own exhibition routines.

Hobie was an NCAA champion who went to Ohio State and then on to coach the Indiana Hoosiers swimming and diving team to scores of championships between 1959 and 1989. He was the glamour coach of the era. He wrote several books and had so many successful teams. He was a mentor to me when I became a coach at the University of Miami in the 1970s.

Similarly talented, Bruce was an Olympic and NCAA champion who also went to Ohio State. The Greg Louganis of his era, he went on to coach at the University of Michigan and was a much-heralded, up-and-coming coach poised to steal some of Hobie's thunder, although the two were great pals and worked so well together.

They didn't make much money coaching, so it was the diving exhibitions and aquatics shows where this dynamic duo made the bulk of their living. They'd honed a particularly entertaining comedy diving routine that was wildly popular, and they traveled quite a bit doing shows. Over the course of several years, I must have seen them at least 10 times just in the Dayton area.

As a young kid, I was utterly captivated by their abilities and wanted to be able to do what they did. Looking back, this desire to emulate them and to experience the aerobatic freedom they enjoyed, not to mention the adulation of audiences, was formative. It was more than just that their performances spoke to my 7-year-old self, diving for applause at that summer pool in Dayton. A lifelong desire to fly was already permeating my being. Their complex and funny routines hinted at a future I might be able to make my own someday, in some way.

Both men became personal friends of mine over the years and both tried to recruit me for their collegiate diving programs. Bruce, especially, wanted me to wear the Michigan maize and blue. From the time I was a sophomore in high school, Bruce all but assumed I was a sure thing to join him at the University of Michigan, and when I was a senior in high school, I received a formal scholarship offer from UM.

But it was a gymnastics scholarship.

As it turned out, Bruce had struck a deal with the gymnastics coach who had an extra scholarship he wasn't going to use that year. Bruce asked him to offer me a full ride as a gymnast so he could preserve another slot for a swimmer he wanted to also bring aboard. I was good enough in both diving and gymnastics to garner a scholarship for either sport, so it made sense. Make the offer under the gymnastics header, and once I was there, I could do both or either sport as needed.

But I didn't want to be a gymnast. I wanted to pursue diving, and I didn't really understand the deal Bruce and that other coach had worked out. It hadn't been fully explained to me, and so I sat on the offer.

I ended up running out the clock. In addition to being unsure about going in as a gymnast, I didn't entirely understand how the whole scholarship-offer-acceptance dance worked—I was under the impression that the deadline could be extended. Because I was expecting to get an offer from Coach Mike Peppe at Ohio State at any moment, I wanted to compare them. But I waited too long on the Michigan offer and found out the hard way that there wouldn't be an extension.

Fortunately, a day or two later, Mike came through with a full scholarship to OSU, and it was for diving, not gymnastics. So, it was an easy decision to stay in my home state, dive for the renowned Coach Peppe, and compete on the gymnastics team under Coach Joe Hewlett, too. I was about to become a Buckeye in both sports. I was thrilled.

But I worried that I'd offended Bruce by not joining him at the University of Michigan. Bruce had graduated from Ohio State, and I'm sure in some way he understood why and how I ended up there, though I'm not sure he ever really forgave me for that. He had planned on my coming to the University of Michigan for a long time, but he didn't really talk to me about the offer, and we never really had another conversation after the scholarship offer expired.

Don Harper, another diver friend of mine, knew Bruce and told me afterwards that Bruce would get over it and that he understood that Ohio State was the right place for me. I hoped he was right and moved on with my diving at OSU. I figured that eventually, Bruce and I would be able to reconnect.

But it wasn't to be. Bruce died unexpectedly in 1959 when I was a sophomore in college. While disassembling the scaffolding of the diving tower after an exhibition show, he slipped and fell about 30 feet to the pool deck below. He passed on before we could really reconcile.

I've come to accept that life is strange like that sometimes. I was truly sorry to hear about the tragic accident that killed one of the sport's brightest stars and most promising coaches. His death meant that I wouldn't have had much time to work with him and benefit from his tutelage at Michigan. So as cold as it may sound, pragmatically it meant I'd made the right decision in choosing to attend Ohio State.

When at last I signed the papers to attend OSU, I finally allowed the excitement to creep in. I'd done it. I would actually be heading off to college—the first person in my family to do so—on a full scholarship, no less. I might have struggled to pay for my education if I hadn't had that support from the athletics department, and I do sometimes wonder what I might have become of me if I'd followed my father and brothers into the trades.

But my coaches at the YMCA had been right: If I stuck with it, diving would take me so many places. Leaving Dayton for Columbus was just the first step on a long journey that, thanks to diving, would take me around the world many times over.

When I arrived at The Ohio State University in the fall of 1957, I began diving and also continued my competitive development as a trampolinist and gymnast. I worked out daily with the other divers, and soon learned what coaching at this higher level really meant. It wasn't the type of coaching you see today, where a coach guides—and sometimes controls—an athlete in many areas and spends copious amounts of time teaching technique and discipline.

No, back then, Mike Peppe—who was in his 60s and already considered a legend—cut a more avuncular figure. He encouraged and supported us. He set up meets and recruited team members. He managed the whole program, providing the finances—scholarships or jobs—for divers and swimmers to attend the school. And he provided the facility and equipment, including suits, towels, and the latest diving boards. But he didn't meddle in our day-to-day affairs or coach us divers in the sense we know it now.

Indeed, I soon learned that I had to be self-motivated, and I'd have to be responsible for my own progress in the sport. Mike never told me when I had to be at the pool or that I had to work out. He didn't teach any new dives or provide much insight into how to improve my diving. He would occasionally critique something I was doing, but as far as teaching, or requiring me to do, well, anything, that wasn't the role he filled.

This hands-off approach suited me superbly, given my earlier self-raising and my own tendency toward self-reliance. Nevertheless, like most kids, I craved his praise and everything I did was designed to impress him. He was like the favorite uncle or grandfather I never had. He was getting older, and everybody wanted to please him. He trusted us to do the work we needed to achieve our potential.

Being the best you could be for Mike was a tremendous incentive and source of inspiration. And the work of coaching on technique and learning new dives largely fell to other divers.

Yes, we were competing against each other, but we were also a family supporting and helping each other. All the divers had various experience that could help a teammate learn to do a dive better or teach another diver a particular skill that could elevate their game. We would critique each other and point out where we might have messed up—an elbow angled too wide or an approach that needed to be shortened just a smidge. We worked hard, did our best, and helped each other. That seemed to make Mike happy. It also helped us become the best divers we could be.

It was this teamwork that got us through at Ohio State. At other schools, some of the coaches were more hands-on and demanding. They did a lot for their teams. At Ohio State, we divers dived on pride and teamwork. And frankly, we didn't lack for anything.

While I was at Ohio State, 13 different individuals I encountered were national champions in one event or another. It was an incredible environment where we were encouraged to thrive. But if a diver wasn't self-motivated, he would fall behind. This was a good lesson for later in life in other areas: Victory is often awarded to those who simply show up and put in the work.

Similarly, as the adage notes, "fortune favors the brave," and my innate desire to learn the most difficult maneuvers—that had surfaced when I first climbed the ladder at the summer pool when I was 5 or 6—served me well at Ohio State. My goal was always to be able to do the hardest tricks, the most complex stunts, and incorporate them into my dives.

In training, we would often start out learning new dives using old-school sand pits. This was before Hobie Billingsley had developed his foam pit for dry diving and Dick Kimball's kipping harness that now helps divers learn to execute new dives safely. These innovations were a few years in the future yet but would eventually become key elements of any training program.

At OSU, we were still using sand pits to practice our approaches and take offs, and Don Harper and I would practice dives on the trampoline by doing an approach and hurdle onto the trampoline bed.

With all this practice and progression, I never tried to be just a consistent performer of medium-difficulty stunts. I pushed for harder tricks, and that was, at times, a drawback, in both trampolining and diving. In trampolining in particular, I practiced several stunts that had never been done before. I didn't always land these new stunts right, and sometimes I lost points in competition for trying to reach for more. But in 1961, I became the NCAA National Champion in trampoline, so I was eventually rewarded for my ambition.

But ambition alone is a hollow promise. For success, there must also be a willingness to innovate—to set aside ego and work with others. Having a coach who permitted us to experiment and encouraged us to push ourselves made the difference. Mike gave us the freedom to fail, but also to succeed—together. We always wanted to help divers who were pushing out the limits of the sport get the scores they deserved. All these experiences would help inform not only my own athletic pursuits, but also some of my work later as an administrator for the sport at the international level.

Another reason I'm very glad I chose Ohio State was that's where I met Joyce Boedeker. She happened to attend a Sigma Chi fraternity party in October of 1959, and it was a chance encounter that would have an enormous impact on the rest of my life.

I have to credit Harold Dench, a guy I lifeguarded with, for that introduction. He brought Joyce to the party that night. Harold was terribly good looking and that meant comely girls were easy-come-easy-go for him. He had the confidence I felt I lacked in that department.

The moment I laid eyes on Joyce, well, it really was love at first sight. As corny and cliché as that sounds, it's absolutely true. She was far and away the prettiest girl I'd ever seen. She had this brilliant smile and twinkly eyes and these lovely golden curls.

I was utterly enchanted.

"Harold, who is that?" I asked him at the first chance I got.

"That's Joyce," he said, nonchalantly. He was used to getting dates with the prettiest girls on campus, so Joyce was just another of, presumably, many dating options for Harold.

"Does she mean anything to you?" I asked.

"Nah," he said. "I just met her at the student union at a meet-and-greet. She didn't have anything to do, and I needed a date, so I asked her to come here tonight." How simple that sounded! I was thunderstruck.

As the night wore on, I determined to find a way to make a date with her, post-haste.

Harold understood I was keen, and he was amenable to stepping aside. I maneuvered things so I could drive Joyce home from the party.

As it turned out, we had a lot to talk about because she was from Trotwood, Ohio, which is right outside Dayton. She had transferred from Otterbein College in Westerville, Ohio, and we met during her first week at Ohio State. She'd enrolled in the two-year dental hygiene course—perhaps the secret to that megawatt smile was knowing how to take care of her pearly whites.

I never tried so hard to impress somebody in my whole entire life. I was so infatuated with her from that very first moment. And I just wanted her to love me back.

But getting Joyce to be my girl wouldn't necessarily be an easy process.

One day, I returned to the fraternity house after a long training session at the pool, and one of the guys said, "Hey, Tom! I saw Joyce out with one of the famous football players on our team."

That casual comment felt like a gut punch.

It was clear I had my work cut out for me in winning her over. I might have been a hot-shot diver, but I couldn't hold a candle to some of the super handsome football hunks and other guys who had also clearly noticed what I did in Joyce. She was a catch, and I'd have to step it up if I wanted her to be my girlfriend.

But I worked my charm, bit by bit. School had started the first day of October and by December, I had "pinned" her. As a Sigma Chi fraternity brother, I was eager to use my fraternity pin to claim Joyce as "my girl." The tradition was that you'd give your pin to the girl you were going steady with as a sign that you were a couple. It's a bit silly, and probably quite antiquated now, but it meant a lot in those days—not least because a pinned girl wore your badge right near her heart. Which is exactly where I wanted to be with Joyce.

What's more, when I met Joyce's family, I fell in love with them, too. They were the perfect embodiment of a loving, supportive family—exactly the kind of family I'd never had. She had an older brother who became one of my best friends and a fishing buddy. And her parents were just wonderful in that Ozzie and Harriet kind of way—the family all gathered around the table for the evening meal to talk about what they'd done that day. It was a revolutionary concept to me, seeing as I'd come from having virtually no family life in high school. It was quite a reversal, in that I had now found not one, but two families—the traditional family I needed with Joyce and her family, and a supportive and extended family of divers.

I was head-over-heels, and Joyce was quick to win over all the other fraternity brothers at Sigma Chi and my friends on the diving team, too. Everyone, universally, loved Joyce—it was a hallmark of who she was. Everyone who ever met her liked and respected her. She was sweet, and vivacious, and smart, and stunningly beautiful, so it was inevitable.

What I'd done right to deserve her, I'm still not sure. But all the fraternity brothers agreed with me that Joyce was topflight. They named her sweetheart of the fraternity, and her picture hung in the entryway of the house for over a year. She was also named May Queen at OSU. I couldn't believe she had picked me.

Once we started dating, we never broke up. Despite my military service, airline work, and diving career sometimes taking me away from her for months at a time, we stayed together. She was by my side through all of it—children, a million air miles, my volunteer work, heartbreak, and joy. I couldn't have asked for a more supportive or perfect partner in all things near, far, and in between.

I don't know exactly when I initially realized that I would so thoroughly join the ranks of "world traveler." But I got my first really good gander at the wider world beginning in 1960 when, as a junior in college, my good friend and fellow OSU diver Lou Vitucci and I were asked to go on a State Department tour of the Far East with a synchronized swimming group. We figured we would take the opportunity, as neither of us thought we stood a chance of making the 1960 Olympic team. So why not tour Asia, see the world, entertain troops overseas, and have fun diving—while getting paid for it?

OK, so we didn't make much money, maybe $5 a day, but with all our meals and transportation taken care of, it was more than enough. Essentially it was all pocket money we were earning.

Our trip to the Far East was a good example of how friendly rivalry and collaboration in performance can enhance the skills and abilities of all involved. The sum is greater than the parts, after all, and Lou and I worked toward that end, developing entertaining artistic and acrobatic diving routines interspersed between the synchronized swimming segments. In addition to some straight diving demonstrations, we also did a whole routine of comedy dives. We borrowed heavily from Hobie and Bruce's routines and the sorts of comedy dives Larry Griswold had perfected. If there was a trampoline on deck, we'd do a trampoline act, too.

At the start of the six-week trip, we all assembled in Hawaii and put our sequences together and performed at all the military bases in Hawaii. After a week of that, we went to Japan where we did a show and exhibition for the Japanese. We went on to Korea and China as well.

To say we had a ball would be an enormous understatement.

During the day, we'd rehearse and perform, and in the evenings, we'd be off by ourselves frolicking in the streets of Japan and other exotic locations, just having a good old time, and learning what it's all about being an American abroad. Two young men in the prime of life getting to live and learn overseas. It was an eye-opening experience and a chance to experience the wider world well beyond Ohio State.

Our diving skills definitely improved while we were overseas, both because of the more straight-laced diving and the comedy routines we put together. The demanding practices and the rigorous schedule of rehearsals and performances meant we were in tip-top shape and peak performance fitness.

We also became great friends during that trip, and wow, did we laugh a lot along the way. During a shopping visit at the base exchange at Hickam Air Force Base in Honolulu, we decided to acquire some uniquely Hawaiian items. So, we each picked up a ukulele, and we tried our best to learn how to play. We weren't terribly good, but we sure had fun pulling out these treasured ukuleles during the trip to serenade the synchro girls and locals with our terribly off-key crooning.

Unfortunately, one of the synchro girls sat on one of the ukuleles—we'd leave our stuff on the seat of the bus, and I guess she didn't see it when we clambered back aboard after a show. The other one went missing somewhere along the way. I hope it's being appreciated somewhere by a more talented musician than I was. But we thoroughly enjoyed these instruments while we had them.

In addition to their performances, the synchronized swimmers also held clinics for local swimming clubs—they were trying to help the sport become recognized as an Olympic event at the time. These exhibitions throughout Japan, Taiwan, and China helped construct the sport's case for inclusion in the Olympic program.

We were helping build history while also honoring it. One of our stops was at Iwo Jima, an island located 750 miles off the bigger islands of Japan. You surely know it as the site of the iconic photo of six Marines raising the flag atop Mount Suribachi after a rancorous skirmish in 1945.

When we visited in 1960, there was still a small base located there with what was essentially a maintenance crew. The men stationed there were really excited to see the show—I mean, really excited. Most of them had been there for almost a year, and this bevy of bathing beauties we had in tow was certainly appealing to these guys. Some of the men couldn't get close enough to the pool for the performance, so they climbed telephone poles nearby to get a better vantage point.

We were excited to be able to perform at this base, but there was a small problem. When we got to the pool, we found that their diving board was broken. So, we made a makeshift board out of a couple of two-by-twelves lashed together. There was no nonslip surfacing to be had anywhere on the island, so instead, we tacked some military blankets to the top of the board. It was soggy and strange, but it worked. We were lucky to be able to execute any good dives from that homemade thing, but we put on a pretty good show. It was well received because we put in a lot of local color from other stops we'd made in Korea and Japan.

Being able to call in at Iwo Jima was a special thing for me, especially knowing that I was going into the military. Iwo Jima and the huge battle that took place there claimed an estimated 21,000 Japanese and nearly 7,000 American lives. Most of them were killed on the beach landing. It was one of the worst but most famous battles of World War II, culminating in that most famous of combat photos of the Marines raising the flag. That image has such significance for anyone who served in the military.

The reason we were fighting there was because the Allies needed an emergency landing field for planes coming out of the South Pacific when they bombed Japan. At the time, the Japanese held the island and had three airfields there. These airfields would make the perfect staging area for invading Japan. Planes were limited in how far they could go in between refueling stops, but Iwo Jima offered the perfect take-off and landing spot for these missions over Japan.

There were something like 350 emergency landings made there during the World War II bombing campaign.

While we were on Iwo Jima, we got to tour Mount Suribachi, and they took us to the chapel next to the runway where they showed us the original military films of the invasion. Those reels had been classified for years, and the carnage they captured was absolutely horrendous. It was revealing and memorable and really meaningful to have this opportunity to learn about Iwo Jima and the soldiers who'd sacrificed so much there.

During another stop, this time in Korea, we nearly caused an international incident. At the time, Korea was just emerging from a bitter civil war. Evidence of the horrific war— bombed-out buildings, broken roads, and squalor—was everywhere. Today, South Korea is one of the most modern places in the world with better Wi-Fi and electronics than we have. But back then, it was still recovering and was a very different place.

We were set to perform on a military base in the Demilitarized Zone, the 2.5-mile-wide border region that separates the Korean peninsula into the communist North and the democratic South. We were given a VIP tour of Panmunjom, a village just north of the DMZ where the Korean Armistice Agreement that paused the Korean War was signed just a few years before we arrived. We got to go into the building where that armistice was made, certainly a significant place for any student of military history.

During the tour, our Swedish escort took us right by a North Korean guard house. They had a pigeon coop there, as the North Koreans didn't trust any radio or telegraph transmissions. They thought their messages would be intercepted, so they were using old-fashioned and decidedly low-tech passenger pigeons to send missives.

One of the girls on the tour didn't understand the significance of these animals. She was just taken with the pigeons (pigeons are just dirty doves after all) and stopped to cluck over them in their coop. That immediately summoned a North Korean guard. He ran out of the hut, weapon brandished, and got right in her space, yelling at top volume. She cowered and nearly fell as she moved back away from the coop and this rabid officer who was, frankly, just doing his job.

One of our South Korean military escort guards stepped in to defend her, and the two men were face-to-face, tensely sizing each other up. It seemed, for love of some pigeons, this swimmer nearly reignited the Korean War all on her own.

So much for doves being an enduring symbol of peace.

The swimmer was absolutely mortified and totally caught off-guard; she was so young. She probably barely even knew about the Korean War and had no idea these pigeons were such a sensitive military instrument. And, well, homing pigeons are pretty neat. It really wasn't her fault that the peace between North and South Korea was so uneasy.

Not long after that episode, I read in the newspaper about a similar incident where an American serviceman and a North Korean solider got into a fistfight in the DMZ over something similarly trivial. Luckily for us, it was patently clear that the young woman had intended no harm, and we were allowed to go on our way.

I've been back to Korea many times over the years. During my tour of duty in Vietnam, I flew many flights into and out of the split country, ferrying wounded Koreans to hospitals in South Korea. I also returned for several diving competitions, including the 1988 Olympics in Seoul and other championship events more recently. It's been amazing to watch South Korea transform itself from that war-torn country I first visited in 1960 to the thriving society it is today.

We had a few brushes with fame during our tour of Asia, too. We did a show in Taiwan for Madame Chiang Kai-shek (Soong Mei-ling) at the Chinese Officers Club, and it was very well received. Lou and I hammed it up to get the audience involved and lighten up the crowd. At the time, Taiwan was engaged in a not-so-cold war with China, following bombings of the islands of Quemoy and Matsu. Things were a little tense to say the least, so I dedicated one of my dives to the Chinese officers in the crowd there, noting their courage and abilities.

I did a back somersault and landed back on the diving board and then did a forward two-and-a-half somersault. It was something they'd likely never seen before—this was one of those dives that wasn't recognized in Olympic competition yet, and as such, seemed totally new and nearly impossible to many spectators. The audience cheered and yelled and threw their hats in the air when I surfaced. This particular dive wasn't the most difficult one I could do, but it took a lot of skill and clearly made an impression.

The audience's response really stuck with me and helped inform many of my administrative efforts later. Spectators go wild for the really complicated dives, and Olympic competitions needed to start recognizing some of these new dives we were developing if international meets were going to remain relevant.

But that fight would come. In the summer of 1960, we reveled in being young, fit, and having a ball as we tore across Asia. We learned a lot, and it's an experience we'll always treasure. Lou and I have been close friends ever since.

The 1960s weren't just a heady time for me. It was also a period of intense growth and innovation for the sport of diving, too. We'll probably never know who the bright spark was who first decided to try extending a plank beyond a rocky ledge to make a cleaner dive into the water below, but as far back as that ancient Greek diver in the Tomba del Tuffatore, people have built structures for diving. Whoever first decided to extend a plank for diving created an innovation that would stand for millennia—and the planks probably didn't budge, given that these early boards were likely made of stone, metal, or thick wood that didn't offer much, if any, bounce.

But over time, divers have experimented with different materials to provide a safer and springier surface to jump from. Different kinds of wood provide different energy return, and as the sport of fancy diving began taking off in the first half of the 20th century, the quest for more flexible boards began.

By the 1950s, diving had begun advancing in exciting ways that I couldn't fully fathom at the time. But during the era I was coming up and diving in college, the sport had begun changing, taking on a more modern look. It was slowly evolving into the sport we know today. The types of dives we mastered in the '60s were a catalyst for elevating the sport amongst the most-watched of all the Olympic events today.

Some of these innovations, particularly with relation to their inclusion in international competition, would come just a little too late for my own gold medal dreams. Given my extensive tumbling and trampolining background, I was always better at executing the more complex dives than the clean, simple, required dives that ruled the day then. But many of these more complicated dives weren't "in the book" yet, meaning that they weren't officially recognized dives according to Olympic competition. The rules lagged where we were in the sport's development.

But it was exciting to be pushing the envelope and contributing to the ever-growing list of dives that other athletes could add to their repertoires whether for competition or exhibition.

One of the most important innovations that was helping us divers create a new and exciting chapter for the sport was the very platform from which we dived. And we have Raymond C. Rude, who I think of as the patron saint of springboard diving, to thank for that. Ray's innovations revolutionized diving's most important piece of equipment. His efforts allowed us up-and-coming divers to finally achieve our ambitions.

Ray was born in 1916 and grew up poor in North Dakota. He ran away from an abusive father when he was 16, landing in California. Lacking a high school diploma but possessing an inventive, engineer's mind, he eventually took a job tooling aircraft parts for Lockheed.

There, Ray began working with aluminum, building tools and machines to cut wing panels for airplanes in the 1940s. Fabricated from a single sheet of aluminum, these panels were amazingly strong, light, and flexible. Though Ray wasn't a diver himself, a chance conversation about an inauspicious rainstorm preventing the varnish on a coworker's newly refurbished wooden board from curing in time for a scheduled pool party led Ray to consider repurposing an incorrectly cut wing panel as a diving board. And thus, the Duraflex board and company was born.

Prior to the development of Ray's Duraflex board, most diving boards were made of wood and covered with cocoa or hemp fiber matting to prevent slippage—wood can get super slick when it's wet, and even with the mats, these boards could still pose a safety risk. The wooden boards also didn't have much give to them, and the amount of spring you could expect to find in a diving board could vary greatly from one pool to the next.

Fiberglass boards are lighter and stronger, but tended to break more easily, especially when installed in sunny, outdoor pool areas. The UV light wreaked havoc on the fiberglass, leading to cracks that could cause serious injury to a diver if the board broke mid-dive. Fiberglass laminated wooden boards could be heavy and were often too stiff to be of much use to divers who wanted to really soar.

Each one of these boards had different characteristics, and divers were having to constantly adjust their approach and timing to be able to dive safely depending on the board found at each pool.

By contrast, the highly engineered aluminum board Ray developed was an astonishing technological breakthrough. That board offered a springier, more controlled way of getting height above the water, creating space for fancier, more acrobatic dives.

Prior to the release of the Duraflex board in the late 1950s, divers doing back, reverse, or inward dives would only be able to execute up to one-and-a-half somersaults. Front takeoffs could result in up to two-and-a-half somersaults. But the Duraflex boards added enough bounce to the takeoff that divers could now safely and easily add a full somersault to their somersaulting dives, regardless of direction of takeoff. Each subsequent tweak to the Duraflex design added more height to divers' takeoffs and thus offered more room for these athletes to add twists, turns, and tumbles.

This new board was the talk of the town. You had to try it. You could do dives on it that you couldn't do on old boards. The cutting edge, more complex dives that spectators love came easier. One dive, and every athlete I knew fell in love with it.

I was lucky to meet Ray while in Los Angeles for a diving event in the early 1960s. We were both at a party thrown by Sammy Lee, the extraordinary diver who became the first Asian-American man to win an Olympic gold medal when he won the 10-meter platform at the 1948 London Games. He owned platform diving in the late 1940s and early 1950s and was a diving coach in southern California. He invited everyone to his house after the meet. Ray and I spent the whole evening talking about where diving was going, and he ended up sending me one of these new boards.

Putting this new, more flexible, and reliable board through its paces, I saw it was clear this board would be the future of the sport. I was thrilled to have it and took it with me to competitions. I'd call ahead to the pool hosting any event I was going to drive to, and if they didn't have a Duraflex on site, I'd strap that thing to the top of my car and bring it with me. I'd change the board out at the pool before the event, so we'd have a better board. Everyone diving there benefited.

That board was installed at the YMCA in Dayton for a while, and it made the rounds. It ended up with a diving club for several years. After that, I lost track of it, but I know it lasted a long time. Duraflex boards are quite durable, and the company will resurface them when needed. With some care and regular maintenance, they can last decades.

Over the years, Ray honed his design based on feedback I and other divers gave him that would make the board lighter, more flexible, and safer.

Taking a page from my trampoline days, I had noticed that webbed trampoline beds are better than solid beds because there's less air resistance. Adapting that idea to the board, Ray added slots at the front of the board. Those added perforations allowed air to flow through, making it more responsive to the diver's movements. But they also increased safety, as they offered standing water a way to drain off the surface. These gaps also made the board much lighter—to the tune of about 10 pounds—which also made it easier for divers to compress to get higher jumps.

Ray also tapered the board at the fulcrum—going both forward and backward—and added ribbing, two design enhancements that further reduced the weight and increased the flexibility of the board.

Over several iterations, the board became ever more precise and attuned to what the diver needs to generate high jumps, thus creating the vertical space necessary to perform audience-adored aerial acrobatics.

Duraflex boards represented a colossal step forward in making diving a more entertaining and athletic event. Precision tools, these boards are astonishingly consistent in performance from one board to the next, and thus quickly became the market leader. Since the 1960 Games in Rome, Duraflex boards have been the only diving boards approved for Olympic competition.

✶ ✶ ✶

As I was nearing the end of my college career, I realized that if I were to have any hope of making the Olympic team in 1964 or beyond, I'd need to pick a career that would allow me to continue training and competing in some capacity while also supporting myself so I might be ready. The military fit all those requirements.

I'd enrolled in the Air Force ROTC when I entered college because I knew I had an interest in flying, and I wanted to serve my country. What's more, I also knew that the military was encouraging of athletes pursuing their passion. As graduation from college loomed, so too did my entry to the U.S. Air Force.

Many people these days don't realize how supportive the armed services were to athletes once upon a time. But there's a lengthy, lengthy history of Olympic athletes who also served in the armed forces, from Bruce Harlan, who was a Navy man in the 1940s to Leon Spinks, the boxer who served in the Marine Corps in the 1970s, and of course, Louis Zamperini, the famous runner and Air Force pilot whose incredible story of survival captivated the world in the book *Unbroken*.

Lots of divers, in particular, have leveraged their love of flying to serve America from the cockpit of a military plane. There's so many of them, it's hard to keep track. Frank Kurtz, the Olympic bronze medalist in the 10-meter platform in 1932 and Marshall Wayne, who took gold in the same event four years later, both boxed out German divers before lending their efforts to defeat them in World War II.

Miller Anderson's college education at Ohio State was rudely interrupted by the outbreak of World War II. As a freshman in 1942, he won his first AAU championship gold, but he put his studies and sports career on hold to serve in the war. He enlisted in the Army Air Corps and was commissioned as a pilot in 1943.

Miller Anderson and Sammy Lee were best friends when the war broke out and they both served. Before they headed off for their respective assignments, they promised each other that if they survived the War, they'd go to the Olympics and Miller would win the springboard and Sammy would win the platform. It was a promise both intended to keep.

Miller served in several campaigns and was awarded a stack of flying medals and honors. But during his 112th mission over Italy, he took heavy fire and had to parachute out. As he fell, the tail of the plane clipped his leg, nearly ripping it from his body. Finally on the ground and in agony, he was caught by the Germans. He somehow talked his way out of being shot by the German who picked him up and was taken to a hospital as a prisoner of war. His leg was set poorly, and it looked like he might never walk again, let alone keep that promise to Sammy.

Luckily, U.S. forces captured the German hospital where he was convalescing about a month later, and he was flown to Rome for leg-salvaging surgery. His recovery was long, but incrementally, he began diving again with one major change: He began using his right leg for take-off instead of his habitual left to avoid putting too much pressure on the damaged leg. Despite those long odds, Miller Anderson staged the ultimate comeback, winning silver medals in the 3-meter springboard in both the 1948 and 1952 Olympic Games.

David Browning, better known by his nickname Skippy, was a University of Texas diver who claimed the gold medal in the 3-meter springboard event at the 1952 Games in Helsinki. He was so excited about his win that he climbed a flagpole to steal an Olympic flag. He got himself arrested, but Mike Peppe bailed him out.

He earned his wings as a Navy pilot in 1955, but sadly, the following spring, he was killed in a plane crash in Kansas. This was just a couple weeks before he was scheduled to be reassigned to Los Angeles so he could begin training for the 1956 Games. He was the favorite to win gold again, and likely would have been the first man to win back-to-back Olympic springboard titles.

I never met Skippy, but I did know his younger brother Dickie. Dickie Browning, who served as a U.S. Navy pilot and then flew for American Airlines for a quarter century, was the national champion in tumbling and was a sensation in the early 1950s. He could do a tumbling pass and a back somersault over the 7-foot bar. He did this with no problem in tumbling exhibitions, and he could have done it in track and field, which would have been a record at the time. But he wasn't allowed to because the rules said he couldn't go over the bar headfirst and he took off with both feet, rather than just one. He experimented with taking off with just one foot and went nearly as high, but he wasn't allowed to jump in competition. This was years before Dick Fosbury pioneered his famous Fosbury Flop, which is basically a back somersault over the bar. Dickie might have been the top high jumper of his day if he'd been allowed to give it a go.

Across all these stories, it's clear there's a deep connection between diving and flying planes. And it really shouldn't be surprising: there's just something about being airborne, whether off the end of a springboard or in the guts of a jet in service of one's country, that speaks to the soul of the diver.

Chapter Four: In-Flight Service

"I am fighting to protect and maintain what I believe in, and I want to live in a democratic society. If I am killed while carrying out this mission, I want no one to cry or mourn for me. I want people to hold their heads up high and be proud of me for the job I did."

– Quote from an unknown Vietnam veteran, inscribed at the Vietnam War Memorial in Ocean Springs, Mississippi.

You could say that December 15, 1961, was a busy day for me. It was also a truly a momentous day. That was the day I graduated from college, was commissioned as an officer in the Air Force, and got married to Joyce. Any of these events taken alone are incredibly significant, but all three in the span of 24 hours? Phew. It was an eventful day, and one that flung open the doors to the rest of my life.

I started my active-duty career at Williams Air Force Base in Arizona, where I spent a year working through pilot training. This one year of rigorous, full-time training was more intense than all four years of college, but I was also able to dive occasionally with Coach Dick Smith. Dick was one of the top diving coaches in America at the time, and I would sometimes make the 30-mile trip to Phoenix where his swim-gym was located.

Diving definitely took a backseat to training to be an Air Force pilot, though. I started training on the T-37 twin engine jet trainer and moved on to the T-38 supersonic trainer. The T-38, especially, was the very archetype of a jet—the sort that a little kid with a crayon might draw—all long, sleek lines and a needle nose. It's still in service with the Air Force today, which underscores its value as a training tool. It was in the cockpit of one of those "white rockets" that I completely fell in love with flying.

When I was in an airplane, I felt like I was part of it. I didn't just move the plane around—it was like it was an extension of my body. The plane became part of me.

I loved everything about flying. I loved the smell of the airplane and the jet fuel they used to fill the tanks. In the scant seconds between maneuvers and watching my instrument panel, I loved looking off into the clouds or down at the ground that was seemingly miles away. I loved the flight suits we wore and being airborne. I just loved the whole idea of soaring high above the earth. And I couldn't wait to finish training and start flying for real.

When I'd had my interview for advanced ROTC back in college, they had asked me what I wanted to do. I told them I wanted to fly jet fighter interceptors, the F-102 and the F-106—supersonic, super-duper jets.

I was keen to be a fighter pilot, but truthfully, I would have taken any kind of assignment. I just wanted to fly.

As it worked out, I got the fighter pilot assignment—it seemed I'd achieved my goal. However, it soon became clear that this thing I'd aspired to do would have to be set aside for another thing I had aspired to and wanted to be even more—an Olympic diver.

I had to turn the fighter pilot assignment down because flight school would have happened at that same time as the 1964 Olympic Games. It was a stark choice: jet fighter training or the Olympics. And there was no way to do both, because once I started fighter pilot training, I wouldn't be able to leave for the competition. So, I declined the assignment and turned my attention to becoming a C-130 pilot instead—certainly not as glamourous as a fighter pilot's career, but sure enough, just as important.

I graduated basic pilot training in Arizona in May of 1963, and Joyce and I took off for a short, joyful vacation to Hawaii. Upon our return, I was to report to Sewart Air Force Base in Smyrna, Tennessee.

Sewart was constructed shortly after the U.S. entered WWII and was named in 1950 for Allan J. Sewart, Jr., a Nashville pilot who died in a bombing mission over the Solomon Islands in 1942. That central-Tennessee installation would be my home base until I left the service. There, I entered the initial two-month C-130 combat crew training school for transport pilots.

In August, my squadron was in France on temporary duty, but I stayed behind by special permission. I'd finished up my training, so I was able to go to the AAU national championships in Chicago instead. I won the 10-meter platform championship and took third in the 3-meter springboard, with barely any training to justify that win.

The rest of my squadron returned soon after and only found out via newsreel that I was the reigning national champion in the 10-meter platform event. And I was off to the CISM Games, better known as the Military Olympics, in Barcelona.

But the demands of my military training didn't stop just because I'd had some success in the pool. No, my first duty was to finish combat crew training, and I began more specific training on the venerable workhorse aircraft called the C-130 Hercules, a four-engine turboprop aircraft with a 132-foot wingspan.

A super versatile mainstay, the C-130 was first built in the early 1950s and can transport anything and everything from troops to cargo. It can also act as a gunship when a 105mm howitzer is mounted on it. It's a colossal machine but fast and maneuverable. A steady ship of all trades in the sky, it's still being manufactured today and was used extensively in the wars in Afghanistan and Iraq. It's ubiquitous at most air bases around the world.

But learning how to maneuver the C-130 without incident took some doing. Being able to take off and land this plane—a bird that weighs 155,000 pounds when it's fully loaded—in the very short distances of the sometimes-makeshift runways we'd have in Vietnam—took a lot of training.

But the plane was agile and responded well, and I felt really at home in the cockpit. I loved that plane, just like all the airplanes I've flown during my career. But you never forget your first time taking control of something that big. After learning how to handle the C-130, I knew I was in for a lifetime of flying.

One of the most defining moments in my life was when I graduated from pilot training in the United States Air Force, because

I knew from that moment on, I now had a career, whether it be flying in the Air Force or flying with the airlines. I had a place in the world and a purpose. I would eventually go on to have a lengthy and rewarding career in commercial piloting. But first, I discharged my duty in service to my country during the Vietnam War.

✷ ✷ ✷

Right after I came back from the 1964 Olympic Games, I was sent on temporary duty to Southeast Asia for three months. I was based at Clark Air Force Base in the Philippines and flew missions within Vietnam as part of the 314th Troop Carrier Wing. When I finished that tour, I qualified for a diving tour of Europe, immediately after which I was sent back to Clark for another short stint of temporary duty. Finally, in January of 1966, I was given a permanent change of station to Ching Chuan Kang Air Base in Taiwan. They sent three wings of C-130s over there, and Clark became too crowded. So, my unit moved up the road to Taiwan.

We were based in Taiwan because we needed to keep the C-130s out of Vietnam itself, where they were vulnerable to attack. Being based in Taiwan allowed us access to all of Southeast Asia, and maintenance was much easier to manage there. We'd shuttle to and from Nha Trang, Vietnam, our unofficial base of operations, regularly. From there we could conduct missions throughout Vietnam. I also flew frequently to Cam Ranh Bay and Bien Hoa, both in Vietnam, that became sort of home bases during the many months I was flying throughout Southeast Asia.

As a transport pilot, I didn't see much direct combat. Nevertheless, the military considered every takeoff and landing made in a combat zone to be part of a combat mission, and I earned extra hazard pay for being in harm's way. I received the princely sum of $100 extra a month for combat pay and got a tax exemption on all monies made during the time I was overseas. It was a nice perk, and one that on occasion, I felt like I really earned.

Like the one time when we landed at a forward base in the Mekong Delta, a hot zone that was constantly under threat of attack. We'd stowed and secured the cargo at the base and were preparing to return to Nha Trang. During the pre-flight check, we discovered that one of the four engines wouldn't start.

An engineer I am not, but the essential idea for how the starter works is this: in a functional system, the starter directs air pressure to the turbine of the engine, which will rotate the prop to a certain speed. Once the prop hits that speed, you can push fuel to it and light it off, thus cranking the engine up to 100 percent.

A starter shorting out on a C-130 engine was a pretty common problem back then, and we had developed various creative workarounds to bypass the problem that would get the prop turning without it. Short of being able to replace or repair the starter, we could achieve the same level of air pressure across the propeller by positioning another plane behind the one attempting to take off. The rush of air movement generated by the other plane's working props would provide the force necessary to get the engine with the bum starter cranking. But there wasn't another plane on the tarmac that day in the Delta.

In other instances, getting the plane aloft would similarly create enough airflow around the propeller to jumpstart the engine with the dud starter. That meant lightening the load to allow the plane to slip gravity's sticky grasp with only three of its engines working—no small feat.

Whatever we were going to do, we needed to do it quickly. Daylight was fading fast, and darkness always posed a threat in the Delta.

"Captain, you've got to get this plane out of here, because we'll have a mortar attack for sure if you leave this one on the runway tonight," the base commander told me.

The sheer physics of it screamed impossibility with only three engines and no external force to jump the engine. Our plane was too heavy, and we had just 4,000 feet of runway to work with—10,000 feet would have been a more appropriate number for the size and weight of plane and cargo we were attempting to move. The longer the runway the more time you have to gun the working engines to achieve enough thrust for takeoff, the better your chances of success. A short runway combined with a heavy plane at only three-quarters engine capacity made the prospect of liftoff seem especially unlikely.

We didn't have the tools or expertise to repair the engine on the runway where it sat like a wounded bird, amidst a jungle clearing surrounded by the threat of would-be predators looking to make a meal out of her. We had to lose weight somewhere.

We set to work, dumping cargo, and casting out anything that wasn't essential. If it wasn't mission critical, out it flew—so that we might, too. We worked quickly and ruthlessly, all with one eye cast toward the jungle.

Watching the sun sink lower toward the tree line, we hurried to prepare for a potentially catastrophic takeoff. Holding our collective breath, the crew clambered aboard, and I gunned the engines, devouring the distance to the end of the runway. I could feel the tension in my body as the runway zipped away beneath the plane. Eager to feel the exact moment when I could take us up, I focused. At the precise instant, instinct and training came together, and I pulled back hard.

An anxious, interminable moment passed between my action and feeling the force of lift that made us weightless. Suspended in that breath was the fearful hope of survival.

We cleared the trees with mere feet to spare.

Though we were leaving the jungle behind, we weren't wholly out of the woods yet. The elation of getting airborne rapidly dissipated as we turned our attention to getting the fourth engine started.

The theory of getting airborne to jumpstart the engine was sound, but it took a few (nervous) moments for the practice to shake out. But Luck did her thing—the fourth engine began turning, and we safely made it back to Nha Trang.

This isn't the sort of thing that would ever happen on a commercial airliner—you'd change planes or cancel the flight before trying to take off with an engine not starting. But combat flight is a different animal, and this was just another instance of having to get creative and improvise on the fly. War, as has been recorded extensively elsewhere, is indeed chaotic. Vietnam was not exempt from this rule.

Landings could be equally perilous. Again, the short runways rimmed with thick, hostile jungle, meant we had to become especially skilled at stopping short when putting the plane on the ground. These short landings were in some ways more akin to placing a helicopter on the ground than a large, heavy cargo plane. But I adjusted and became quite skilled at what we called the Vietnam Approach with the Herc.

In the early years of the Vietnam War, the runways were exceedingly short and often largely unprepared. Not like the sleek long thoroughfares of modern airports in most developed nations around the world today, these combat airstrips were tiny, rarely paved, and subject to harsh environmental conditions—not to mention the occasional mortar attack. This all made for anything other than a smooth landing, especially when taking fire.

To avoid attracting the attention of Viet Cong—who often worked the rice paddies around the area one minute but might be picking up a rifle and shooting at a plane coming in overhead the next—I would approach the base and stay at about 4,000 feet until I was just short of the end of the runway. By then, all the gear and flaps would be down as for a normal landing, but I would point the nose of the aircraft straight down toward the end of the runway. I'd slow to idle speed with gear and flaps hanging as we slipped toward the end of the runway. Then, at the last minute, I'd plunk it on the ground. Throw it into full reverse, and we'd come to a stop on the few feet of remaining runway.

This maneuver isn't for the faint of heart. If you ever experienced such a landing on a commercial airline, you'd get off that plane as quickly as possible—likely shaking with fear, throwing up, complaining, or all three—and never get on another one. But in Vietnam, it was a necessary skill that was critical to survival, preventing us from being exposed to enemy fire for a long time at low altitude as we approached the runway.

Most of the C-130 fleet had a few bullet holes and we frequently saw Viet Cong shooting up at us as we landed. Despite all that, I never felt exceedingly threatened. And we cargo transport pilots were really the only means of getting goods and supplies around to the soldiers on the ground who needed our support. We had so many airplanes in Vietnam when I was there because we didn't own any of the roads. Our work was critical to the mission in country, so we just got on with it. Just as I'd done as a high school kid, I found ways to adapt and improvise to get through the day.

Everything was transported by air in C-130s or C-123s. (The C-123 looks like a baby C-130. It's got the same body shape but has just two engines.) Even vehicles got a lift from us. Occasionally other unexpected items—or passengers—came along for the ride, too, as I discovered one day before a mission while checking the logbook on the plane I was to take command of. A note in the book indicated that there was a "suspected cobra onboard aircraft."

OK, so, now I'm on alert. We're talking about one of the deadliest snakes in the world, and the write-up says it might be on the airplane. Might? What kind of note is that to leave for the next captain?

You can probably imagine the way we felt at just the prospect of having to fly this plane, particularly at night, thinking that maybe a snake would come crawling out of the metalwork somewhere and land in our laps. It was the kind of stowaway no pilot or crew ever wanted to discover onboard.

I imagine the snake wasn't too fond of its new home, either. It had come aboard with some cargo picked up in Thailand, which is known for its extant population of king cobras. Presumably, the snake had been attracted to warmth or shelter offered by some boxes sitting on the tarmac and had crawled in and settled down, not realizing that it would soon wake up far from home in the midst of a very human conflict.

It wasn't noted in the logbook, but I later learned that when the plane landed, the loadmaster opened the troop door and looked in. Staring him right in the face was this large and rather unhappy king cobra, ready to strike. Luckily, the airman knew to stand fast and not move—those snakes go after fast movements. He shouted for assistance and one of his fellow airmen came and pulled him out of the way. They gave the snake the run of the plane for a few minutes while they caught their breath and figured out what to do. They then went back in looking for it, but they couldn't find it.

Uncertain whether it had recoiled deeper into the aircraft or somehow slithered out into the nearby jungle, they alerted the maintenance crew. Obviously, no one was going to fly that plane until it had been inspected. The maintenance crew carefully tore that plane apart, looking for the creature. They found no sign of it and tried to lure it out with various enticements. They gave it a couple days, but they never did find that snake, and the war continued around us. So, the plane was put back into service with a note that an errant cobra might still be onboard. Captain and crew beware.

We flew the plane without incident and figured the snake must have found its way to a safer place. About a month later, the maintenance crew was conducting routine service and removed a panel in the cargo track where we'd roll pallets in and out of the hold. There, they found the cobra, curled up and, mercifully for them, unable to inflict its venomous bite on anybody. It was dead.

That poor creature ended up in the wrong place at the wrong time and perished aboard that plane. Sadly, it was not my only brush with the dead, and far from the worst incidence of death in the cargo hold of a plane I helmed in Vietnam.

No, that experience came toward the end of my time in Vietnam. I was nearly finished and eager to return home to Joyce and my young son, Tim, who'd been born in August of 1965. Thinking I was in for just another routine flight, I landed at our base in Pleiku, Vietnam. My original orders had me ferrying goods onward to another base, but the base commander came out to speak with me.

"We know you're supposed to take this aircraft onward, but we've diverted your plane for a special mission," he told me. "We had a firefight here last week, and 12 Americans were killed. They've been put in a field freezer until they could be put in body bags and shipped off to Saigon for preparation and repatriation back to the United States. It's your job to fly the bodies to Saigon."

My heart sank. For most of my time flying in country, I'd been conveying supplies, ammo, and live troops from relative safety. This buffer created a sense of detachment from the war's day-to-day carnage. But this flight, transporting these dead servicemen, brought the reality of the conflict into unavoidable, visceral focus.

To make matters worse, the dead had been laid out onto four pallets to be loaded into a different plane that had been scheduled to depart hours earlier. But that plane had broken down, so the entire time, the bodies of those fallen servicemen had been lying on the ramp in 90-degree heat and full glare of the sun.

They loaded these pallets into the plane and the stench... I don't have words to describe it. It was sickening, physically and emotionally. It invaded my senses. I felt ill, not just because of the stink of death, but also because these were my fellow soldiers who'd been left to rot in the sun like so much discarded meat. It just didn't seem right to any of us.

I considered refusing the flight because we didn't have our normal oxygen system. Typically, if we had need for supplemental oxygen, either because of altitude or because we were transporting a potentially toxic load, we could don masks that dispensed pure oxygen. But because this was an emergency, we didn't have time to top up the oxygen tanks. We were told to go immediately from Pleiku to Saigon.

So, we did.

C-130 planes were usually equipped with a couple of small bottles of oxygen that you could use in emergencies. These hand-held tanks allowed you to walk around with your oxygen, which you can't do when tethered to the larger system on the plane. But there was only one canister of oxygen on this particular plane that day.

We did everything we could to circulate air through the plane. We couldn't pressurize it, and we had to stay at low altitude, so the air didn't move very well to disperse the stench. We even tried blocking off the hold from the flight deck with blankets to try to stop the smell from creeping in as best we could. But the cloying reek was still so bad that the copilot, the navigator, and the flight engineer all vomited repeatedly.

I had to keep my lunch down in order to get us safely to Saigon, so as captain of the aircraft, I used the one tank of oxygen so I could remain in control of the aircraft. I felt awful that there wasn't enough to go around for my crew, but if I fell ill, too, we'd likely go down as a whole.

We finally landed in Saigon, glad to be able to leave that confined space, but with a growing sense of doom. There, we were instructed to drop the bodies, refuel, and go onward to Taiwan. With an odor-filled plane.

I refused.

A colonel came out to see what the problem was.

"There's no way we can fly without all of us being on oxygen," I explained.

"But Captain, the liquid oxygen at this base is reserved only for fighter aircraft," he replied. As a cargo plane, we were very low on the priority list.

Undeterred, I leveled with him.

"Colonel, you can say what you want, but this plane is not gonna move unless we can go on oxygen. The flight to Taiwan is about four hours. We'll all be sick. We'll be a safety hazard."

"You mean to tell me you're not going to take the plane?!" The colonel was incredulous that a lowly C-130 captain would refuse a direct order from him.

"Well, Colonel. If you walk over and stick your head in the door there and can truthfully tell me that it would be safe for me to take the plane without oxygen, I'll take it."

Clearly irritated, the colonel marched over and stuck his head into the troop door. His reaction was swift and decisive. He turned around gasping, nearly vomiting on his shoes.

He staggered a few feet away from the plane and hoarsely said, "I'll get you your liquid oxygen as soon as possible."

Once the oxygen had been delivered, we were on our way to Taiwan. That C-130 remained grounded in Taiwan for several days as maintenance tried to clean out the smell. But the stink of death just wouldn't budge.

The walls of the C-130 are insulated with blankets that prevent noise penetration, and there's plenty of other soft fabrics and furnishings inside, from seatbelts to canvas seats, that absorbed the stench of those fallen service members. Multiple maintenance crews went in and tired cleaning every inch—scrubbing, spraying, disinfecting—to remove the smell. Despite these efforts, the first crew that took the plane up to altitude and pressurized it all got sick.

It was just a horrific situation, probably the worst experience I had while in the service. It's hard to imagine anything that smells more unsettlingly awful than rotting human flesh, and it's difficult to describe that odor to someone who hasn't smelled it. The lingering stink just penetrates everything. There's little worse than having your whole crew sick on an airplane, but what that stubborn stench represented was even more horrifying.

Though it was my most gruesome experience while serving in the Air Force, it wasn't the only time I went toe-to-toe with a commander demanding something unsafe or unrealistic.

There was one incident when President Johnson was set to visit Cam Ranh Bay airbase as a morale booster for the troops who'd been injured in battle. The Air Force decided it would be wise to take a couple C-130s and load them up with wounded soldiers from the hospital. The soldiers were placed on litters in the back of the plane, and I was selected to be one of the pilots who would fly them over to the base so they could maybe get to meet the president.

All well and good, except for that god-forsaken heat. These guys were recovering, wounded soldiers. They weren't exactly fit for travel. And in the back of the C-130, even if we opened up the ramp, it was probably 90 degrees or hotter with so much humidity.

Of course, safety protocols surrounding the president's visit meant that no planes could fly in or out of the base within an hour of Johnson's arrival or departure. So, we ended up sitting on that ramp for about three hours in this tremendous heat, with the wounded soldiers languishing, waiting for President Johnson to arrive.

When he did finally turn up, Johnson walked off Air Force One, shook hands with a couple commanders and maybe peeked into one of the C-130s loaded with soldiers. He then ran back to his plane and left. Our guys had been lying there very uncomfortably, and we were supposed to wait another hour before take-off.

Well. Another C-130 pilot and I decided that was bogus. We decided these men needed to get back to the hospital as quickly as possible or we'd likely have some additional casualties to add to the rising death toll in country. We cranked our engines and went to get taxi clearance on the runway.

"You can't take off for another 45 minutes because the president's only been gone for 15," the tower responded.

"We're declaring a medical emergency," the other pilot announced. "We want take-off clearance now."

We got that clearance and took the men back to Nha Trang Base where they could recuperate in more comfortable surroundings.

Strange things happen in wartime, I guess you could say.

In Vietnam, we used VFR, visual flight rules, which means you're flying pretty much on your own without the assistance of air traffic control. In those early days, we didn't have the kind of air traffic support that most pilots have become accustomed to or that are typical of commercial flying. Instead, we had to make our best judgements and try to avoid inflight collisions, incoming fire, and other near calamities with our own eyeballs and wit. Fast reflexes sure didn't hurt either.

I had to apply all of those skills one day when I was scheduled to do several flights in and out of the base at Kon Tum, an inland, highland province toward the northern end of South Vietnam.

As we've already established, long, broad runways were not common in Vietnam. The installation at Kon Tum was situated at 4,000-feet altitude, and in the mountains, there wasn't much space to build the roomy runways we would have preferred. No matter, but this particular 4,000-foot-long runway had the added bonus of being perched atop a mountain surrounded by a deep valley on all sides. We didn't exactly have a large margin of error if something went wrong coming into or leaving from this base.

Because I had orders to shuttle troops and gear over several trips, I went in with full fuel tanks. Fuel is heavy, but it's the price of admission when flying any kind of large craft, especially one that needs to haul a lot of weighty supplies and people.

I landed, and the officer in charge came out to explain what they needed.

"Captain," he said, "we're doing a unit move. We're going to give you a two-and-a-half-ton truck and 20 troops with full armor and gear to take to this other base. Then you'll come back, and we'll shuttle another load." And another, and another, until the unit had been fully relocated.

There was nothing extraordinary about this, as we did a lot of shuttling and moving of resources. But this initial transport would be too much.

"We have a full fuel load, which makes us already quite heavy," I said. "And you're talking about a 5,000-pound truck that's loaded with stuff and a full troop of men. We'll have to do a weight and balance check to determine whether we can do it," I explained.

The flight engineer got to work crunching the numbers and discovered we'd be more than 10,000 pounds overweight. That may have been a conservative estimate.

I turned back to the commander. "We can't go," I said. "We'll be too heavy."

That wasn't the right answer, apparently.

"I've been told that you could do this, so I'm ordering you to take this plane out of here because we have to get this unit gone," he said. He was an Army officer, not a pilot, so he didn't fully grasp the implications of our being so greatly overweight.

"I understand that," I replied. "But Colonel, you're ordering me to fly a plane beyond its capability. And I'm not going to do that."

The military is not the best place for a young man to push back against an authority figure. But we'd reached an impasse—I was not going to jeopardize my flight crew to suit his schedule or placate his sense of hierarchy. I paused, thinking, as he grew redder in the face.

"How about we make a deal?" I suggested.

"First of all, a two-and-a-half-ton truck is not supposed to have cargo in it, because that makes it heavier. It's about three times the weight it's supposed to be, and we don't even know exactly how heavy it is. So how about we take the truck without its payload? And we'll take half the troops and come back and get the others later."

The colonel shook his head. "But I was told you could take a full troop and truck load," he replied.

"And I'm telling you what I'm going to take," I said. "You can write me up or do whatever you want, but this is what I'm going to do." I was polite but firm. And took a deep breath realizing I was risking disciplinary action for insubordination.

Naturally, the Colonel was very upset with me, but he agreed to my terms. We took as much gear as we felt we could, getting right up to our maximum takeoff weight of 155,000 pounds. I instructed the crew to turn off bleed air to the engines to give us a few thousand pounds more thrust to clear the end of the runway.

Beyond the edge of the runway the terrain plummeted into a river valley thousands of feet below. If we hadn't calculated our weight correctly or couldn't get airborne before the end of the runway, we'd go plunging down the side of the mountain into the ravine where we'd surely be killed, and some other poor soul would have a heck of a time retrieving what was left of us from down there.

Taking off toward the cliff's edge, I felt reasonably confident that we'd make it. But I was certain it would be close. And it was. We just barely achieved liftoff in those last few feet of runway.

Accounting for the updraft from the valley below, I pushed the nose downward a bit to help stabilize the plane and move us in the right direction to catch better air for our necessary climb to altitude. I knew I had the plane, but it appeared to those watching us from the runway that we'd gone right over the edge and crashed into that yawning canyon.

For several moments, the plane sank down into the valley before I was able to maneuver us upward and clear the horizon where those on the ground could see that we were actually flying. Cue the cheers as we soared up into the clouds. We made it to our destination, dropped off our cargo, and returned to the mountain top runway a few hours later.

When we landed safely back at the base, the Colonel strode out to greet me. Breathlessly, he nearly shouted, "just tell me what you want to take!"

Much relieved to see me in the flesh, he pumped my hand vigorously and added, "I thought you were gone on that last take-off. I saw my whole career passing before my eyes as we watched you dip below the edge of the runway," he admitted. "And I felt just awful, because I thought you'd all been lost because I told you that you had to take that load."

It was a victory of sorts for me, not just because I'd been right. But because I'd stood up for myself and my men. I was a very young captain and held my ground against a much higher-ranking officer. But because I'd looked out for my crew and the troops we were transporting, we all made it where we needed to be that day in one piece.

Another near miss came one day when I was flying from a base on the coast where the Army had a fleet of helicopters stationed. I was readying for takeoff and communicating with the tower over the UHF radio. We were carrying a fairly heavy load, as usual. We were less maneuverable than we would have been with a lighter load, but we were cleared for takeoff.

We got up to speed on the take-off roll, and at the right moment, I began pulling up to clear the ground. At that exact instant, 12 helicopters popped up right in front of me.

They appeared out of thin air, returning from an operation. They were coming in quickly at low level, just above the treetops. They materialized as they approached the runway to be able to communicate with the tower, and surely didn't expect to see me in my big, lumbering bird barreling right into their flight path. The immensity of the C-130 meant there was absolutely nothing I could do to get out of their way.

"Hang on!" I shouted to my crew, adrenaline surging as I braced for the absolute worst kind of bird strike.

I blinked and all I could see was the underside of a dozen helicopters careening off in every direction as quickly as they could to get out of my way. As with the water-skiing elephant, though, somehow, mercifully, we avoided a catastrophic mid-air collision.

The problem was the Army uses FM radio frequencies while I was on UHF. We couldn't hear each other. Thankfully, that sort of issue only happened once for me, but I know mid-air collisions were a fairly common occurrence during the War, especially in those early, Wild West–like days.

Despite all these high-adrenaline incidents, most of my missions weren't terribly exciting—just a lot of routine flying with the occasional close call interspersed. On one of these, I was flying six pallets of bombs from Huế Phu Bai Combat Base. It was one of the bases that would be overrun by the Viet Cong during the Tet

Offensive in 1968 after I'd left the service. I was flying on to Cam Ranh Bay where a fighter group ran bombing missions.

The airstrip at Phu Bai was temporary—we didn't have solid land to get the plane off the runway to a loading area, so a neoprene layer had been put down over the sandy taxiway to help keep the sand where it needed to be. We'd taxi over the neoprene for a smooth surface.

Usually no problem, but on this particular day, an air bubble had formed under the neoprene in the middle of the taxiway. We managed to navigate over it, and I carried on with our bombs, not even really registering the bubble as a potential problem.

A couple hours later as we prepared to land at Cam Ranh Bay, I discovered that the nose landing gear wouldn't come down. I was up there circling with no nose landing gear and 3,500 pounds worth of bombs in the payload. It was a scramble to figure out how to get the plane on the ground safely—without blowing up the base and ourselves.

The flight engineer went down into the electronics department just behind the nose landing gear well and he chopped a hole in the aluminum wall between the compartment and the landing gear to see what was preventing the gear from descending.

There, he found that when we'd bumped over the bubble in the runway, it bent the nose gear door. The door was getting caught and wouldn't let the wheels down.

With the problem diagnosed, this very clever flight engineer had a plan. He reached out with a long aluminum pole to nudge the nose gear door open. He wedged the pole between the gear door and the fuselage to prop it open.

This procedure he invented saved us from having to make a landing with no nose gear on the airplane—when that happened, you usually lost the whole nose, so he saved the military a lot of money for repairs. He also quite possibly saved all our lives, as it's entirely possible the bombs on board could have detonated if we'd had a rough landing.

The choice mission when I was in country was to go to Bangkok. All the transport pilots wanted that duty because it meant flying to Thailand for five or six days to shuttle cargo around the various bases we had in Thailand. That's where we'd stage the fighters that would go up to North Vietnam for bombing sorties.

Those missions in Bangkok always meant staying in a nice hotel downtown that had really fine food and comfortable beds. But even more importantly, there'd always be a swimming pool. The workdays were shorter and less onerous because the bases were more secure, and then you'd be able to go back to the hotel for a nice dinner. For me, I'd also spend some time at the pool lounging, swimming, or maybe even diving.

There was one hotel in particular in Bangkok that had a U-shaped swimming pool in the middle of it, as though the pool were the courtyard of the hotel complex. The hotel rose up around it, four stories tall. One of the days I was staying there, I had a late takeoff, so I headed down to the pool in the morning for a swim.

While I was doing some laps just to stretch out and enjoy the water, I noticed that it might be possible to get up to the fourth floor and dive from there into the pool. It wasn't terribly deep—maybe 8 or 9 feet at best—but it struck me as being deep enough to accommodate a dive from the roof. And I needed some excitement, because flying around in a warzone apparently wasn't doing it for me.

I did a lot of crazy, dumb things at that time, and this was certainly among them.

I was young. It seemed like it would be fun. And I managed to get myself up to the fourth floor and creep to the edge of the railing on a balcony that overhung the deepest part of the pool. I positioned myself, paused for a breath, then executed.

Tumbling and turning, I landed in the water just as I'd hoped, to gasps and applause. Apparently, I'd attracted a lot of attention not just from people in and around the pool but from people walking along the hallways at each level of the hotel that rimmed the small pool. That dive wasn't that big a deal—I was launching from a height that was very similar to the 10-meter tower I had so often competed from. But it was far more satisfying than bouncing off the 1-meter board they had at water level.

Feeling refreshed, I dressed and headed to the base for my work. When I got back to the hotel later that evening, I saw a KC-135 refueling crew that was also staying in the hotel. They all came out and sat around the pool, no doubt enjoying a few beers.

Unbeknownst to me, one of my own crew members—that same very clever sergeant who saved our landing in Cam Ranh Bay—was also there and got to talking with these other guys.

"You know," he said, "my captain can dive off this hotel roof into this pool without any problem."

They all looked up at the roofline, then back at the tiny pool and shook their heads.

"There's no away anybody can do that without killing themselves," one of them responded.

"Oh, but Capt. Gompf can!"

Very naturally, a wager was made. I mean, if the tables had been turned, I probably would have taken the bet, too.

The first I heard of any of this was when my sergeant came knocking on my room door, telling me I had to come put on a show.

"Captain," he said, "have I got a deal for you! I've got enough money bet on you being able to dive off the roof into this pool that we can go out and have a really fine dinner tonight."

That was all I needed to hear.

I climbed up onto the top of the hotel roof while the other servicemen looked on from far below. I could barely make out their faces as I lined up the dive. I paused for dramatic effect, making it look like maybe I was losing my nerve. Those summer days at the pool in Dayton had honed my sense of timing to perfection.

When I felt the audience was at the very edge of their seats, I pushed off and executed a perfect dive into the pool.

I held my breath underwater and crossed to the side of the pool where the men who'd just lost their bet were seated. I popped up and said, "Hi, guys!"

They about fell out of their chairs; they couldn't believe it. Not only that I'd done it, but now they owed my sergeant a pile of cash for our dinner—several beers and a steak each for sure.

While I was stationed in Taiwan, the Chinese Air Force apparently caught wind that I was in country again. Someone remembered that fancy dive I'd done at the Taiwan Officers Club back in 1960 when I was on the State Department tour with Lou Vitucci. The U.S. Air Force received an invitation from the Chinese Air Force for me to come perform during the 30th anniversary of the founding of their Air Force. We were allies with China, so the request was granted.

There were thousands of people there, and the show was well received. I expected to be dismissed after the exhibition, but an escort officer invited me to attend the ceremony in the Chinese Officers Club.

All the top brass of the Chinese and Taiwanese Air Force were in the club. I was escorted by Captain Lee, who introduced me down a long receiving line of officers. We got to a very senior member of this coterie, a general of some sort. This general had been trained by Claire Chennault, an American Air Force pilot who went to China in the late 1930s at the behest of Madam Chiang Kai-shek. China was under daily attack from Japanese forces, so Chennault was charged with helping them protect themselves. He founded the Flying Tigers, a volunteer air force of American pilots who fended off the Japanese in China before the War. They were an extraordinary unit and the most successful and famous pilots in the world. They knocked out something like 20 Japanese planes for every one that they lost. It was the most successful air combat ratio ever.

I grew up watching the movie *The Flying Tigers* starring John Wayne. So, I knew all about this and was thoroughly impressed that this man had trained with Claire Chennault.

Looking around the room, it became apparent that he wasn't the only person who had a connection to the Flying Tigers and that the super senior officers I was meeting were all there at the founding of the Chinese Air Force in 1936. It was an incredible honor to get to meet and interact with these venerable Air Force officers. It would not be the last time the Flying Tigers appeared in my life.

Everywhere in Southeast Asia—whether we were flying over Thailand, Vietnam, Taiwan, or somewhere else—it was hot and steamy. It was the jungle after all.

Despite the heat and cloying humidity, we pilots would wear flight suits—you've seen them. They're those olive or brown jumpsuits with lots of pockets that the fly boys in *Top Gun* somehow made look cooler than they actually were.

But in Vietnam, it was a lot of heavy fabric that sometimes made for an uncomfortable uniform, just because it was so dang hot and sticky in the jungle. So sometimes when I was flying at night, I'd take off my flight suit and fly in my underwear. It was just cooler that way. And typically, it wasn't an issue.

But there was that one time.

We were told we'd have to take a couple of passengers. I didn't think anything of it, as we often gave soldiers a lift from base to base. I assumed it would be another soldier or two just base hopping.

Turned out, it was two women.

I was sitting in the captain's seat in nothing but my skivvies when they came aboard and introduced themselves. My flight suit was lying where they were going to be sitting.

I must have turned eight shades of scarlet. But these two journalists were completely unfazed and insisted that I stay comfortable. *Why dress for their benefit?* They could appreciate just how unpleasant it was to be clad in canvas in that heat, too, and they didn't mind. I was used to walking around in next to nothing from all those years diving in briefs, so I figured if they weren't bothered, *why should I be?* A little friendly banter later, we got on our way.

Toward the end of the flight, one of them leaned forward and said, "You do realize we're going to have to write about the time we flew with a pilot in his underwear, right?"

I chuckled but gulped inwardly, hoping it wouldn't mean trouble for me with my superiors. But I figured it would probably be fine—indeed, it seemed unlikely anyone would even notice or read their article or figure out they were referencing me. It was Vietnam after all. A little bit of chaos was always to be expected, and decorum had largely left the building. You needn't always be dressed to the nines to impress.

As any good diver knows, sometimes you barely need to be dressed at all to make a statement.

I'm proud of my military service and feel like I could write a whole book about what I saw and experienced in training and while serving. After every 35 missions, I'd qualify for an air medal, and I earned quite a few of those. I got to the point where I didn't even put in for them anymore because I'd already gotten three oak leaf clusters and additional qualifications. I felt I would probably opt to get out of the service when I reached the end of the five-year term I committed to when I was in college. I didn't see myself staying on as a career Air Force officer; I didn't want to get promoted to a desk job and cease being able to fly every day, so I wasn't trying to fatten up my air medal count. Before I left, though, I did receive the Distinguished Flying Cross and an Air Force Commendation Medal. They're now proudly displayed in my home office alongside my diving accolades.

But while I was still in the service, I was frequently aware that there's always a catch-22—a confounding convergence of opposing and often nonsensical factors and rules that make forward progress difficult at times.

For me, this catch-22 came in the form of trying to put in my resignation papers at the right time so that I could leave the Air Force at the end of my 15-month tour in Southeast Asia. The timing was such that the completion of that tour matched up with the completion of my five-year commitment to the Air Force that I had made while I was in the ROTC program in college, so it should have been a simple case of filing the paperwork and getting discharged.

But it wasn't. The timing was actually off just enough to make my extraction a very complicated affair.

The rules dictated that I couldn't put in for discharge until I was at a precise point in time within the current assignment, a point that given the timeline of this tour was quite impossible. I tried to submit my papers anyway, but that request was denied. Before I knew it, another assignment was being prepared for me at McGuire Air Force Base in New Jersey to commence at the completion of my 15-month tour in Vietnam.

I did everything I could to avoid being officially given that new assignment because once you get an assignment, you can't get out of it until you've met the minimum obligation, which is usually a year or more. In this particular case with training and so forth, I was looking at an additional 18 months to two years in service if I was given that assignment. While I admire the people for whom the military is their career, it wasn't for me, so I cast about for ways to fulfill my commitments but conclude my service and move on.

As it worked out, I actually had to extend my tour in Southeast Asia by three months to make the timing for putting in my resignation papers work out. I can't say I was all that eager to spend another three months in country, but if that's what it took to check all the boxes and gain an honorable discharge, then so be it.

But, as Luck would have it, I discovered that I could leave my post 90 days early if I'd been accepted into a university course that was scheduled to commence within 90 days of my scheduled completion of service. If I could work it out to get back into a session that would start right at the end of my tour, I might be able to keep to the originally planned 15 months.

So, I wrote a letter to Ohio State and said I'd like to come back to school in the spring quarter. They sent me a letter of acceptance that I used to leave the service on time to make it to that class. Sure enough, this brought my tour back to the initially planned 15 months, and I was able to get discharged at the end of my five-year commitment to the Air Force.

It took a lot of paperwork and research to satisfy the bureaucracy, but I was glad to be on my way home in the spring of 1967 with the war and Vietnam in the rearview mirror.

Chapter Five: The Olympic Dream

*"We all have dreams. But in order to make dreams
come into reality, it takes an awful lot of determination,
dedication, self-discipline, and effort."*

*– Jesse Owens, American track and field
athlete and four-time Olympic gold medalist*

During my service in the U.S. Air Force, I spent a lot of time in the air. But I also dived a lot, too. In fact, it was during my time as an active-duty pilot that I qualified for and competed in the 1964 Olympics in Tokyo.

The Olympics had long been a dream of mine, as they are for many a young athlete. Growing up a diver and a tumbler, I hoped one day to represent America on the world's greatest athletic stage, and I worked hard to bring that vision to reality.

I first went to Olympic Trials for the 1956 Melbourne Olympics. That event was held in Detroit in August of '56. I finished 31st in the springboard competition and didn't even qualify for the 10-meter platform, so I didn't make the cut any way you slice it. I wasn't unduly bothered by that, though. I figured I was still in high school, still developing my skills, and had plenty of time.

When the 1960 Trials rolled around, I was pretty sure I wouldn't make the team then either, and thus took the opportunity to tour the world with Lou Vitucci and the State Department instead of trying to qualify.

But I was aiming for '64, and it looked like it could be a viable year for me. During my time training with the Air Force in Arizona, I was sometimes able to arrange to go work out with Dick Smith and his crew at the Dick Smith Swim Gym—say that five times fast!—in Phoenix.

Dick was world-renowned for his ability to build great divers. He'd established his world-famous swim-gym about 40 miles from Williams AFB—a relatively quick drive, and well worth making, especially when first-class coaching and facilities were waiting at the other end of it. Dick's swim-gym was always open to divers and swimmers at various stages of development from across the aquatic disciplines.

Though he was small in stature, Dick was a giant in the sport of diving. In the 1930s and '40s, he was a near-constant fixture atop podiums in competitive diving. But his achievement as a diver was unlikely, not least of all because at age 13, Dick took an ill-fated high-dive from 48 feet that saw him crash into the bottom of a rocky quarry. He landed with a concussion and fractured neck that left him paralyzed for several months. Though his doctor advised him to get used to the invalid lifestyle, Dick wasn't having it.

In a move I can completely relate to, Dick began sneaking to the local pool to reteach himself how to swim. So keen was he to continue diving, he stealthily—and against doctor's orders—rehabilitated himself on his own in secret sessions at the pool.

Within a year of the accident, he was diving with relative ease. By age 16, he'd completed his recuperation and demonstrated such by claiming both junior and senior springboard titles in the Arizona state championships. He also earned several other amateur championship titles, including the Arizona AAU and Pacific Coast AAU, and won the intercollegiate championships while diving for the University of Southern California.

From 1946 through 1950, Dick managed Buster Crabbe's Aqua Parade, a massively popular aquatic show that toured the U.S., Canada, and Europe. But his greatest contribution to the sport of diving came as a coach, both through his own Arizona-based swim-gym as well as at august institutions ranging from UCLA to the Air Force Academy. He was also the women's U.S. Olympic diving coach in 1964 and the men's U.S. Olympic diving coach in 1968. In 1976, he coached the New Zealand Olympic diving team.

Across this broad spectrum, Dick's coaching efforts resulted in his protégés qualifying for the finals in Olympic, Pan-American, international, and national competitions some 350 times. More than a quarter of his divers took gold medals in those competitions.

In short, Dick Smith produced winners.

And I knew if I was going to have a shot at making the Olympic team—or even entertain the idea of medaling—I needed to visit with the magic-maker at his workshop not far up the road.

I worked with Dick and another diver, Frank Gorman, a Harvard graduate who was in the Navy. We were great friends after being together on the US Military World Games Team in 1963 where I won both events, and he was second. He was a great diver, and we crossed paths many, many times. At the previous 1964 indoor national championships, we decided we would be better off if we worked together and with Dick Smith. It turned out to be a good plan for both of us.

Working with Dick was really good for me, not just for my diving but also because he was a reserve colonel in the Air Force. We had a lot to talk about, and he gave me some pointers for my career. He helped me adjust to life as a service airman as much as he prepared me for the various championships and competitions that lay ahead on the road to Tokyo.

As a kid, my goal had been to win a national championship. I did that first in 1961 in trampoline and diving. In 1963 and 1964, I was the AAU champion in the platform event. Naturally, my focus shifted to trying to make the American diving team going to the Olympics.

Being able to represent your country at the Olympics is the dream for most athletes from every sport that's part of the Olympic movement. But if you scratch the surface, just making it isn't quite enough. Everyone dreams of winning a gold medal one day. And for me, if I'm completely honest, that was the real goal all along.

But first, I had to get on the squad, and that meant competing regularly to hone my competition repertoire and to establish myself as a viable candidate for the U.S. to bring to the Games.

That meant getting creative to get time away from my pilot training and other Air Force duties to be able to attend meets. It wasn't always easy to do that.

In 1962, I went to the national championships in Philadelphia on my own time and my own dime without the Air Force breaking up my training. No one was allowed to leave the base until training was over, and you couldn't break it up for the whim of competition, but I had a supportive flight instructor named Daryl Lemon who helped me get ahead on my training so that I could have a four- or five-day period of leave. You'd get occasional days off, and with Daryl's help, I was able to save them up to so I could attend the meet in Philadelphia without disrupting my flight training.

Few of the other men in my squadron even knew I was headed off for the championship.

I entered the contest citing my affiliation with the United States Air Force and dived well. I earned second place on the 3-meter springboard and a third place on the 10-meter platform, all with very limited training.

No one at Williams AFB would have known I'd even attended the meet, except for the fact that the event was covered on ABC's *Wide World of Sports*, and I was featured prominently. The "secret" was out.

Personnel services got wind of the fact that I'd competed and done well, and they also learned that I was juggling my diving around my professional duties and had gone to the meet on my own time. They decided to come to my rescue by cutting temporary orders for that event so I could get my expenses covered. It helped a lot because Joyce and I were just starting out and didn't have much money. This sort of assistance happened a few more times during my time in the Air Force and is a great example of how the military actively helped young athletes pursue Olympic goals once upon a time.

My fellow trainees thought it was very cool that I'd jetted off to compete in the national championships, and they were proud of how I'd done. So were a lot of my immediate superiors. But the reactions weren't universally supportive. There were a couple instructors who didn't back my efforts. I don't know whether they were jealous or just objected to my getting some special treatment. But it made things a bit uncomfortable from time to time.

Although the military largely supported my training and competing and wanted me to win gold while wearing the uniform, not everyone saw what I was doing as being part of the Air Force's mission. Not everyone thought I should be able to pursue both sports and service.

These occasional conflicts arose well into my commercial piloting days, too. Sometimes it's difficult to be visible for something you're good at that many other people aren't; it can make you a target. Turns out, having a talent for something isn't without its downsides.

But I was busy enough that I couldn't spend too much time worrying about how others might be harshly judging my efforts. During pilot training, it was all I could do to keep up with the flying and find even a little time to train at the pool. It took a lot of energy to juggle it all. I simply kept pushing forward.

In the summer of 1963, I won the national championship on the 10-meter platform. It was then that I realized I had a very good shot at going to the Olympics, and I adjusted my Air Force goals to leave behind the idea of becoming a fighter pilot and became a transport pilot instead. That was one of the best moves I ever made, as it changed the whole trajectory of the rest of my life.

That still meant a lot more flight training, and the juggling to fit the diving in around training on the C-130. In September of 1963, the Air Force chose me to go to the Military World Games organized by the International Military Sports Council. More commonly called the Military Olympics, the event was held in Barcelona, Spain, in the same pool where the 1992 Olympics would be staged nearly 30 years later. There, I won the 3-meter and the 10-meter events and felt confident that I was on track to make the actual Olympics in just 12 months' time.

When I got back from Barcelona, I was right back in the cockpit working on tactical training for the C-130. At the same time, I was trying to find the time to practice at Vanderbilt in Nashville or the University of the South in Sewanee, Tennessee. Both pools were more than an hour's drive from the base, and I had to get there to work out on my own time. This hectic pace continued all winter and into the spring of 1964, with occasional competitions thrown in to keep me sharp.

In April of 1964, I competed in the springboard event at the AAU National Championships in Bartlesville, Oklahoma. I happened to come down with the German measles as the competition was kicking off. I was quite ill and didn't perform well. But I started to recover.

There was no 10-meter platform in Bartlesville, so that segment of the competition was set to take place at the Air Force Academy in Colorado, which was the only facility at the time that had an indoor 10-meter platform diving tower. That was important, because the Tokyo Games the following summer would be held in an indoor pool as well, and there's a big difference between diving indoors and outdoors.

Inside, you're dealing with a controlled environment with a ceiling and walls to help serve as visual anchors. When you're diving outside, there's wind that can alter your timing and nothing but clouds and the occasional bird overhead to look at while spinning. It may sound like one is preferable to the other, but they each have their pros and cons. And it takes practice in both environments to get it right.

Upon arrival in Colorado, I was still not well and went to see the Air Force doctor there. He found that my platelet count was very low, and I was internally bruising—an after-effect of having had the measles not long before. He didn't want me competing in the 10-meter platform event; he was worried I'd get seriously hurt. But at the last minute, I got approval to go and dive in the event. That same doctor attended the meet to make sure I was OK.

I did better than OK. I actually won the event.

This ended up earning me an over-dramatized mention in *Sports Illustrated*'s Faces in the Crowd column:

> *Lieut. Tom Gompf, 25, an Air Force pilot and former All-America diver at Ohio State, left the hospital where he was being treated for German measles just long enough to win the National AAU indoor platform diving title at the Air Force Academy, Colo.*

It wasn't quite that sensational, but I did make a quick rebound from a potentially serious illness, no doubt because I was young, fit, and otherwise very healthy.

The *Sports Illustrated* piece did no harm to my reputation either, even if it was a bit overblown!

Additional meets and competitions followed, and by late summer 1964, I was in good standing to compete at the Olympic Trials in Queens, New York. The swimming and diving events were held in the lovely Astoria Pool, an outdoor venue in Flushing Meadows Park. The Trials were staged in conjunction with the New York World's Fair, and all the sports were contested in and around New York that summer. It was quite a big to-do, and sort of a mini-Olympics in its own right.

I had a good meet and finished third, with a score of 806.50, behind Lou Vitucci who earned 825.15 points and Bob Webster who dived beautifully and finished with 826.30 points.

In reporting the results the next day, the *New York Times* called me out, noting that I "won the final berth with the day's most magnificent dive—a three-and-one-half somersault. When the competition had ended, he grabbed his coach, Dick Smith of Phoenix, Ariz., and threw him in the pool. Gompf went along for the bath, too."

It was a joyous day, and I was ecstatic that I had punched my ticket to Tokyo.

What made that day even better was that I was able to celebrate it with my diving friends and my wife. Joyce drove all the way across the country from Arizona with Frank Gorman's wife, Maria, to be there to watch me compete. Maria and Joyce were great friends, and they really enjoyed the road trip to come watch us both make the U.S. Olympic team.

It was so important for me that Joyce was there to see me make good on this dream that she had supported so faithfully and sacrificed so much for. I very much wanted to bring her to Tokyo to see me dive at the Olympics, too, but we couldn't afford her airfare. She was going to watch the Olympics at home in greater Dayton with her parents. That was our plan.

But our extended diving family in Ohio wouldn't hear of it. A whole group of people connected to the YMCA in Dayton where I'd started my career, raised enough money to buy Joyce a roundtrip ticket to Tokyo, so she could be there to watch me compete in person.

I was so humbled that people from my hometown, where I hadn't lived in seven years, would do that for us. It was just an incredible act of kindness that meant the world to us. Dayton is a good place to be from.

Joyce and Lou's fiancée, Joanie, who had been sorority sisters and roommates at OSU, flew over together and shared a hotel room because Joyce couldn't exactly stay with me in the Olympic village. They had fun seeing the sights while Lou and I did our best to be ready for competition.

My date with Olympic destiny took place on Sunday, October 18, 1964, during the finals of the men's 10-meter platform diving event at the Yoyogi National Gymnasium in Tokyo, Japan. It was a state-of-the-art indoor pool with seating for more than 11,000 people. The stands were packed, and the humid air was thick with anticipation, anxiety, hope, fear, and pride. I was more keyed up for that event than I'd ever been for any other competition in all my life.

For years, I'd gone to national championships and accepted the results. Things didn't always come together on the day, but you'd have another shot soon enough.

But with the Olympics, it was "now or never." The four-year cycle of the event can make the crucial difference between optimal condition and being "past your prime." It put a lot of pressure on me that I'd never had before.

That internal sense of pressure was compounded by the weight of expectation I felt. Just about every diver I'd ever admired was on-site watching me compete. Sammy Lee, Dick Smith, Hobie Billingsley, Bob Webster, Dick Kimball, and Frank Gorman—they were all there. And about six of my pilot friends who were on a mission to the Philippines diverted and came by to see the event. The burden of all of their eyeballs, all their hopes and expectations, weighed on me. I didn't want to let them down.

Some of the comments I'd fielded from others in the Air Force and people who weren't on the inside track of the sport got in my head, too. I know they meant well, but a few people said dumb things, like "you've got to do well. This isn't for you. This is for America. We're counting on you."

That's not the sort of encouragement I needed in that moment.

What's more, at the time, I thought that would be the last time I'd ever compete, because after the Games, I planned to retire and just be an Air Force pilot. I think all of that affected my diving.

The pressure was tremendous. But I got up there and took my shot.

All things considered, I had dived pretty well, actually.

In the first several rounds, Italian newcomer Klaus Dibiasi took a comfortable lead. But with two dives to go, he had a less-than-perfect entry on his forward three-and-a-half somersault. That provided an opening for Bob, who answered with a nearly perfect inward two-and-a-half somersault—a dive he was famous for. That super clean and elegant dive pushed him into first place.

It came down to that last dive to decide who would be first and who would be second. Bob nailed it, clinching the gold. Suddenly, the race was between me and Klaus for second. When the tally was finalized, less than one point made the difference.

After two hard-fought rounds of diving, the final standings showed that Bob Webster—the reigning Olympic champion and my friend who dived under the legendary Sammy Lee at Santa Ana Junior College and then transferred to the University of Michigan—had claimed gold for the USA with 148.58 total points. Second came Klaus Dibiasi of Italy with 147.54 total points. And I was third with 146.57 points. It had been such a close event, with all three of us within two points of each other.

I'd earned third place and claimed a bronze medal for myself and the United States of America. I got to stand atop an Olympic podium and hear our glorious national anthem echoing throughout the natatorium. I was proud, absolutely. But the music wasn't being played for me.

The whole experience just seemed a little anticlimactic.

I didn't realize it at the time, but after my Olympic experience ended, I was depressed. I'd just been through this intense experience—one I'd worked for my entire life—and just like that, it was over.

If I'm honest, I was almost a little embarrassed with my bronze medal. Which sounds crazy, I know. But I came very close to winning the gold medal. I just missed it. It was no surprise that Bob Webster won—he'd won the same event in Rome in 1960, after all, and hadn't lost a competition off the 10-meter board since. The expectation was that I would take second. America always took the top two slots.

But this young kid from Italy snuck in there between Bob and me. It was a bit of a shock—prior to 1964, America had more or less owned tower diving. We won everything, and there just wasn't much in the way of star power coming from other countries. Klaus was a sign of how the sport was changing and that eventually other countries would rule the platform.

Klaus was just 17 and pretty new on the scene. He'd been coached by his father, Carlo, and they were both great gentlemen. Klaus was truly a spectacular diver who would go on to become one of the most decorated athletes in the sport and arguably the greatest platform diver the world has ever seen. I finished less than a point behind him, and I had been very much in the hunt for gold, amid some absolutely stellar competition.

But at the time, the loss stung quite a bit. Back then, third place was considered the second loser. It was a different time and people had a different attitude. America should always be the top dog in the Olympics—we were a superpower on the geopolitical stage and that international dominance extended to athletics, too.

Looking back now, I understand that it was actually an enormous triumph—here I was, a kid who'd come from nothing and nobody in western Ohio. I had earned a spot on the podium of the sport's highest stage. But at the time, that success was tinged with a feeling of failure.

On reflection, I came to understand just why my Olympic experience had seemingly left a lot to be desired. It didn't measure up to the expectations I had going in, and it wasn't the idealized sporting event I had anticipated. Helping to fix some of the systemic issues I saw within the sport would eventually spur me on to getting deeply involved in the administrative side of diving.

But in the moment, I did my best to meld back into the rest of my life. When I arrived back at my base in Tennessee after the Games, my commander asked how I did. I don't think anyone in the squadron had watched the proceedings on television. This was before the era of big broadcasts on NBC with the glitz, glamor, and special packaging that makes the Games so appealing to people from all over. Back then, the Games were beamed via satellite around the world in real time. My event went off in the middle of the night, and you probably would have had to hunt for the results in the paper the next day if you wanted to know how I did.

When my commander asked how it went, I said, "Well, I got the bronze medal."

"The bronze medal?" he asked.

"Yeah. Third place."

"If I'd known you were only going to get third, I wouldn't have let you go," he said.

Talk about deflating.

I struggled with this attitude a bit because, on one hand, I sort of agreed with that assessment. I should have gotten first or second.

But on the other hand, I was the third best at something in the world! It would be nice to celebrate that. Maybe just a little?

Indeed, President Lyndon B. Johnson thought I should, and a few weeks after I returned from Tokyo, I received a telegram inviting me to a luncheon at the White House in honor of Olympic medal winners. It's pretty standard now for Olympic and other sports teams to be invited to the White House for a luncheon or a ceremony after a big event like the Super Bowl. But this was the first I'd ever heard of such a thing. It was flattering and exciting to receive a direct invitation from the president.

I almost didn't make it to meet the Commander in Chief, though, mostly because of petty bureaucrats in the military who stood between me and him.

I took the telegram invitation to my squadron commander and showed it to him.

"Commander, I've been invited to the White House for a luncheon with the president," I said. I handed him the paper.

He looked it over, frowned, and looked back up at me. "Well, you can't go."

The luncheon with the president was scheduled for December 1, 1964, which also happened to be the day after a special event where the colonel in charge of Tactical Air Command was coming from another base to ours for what's called "dining in." It's a formal dinner where this commander speaks with everyone, and all the officers pal around with each other. It's a bit of pomp and ceremony, but it's important to be there for the facetime with higher ups.

I was disappointed that I would have to miss the presidential luncheon—being summoned to dine at the White House is one of the more exclusive invitations any one can hope to receive, especially a young man with no pedigree. But pragmatically, I understood that I was needed elsewhere. My squadron commander said I couldn't go, so I figured that was the end of it.

That's the essential foundation of the military—you do what you're told, and there's not much room for discussion.

So, I got on the phone to RSVP to the colonel in Washington who was putting together the event. "I'm sorry to inform you that I will be unable to attend the luncheon with the president," I said.

He went ballistic.

"Lieutenant, don't you have any idea what a request from the president himself means? He's the supreme commander of the military. Any invitation from him is deemed to be a direct order."

I didn't know what to say. I was following my immediate superior's direct order in declining the invitation.

"Let me have your current squadron commander's phone number," he continued. So, I gave it to him, and we hung up.

A few minutes later, I was in the hallway just a little way down from my squadron commander's office and I heard him holler, "GOMPF! Get in here!"

I ran into his office not quite sure what to expect but certain I was in trouble.

He pointed at the chair, so I sat down.

"What did you do?" he bellowed. "You got me right in the shit!"

I hadn't seen that one coming. I thought I was the one in the doghouse after his agitated summons.

"What did you say to the colonel about the luncheon?" he asked.

I explained that all I'd done was RSVP as the telegram instructed me to. "I told the colonel in Washington that I couldn't make the luncheon with the president because of the dining-in here in Tennessee, sir," I shrugged, still confused as to where I'd gone wrong.

My commander glowered.

"You don't understand," he grumbled. "This colonel threatened to have me removed from my position and sent to Vietnam because you're violating a protocol where you have to accept all invitations from the president!"

Unsure of what to say next, I shrank down just a bit in my chair. I had just done what he told me to do, but now, he was visibly upset that I had followed his orders. I wasn't sure how to fix any of that. It occurred to me that all the intricacies of flying a 38-ton plane were far more straightforward than the finer points of military chain of command.

"Sir, I showed you the telegram and I told you I had to RSVP. And I told them I couldn't go," I said as calmly as I could.

"Well, you are gonna go," he said. "We'll arrange special transportation. You are attending the dining-in on Monday evening, and then we'll fly you to Washington for the luncheon on Tuesday."

So that's what I did. I went to the dining-in and met all the officers and then that evening, took a transport flight to Washington.

I checked into the Willard Hotel, a super swanky D.C. institution, located a block from the White House.

We had instructions to wear our Olympic uniforms and assemble in the lobby of the hotel at 11 the next morning to go over to the White House together. So at 11, I was there in my USA track suit, ready to go have lunch with the president.

An Air Force officer approached me. "Lt. Gompf. What are you doing in that uniform?"

"It was in the instructions that I should wear my Olympic uniform," I replied.

He shook his head. "Did you bring your Air Force blues?"

"Yes, I came on a military transport, and I wore them here. They're upstairs in my room."

"Go change into your Air Force uniform," he said. "Quickly," he added.

I hurried back up to my room and got changed. Nothing more was said about it, and we went over to the White House.

During the luncheon, I sat at a table with Lynda Bird Johnson. I still have the menu from that day and a couple of other mementos. But frankly, I wasn't really that impressed with Lynda. She came across as pretentious—she made a big show of using the fingerbowls that seemed like overkill for a bunch of athletes who probably would have been happier with a buffet or burgers—and spent most of the luncheon complaining about her sister, Luci. Clearly, there was a good bit of sibling rivalry at work in their relationship.

Ironically, LBJ showed up late, and we soon found out why. He hurried in, clearly distracted, and made a perfunctory statement about American honor and marvelous athletes or something along those lines before leaving again a short while later. We came to find out that his agitation was related to the mortar attack that had transpired at Bien Hoa Air Base in November. During the attack, the Viet Cong destroyed nearly four dozen aircraft and killed hundreds of U.S. personnel. LBJ had just come from a meeting coordinating retaliation for the attack. Bien Hoa would be decimated during the Tet Offensive in 1968, and it was a flashpoint in southern Vietnam that often saw action.

Nevertheless, the lunch itself was pleasant. It was an enormous honor to be able to meet and mingle with other medalists and get to meet the president and his wife.

After the luncheon, the same Air Force colonel who'd hastened me into my dress blues back at the hotel came up to me and said, "You're going with me and the three other Air Force officers who've won medals."

"Where are we going?" I asked.

"Don't ask questions. Just come with me," he said.

I looked at the other officers who all shrugged in a "beat's me" kind of way. They didn't know either.

We dutifully followed the colonel out to a car that was waiting for us and clambered in. We drove straight along the National Mall, past the Washington Monument and a litany of important-looking buildings. We crossed over the Potomac and soon arrived at the Pentagon. Still bewildered, we dutifully followed the colonel out of the car and into the building. All through that labyrinth of hallways, we followed in silence with no idea what might be awaiting us at the end of this walk.

Finally, we came to a pause outside a door that was marked "Secretary of the Air Force, Eugene M. Zuckert."

A moment later, the door opened, and we walked in. The office was lined with generals, colonels, and other command staff. They were standing in a semi-circle around Eugene Zuckert's desk. He stood up and started reading from a card in his hand.

I don't remember exactly what he said, but the words "meritorious service" and "award" jumped out at me. Turned out, we were being awarded Air Force Commendation Medals.

We were shocked because we had no inclination whatsoever that this would happen.

Zuckert came around the desk and pinned a medal on each of our chests. Up close, he looked ever so slightly like a younger, less rotund Nikita Khrushchev. All the officers shook our hands—and these were important, military big wigs. It was a very big deal.

As fast as that all happened, the important men left the room and we athletes were left standing there dumbfounded, wondering, *now what?*

Another sergeant walked up to us, and asked, "What are your intentions?"

Intentions? Well, I certainly wasn't going to marry his daughter! We didn't exactly have intentions outside of steering clear of any flak. We had to get back to our bases and get back to work.

This sergeant arranged for us to get to the airport and find flights back to where we each needed to be. It was a day replete with strange situations and pervaded by a sense of the not-quite-real. But a proud day all the same.

News about my commendation medal had preceded me to Tennessee, as I found out during the morning meeting the day after I returned from D.C. Every morning we reported at 7:30 a.m. for the commander to make assignments and talk about the missions for the day. That next day, the colonel—the same one who wasn't going to let me go to Washington at first—walked into the briefing with a stack of about eight papers. They were all commendation letters from various levels of the Air Force congratulating and recognizing me for outstanding service.

I still have that stack of letters. And one in particular makes me grin when I recall it. You see, as my commander, this squadron leader, who also happened to be the one who'd told me he wouldn't have let me go to the Games at all if he'd known I would "only" win a bronze medal, was required to attach a letter of his own. He also read it aloud to the squadron that morning, and I'm sure he didn't much care for having to do that. It was mostly platitudes and the party line, but I was struck by the irony of him having to publicly praise me when he'd been so against my diving.

✶ ✶ ✶

I had planned to retire from diving after the Olympics and for the next six or seven months, I put in a lot of flight hours and did all kinds of missions. Our squadron was indirectly involved in the Civil

Rights Movement, including the march on Selma, Alabama. We were on alert and sent to places like Fort Campbell in Kentucky and Pope Air Force Base in North Carolina to be available in case military troops were needed to quell any riots. It amounted to a busy time and many maneuvers as we anticipated that we would likely be sent to Vietnam soon.

As a prelude to my longer period of service in Vietnam, in March of 1965, our unit was sent on temporary duty to Clark Air Base in the Philippines. I had two or three months in early spring of 1965 at Clark, flying missions into and out of the combat zone. It was a short-term assignment, and by the early summer, I was back in Tennessee.

This was good, because Joyce was nearing the end of her pregnancy with our first child, Tim, who would be born in August. After I returned from the Games, we had felt like the timing was good for us to start a family, and Joyce became pregnant a couple months later.

As summer wore on, however, I worried that my Air Force duties might take me away from being there for Tim's birth. My squadron was due to go back on rotation or temporary duty in late summer, about the same time Joyce was due. So, there was a good chance that I would miss the birth. That didn't sit well with me.

But diving provided an opportunity for me to be there. I learned that the AAU National Championships would be held in Maumee, Ohio, just outside of Toledo, in August. The timing and location were beyond perfect to ensure that I could be there when my son arrived. I figured that was my only chance to make sure I wouldn't be deployed at just the wrong time.

I was the reigning national champion and the most recent Olympic bronze medalist in the 10-meter platform event, so it made sense that I would participate in the championships. In July, I contacted the personnel department and asked if I could represent the Air Force in the championships the following month. I also asked for some time off to train, as I hadn't done much diving in the preceding several months.

Though I had considered myself retired from diving after the Olympics, it seems that Fate had conspired to pull me back in. I was excited at the prospect of training for a week or so with Dick Smith in Arizona beforehand and getting back into competition. But more than anything, I was relieved that Luck offered a path for me to be in Ohio at about the same time Tim was expected to arrive.

Joyce went home to Dayton in early August to be with her family while I was in Arizona training with Dick, and a week or so later, I headed up to Toledo for the championship. There, I was just a couple hours' drive from where Joyce was going to have the baby at Wright Patterson Air Force Base. So, with minimal friction, I was able to go back and forth between the pool in Toledo and visiting with Joyce as she neared the end of her pregnancy.

I could compete but still be there for Joyce and Tim. It was the best possible solution and the only way I could be assured of being there when my son was born. Otherwise, who knows what other orders might come down and have me winging my way to another base on the other side of the world on short notice? And it was all courtesy of diving.

I committed to competing in the five-day championship event even though I was not in the greatest shape. I'd not been doing any diving at all since the Games, and I had just seven or eight days of concentrated training to put it all together. It was a tall order, but I was young, and I found that years of hard training and muscle memory kicked in. I was feeling mostly like my old self in short order.

The day before the meet started, I was up on the platform about to execute a practice dive when I was summoned via the PA system to come to the office for an "emergency."

Everyone knew that Joyce was about to go into labor at any moment, so when the call came, the other divers hooted and hollered, celebrating Tim's impending arrival. I ran down to the office to take the phone call I'd been hoping for, and tore out of that pool so fast, I barely even paused to get dressed.

I hustled over to Wright Patterson. I reported to the wing where Joyce was in labor and the doctor said, "It's going to be a while." I was sent to the Bachelor Officers Quarters (the BOQ) where I could wait until they called me back. There was no such thing at that time as the dad being involved in the birth or being in the room during labor. That's not how they did it back then. They thought I would have just been a nuisance and gotten in the way. So, they promised to call me when Tim had arrived.

So, I went to the BOQ and waited. And waited. And waited some more. It was a long labor. Finally, after about 12 anxious hours, I got the call to come meet my new son.

Meeting Tim that first time was one of the most joyous moments I've ever experienced. Better than standing on the podium in Tokyo, better than all the other awards I'd won over the years. I was a dad, and this tiny, perfect baby was ours. Joyce had done an amazing job bringing this new life into the world, and now, we were our very own family. Elation!

Joyce's whole family was there, and she was well tended to, so after some time together as a new family, I went back and competed in the meet. I think I took 6th in the 3-meter, 4th in the 1-meter, and 4th in the 10-meter. Not terrible for someone who hadn't trained a lick in six months and whose wife just had a baby.

My fellow Dick Smith acolyte, Bernie Wrightson, a young and super talented diver, was the talk of that meet. He won both the 1- and 3-meter springboard events for the third year running.

I was less concerned about the meet, and more thrilled I could be there for Joyce and Tim. But my performance there was good enough to punch my ticket for a trip to Europe a week or so later. It seemed I was back on the international diving train, and it felt great to get back to it.

✶ ✶ ✶

A small group of mostly young swimmers and divers was selected after the national championships to represent the United States on a competitive tour in the UK and Western Europe. The team was composed of mostly very young kids—I think the average age of the women was about 18 years old, and the men couldn't have been much higher. I was one of the oldest in the group, at 26.

There were four divers. On the men's side, Keith Russel, a rising star who would compete at the 1968 Games, and I were in attendance. The women were Micki King, who would go on to become one of the most spectacular divers ever and win a gold medal at the 1972 Games in Munich, and Lesley Bush, who took gold in the 10-meter platform in Tokyo. It was a young but talented crew of athletes.

Our first stop was London. We did a little touring there and proceeded to drive on to Cardiff, about three hours west. About 45 minutes outside London, we passed Windsor Castle and marveled at this stately seat of regency, then carried on toward Cardiff.

Once there in the bustling capital of Wales, we got settled in a hotel directly across the street from Cardiff Castle. The Castle sits right at the end of the main commerce streets, and it's very accessible—an unmissable landmark smack in the center of town. The hotel itself was quite posh—so much so that it was frequented by celebrities.

On the morning before the event, we came down to breakfast to find Sophia Loren and Gregory Peck enjoying some coffee and toast. They were shooting the movie *Arabesque* in the area. Gracious and curious about us, they chatted. They wanted to know what this gaggle of young American athletes were doing in Cardiff, and we, of course, were fascinated by them.

We went off to the pool for practice, and afterward, we were permitted to go exploring the city on our own. We were under a strict curfew of 10:30 p.m. because the athletes were so young. I was the old man by comparison—I was in the military and had already served in Vietnam. I was married and had a child. My experience of the world was far different from the 18- and 19-year-olds in the group. But I was still beholden to the curfew, just like everyone else. And that was fine. I didn't have much need to be out all night or to get into (much) trouble.

Still, the chaperons had instructed the group that if it looked like any of us were going to be late for curfew, we should grab a cab and tell the driver to take us back to the hotel across from the castle.

So, I went out that evening and found a pub inhabited by some friendly locals. I fell to talking with them—swapping stories of my life in America and theirs in the UK. The night slipped away as only it can inside the cozy confines of a warm, Welsh pub. Before I knew it, the barman was ringing his bell for last orders shortly before 11 p.m. I'd well missed the curfew.

I hightailed it out of there and ran down to the hotel. In the lobby, I found all the coaches looking rather dour at my lateness.

"Tom, you missed your curfew. What's your excuse?" asked Lyle Draves, a renowned diving coach who was in charge of the divers.

I thought quickly.

"Well, you know how when you said if it looks like you're going to be late, just jump into a cab and tell the driver to take you to the hotel across from the castle?"

Lyle nodded.

"Well, I did that. And would you believe the driver took me toward Windsor Castle? It took me a while to realize he was going to the wrong castle! I asked him to turn around, but by then I was already late." I shrugged and smiled.

The coaches passed a look of confusion between them. Before they had a chance to respond, I bounded up the stairs toward my room with a wink and a wave.

As I was walking away, I could hear them discussing my excuse between them. One rather naïve coach said, "Wow, do you think he really went to Windsor Castle?"

Another responded, "He would have been halfway there to be this late!"

In response, Lyle just laughed and laughed, and the rest of them clued into my tall tale. They let me get away with it, though. I think they appreciated that the rules that made sense for the kids didn't really need to be applied to me. And I'd conjured up a pretty creative excuse to boot.

✶ ✶ ✶

From Wales, we headed onward to the continent, landing in Paris for additional competition events. There, the divers and Lyle and I went to see the Paris Follies, where Larry Griswold was a headline performer. Lyle sent a note backstage to let Larry know we were in the audience. A few minutes later, an usher came and got us. Larry had invited us to watch the show from backstage.

There, we had a perspective on proceedings that we never would have gotten from the seats—we got to see all these show girls coming and going nearly naked, with nothing but feathers in front of them.

Larry brought down the house as per usual, and after his routine, he came over to chat with us. He invited us on an all-night tour of Paris. And when he said "all-night" he meant it. We ended up visiting Les Halles, the massive food market across the Seine from the Cathedral of Notre Dame. There, we had French onion soup at about 5:30 in the morning, a delicious treat made famous by the 1963 movie *Irma La Douce* starring Jack Lemmon and Shirley MacLaine.

The traffic in and out of Les Halles was incredible—the area is well known for its all-night eateries. All these people had been out enjoying the nightlife of Paris and they came in wearing furs and black-tie outfits. They all came to the middle of this antiquated market for drinks and onion soup to cap off the night. And there we were among the glitterati of Paris.

From Paris, it was on to Nice. When we landed, Jack Kelly, an Olympic rowing medalist and the brother of the movie-star-turned-royalty Princess Grace Kelly was there in a convertible. He said, "Tom, come with me."

I was acquainted with Jack Kelly. I'd first met him in 1957 in Philadelphia where I was attending a meet. During one of the early days of diving, he approached Don Harper, who was an Ohio State diving national champion at the time and had really taken me under his wing at OSU. Jack asked him if he and another diver would like to come to his lake home. The idea was for us to perform some dives for Jack's friends as entertainment during a party he was throwing at a lakeside property in New Jersey.

I gladly went along with Don, who was a great friend and an excellent coach. I have no idea where this lake was, just that it was about an hour's drive outside of Philadelphia. When we showed up, sure enough, there were about 50 of Jack's friends with drinks in hand. And there was a three-meter diving board right into the lake.

Don and I performed a routine that included some difficult dives and ended with a series of comedy dives that the crowd loved. After the party, Jack drove us back to the pool where we competed in the national championships. (I would return to that same lake in 1962 for another show for Jack's friends.)

Jack had found out I was touring in Europe and was headed for Monaco with the group. So, he decided he'd pick me up at the airport in Nice so I could do a special exhibition for him and his friends there, too.

While the rest of the team was assembling for photos and collecting their luggage, I took off with Jack and we headed for Monaco and the Monte Carlo Beach Club pool.

When we arrived, I found there was nothing but a 5-meter platform that had no spring to it at all. It was high enough that I could execute some good dives, but I would have preferred either a springboard or a 10-meter. No matter. Jack's friends seemed enthralled with the dives I put together. And Jack certainly seemed to enjoy bragging to them that his friend Tom was able to do all this cool stuff off the platform.

After I'd done a few dives, Jack came over and said, "Tom, come with me. I want you to meet somebody."

So, I followed Jack about halfway down the pool and there was Princess Grace with her children.

"Grace, I want you to meet my friend, Tom."

I was flabbergasted.

"I'm not sure whether I should bow or curtsey," I said. "But it sure is a pleasure to meet you, Princess Grace," I stammered.

"Well, why don't you just sit down and have some ice cream with me?" she said. "I just ordered some for the kids, and we'd love to have you join us."

So that's what I did. I sat down next to royalty in my swimsuit and ate a banana split. People must have been wondering *who's that guy sitting next to the princess?*

Within a few minutes of my polishing off that delicious treat, the whole swimming group, including Micki King and the other divers arrived. Princess Grace gave our girls her cabana to change clothes so they could hop into the pool.

We had a rousing good time, swimming and diving and putting on an impromptu show, observed by royalty, no less.

While we were having fun, Jack said to me, "You know, there's a restaurant on the side of the cliff here that has a balcony that looks like you could dive from into the Mediterranean if you want."

That was all the enticement I needed.

"Sure, why not?" I replied.

We four divers wandered up to the restaurant and climbed out over a railing on the balcony—probably about seven meters above the water—and started to dive.

The waiters came running over protesting, "Stop! Stop! You can't do that!"

Jack Kelly intervened and told them, "These are Olympic divers. They'll be all right."

And thus, we carried on.

We each did about three or four dives as all the café patrons snapped pictures. It probably looked impressive, but at just seven meters, this version of "cliff diving" wasn't that big a challenge. But the restaurant-goers certainly got a heck of a free show they hadn't expected when they sat down to their meals. And Jack loved the little bit of chaos he'd introduced to this otherwise staid Monaco afternoon.

I looked up behind the restaurant. Sure enough, there was another, higher ledge calling to me from there. So, I decided to climb up to the top of the cliff and see if I could get myself into the water from there. Or just into some trouble.

From up there, I found a platform that was probably 55 or 60 feet high. You know me. Being something of a daredevil, I had to do it.

I did a couple dives off the cliff, which really got people's attention. They'd never seen anything like that before. Micki, Keith, and Lesley followed me up there and did some dives, too. I did some somersaults—yes, I was definitely showing off a bit—but it was so much fun.

The next night we did an exhibition swimming show in a competitive swimming pool that the Kellys built for the Principality of Monaco. And of course, they had all the good equipment, with springboards and a 10-meter platform. It had been built in conjunction with some charities that Princes Grace was hosting. She had quite a few celebrities, even some Hollywood stars there, to watch us do our thing. The guests loved the extravaganza.

On our final dive from the 10-meter platform, Keith and I decided we would do a synchronized dive. We ran off together and did side-by-side three-and-a-half somersaults. That absolutely brought the house down. I don't know whether any of the attendees had ever seen synchronized diving before, but their cheers and applause seemed to suggest that they had just seen something out of the ordinary.

We thought we were finished. We took our bows and were ready to leave. But then a man came up to us and said, "Gentlemen, could you please do that last dive again? Princess Grace had turned her head at just the wrong moment and missed the dive. Everyone told her how sensational it was, and she would feel very badly if she didn't get to see it. Would you please do it again?"

And how.

We climbed back up to the 10-meter and did another tandem three-and-a-half somersault to another roar from the crowd. It was such a thrill.

The next day, we were invited to the palace where we were told to bring our swimsuits and enjoy an afternoon by the pool inside the palace grounds.

They had a 1-meter board there, and naturally, we divers began doing our dives. We looked across the pool, and there was Princess Grace with a movie camera taking film of us diving. It was a trip to see the movie star turning the tables and taking pictures of us instead of us taking pictures of her.

Speaking of pictures, Micki and I tried to sneak a picture of Prince Ranier, husband of Princess Grace and ruler of Monaco. He was busy talking to someone else, and I tried to position Micki to the side so we could get him in the same shot. As soon as he saw me with the camera, he came over and said, "May I have your camera?"

Uh-oh. We're in trouble, I thought.

I handed him my camera.

He passed it over to his friend and said, "Here, take a picture of us."

He got in between me and Micki and put his arms around us. We got a photo with the Prince. The Prince! I thought that was really outstanding.

Another famous guest at the party was David Niven. He starred in several popular movies in the 1950s and '60s and was the Pink Panther in the original *Pink Panther* series. He'd also had a career in the military during World War II and was in the secret service.

When I was introduced to him, it was mentioned that I was in Monaco with him at that moment instead of being in Vietnam where I'd been earlier in the summer and would probably be heading back to soon. He was intrigued and had so many questions about my service. I must have spent 15 or 20 minutes talking with him about all that I'd seen while I was flying in Vietnam, and I hadn't even had the bulk of my experience there yet.

At that party, I also met a 19-year-old girl who was a friend of the Kelly family who wanted to be an actress in Paris. She was home visiting her family and attended the party. A dance was planned for later that evening, and Jack wasn't interested in being saddled with this young woman. He had his eye on another girl, so he asked me if I would escort her to the dance.

I hardly knew this girl at all, but I was just trying to be helpful. No sooner had we arrived at the club than she said, "We need to leave."

"What? We just got here!"

"I think my boyfriend is here," she said. "He proposed to me in Paris the other day, and I turned him down. I think he's followed me here."

She grabbed my hand, and we dashed outside and jumped into this tiny Renault car. We took off along the bumpy, cobbled streets.

Her boyfriend spotted her and gave chase in his own similarly small car. We raced through the streets of Monaco trying to ditch him. It was like something out of a movie.

I was quite relieved when she dropped me off at the hotel. I didn't know the jilted boyfriend's intentions. It seemed he was trying to run her off the road; whether to woo or to wound was anyone's guess. In any event, I wanted no part of this drama, despite car chases through the streets of Monaco being a cinema staple at the time.

Many years later, I'd run into Jack Kelly and that young woman again in Montreal where we talked about what a strange evening it had been racing through the famous hills of Monaco—an adventure, indeed.

With the tour of Europe concluded, I went back to Tennessee and spent a week or so with my wife and young son. Then toward the end of October, I went on my second two-plus-month TDY (temporary duty travel) in Southeast Asia.

One day, as I got toward the end of that tour, my squadron commander came to me and said, "Hey Tom. I've got good news and bad news for you."

Oh boy. We'd all come to dread the good-news-bad-news sandwiches that so often got doled out to military men in those days.

"Give me the good news first," I said.

"You'll be home for Christmas!"

That was excellent news, indeed.

"So, what's the bad news?" I asked.

"You'll be back here for a 15-month tour in January," my squadron commander said.

My time for longer service had come.

It seemed unlikely that there'd be much diving for me during a 15-month tour in Southeast Asia, which was OK. I really had intended to retire from competitive diving after Tokyo. Truly, I did. But opportunities kept cropping up. I loved the sport so, and if it wasn't done with me, who was I to refuse its call? Despite being deployed overseas, I managed to continue competing occasionally.

In the summer of 1966, I went back to Tokyo as part of my deployment and while I was there, I looked up my good friend Masamitsu Ogihara, a diver turned businessman. We'd been good friends since I first went to Japan in 1960. I went back for the All-Japan competition in 1961, and again for the Olympics in 1964, so I saw him fairly regularly and we have remained close friends for our entire lives. I don't think a year went by for several decades when I didn't visit with Ogi, and his son and my son are very good friends, too.

While visiting Ogi in 1966, he had a proposition. We were out having a few of beers and he said, "You know in a couple of weeks, there's an All-Japan Championship that's going to be held in the Olympic pool. You should come."

He assured me that I would be welcomed back and that it would be great fun. But I would need a formal invitation for the Air Force to grant me leave to participate.

Well, that was no problem. Ogi had connections. He talked to the Japanese Swim Federation, and they sent a letter to my squadron commander saying how much they would like the Olympic bronze medalist to take part in their championship.

Sure enough, they said I had to go. So, I got a week off and went up to Japan. I tried to get in shape; I hadn't dived much since the summer of 1965. But once I was in Japan, I trained a couple hours a day with Ogi. He wasn't diving anymore, but he coached me. I was training with a group of about 10 young divers called the Tokyo Splashers that Ogi coached. I would demonstrate for them and help them a little bit. They took a liking to me and gave me a patch with their team logo on it.

I had it sewn onto my suit and when I came back to the pool the next day, they were so happy I was diving with their patch on my suit. When it came time for the competition a few days later, they brought all their friends and family and teammates to the pool to watch the American dive in their championship with their Tokyo Splashers patch on. I guess it was just lucky because I put together one of the best lists of dives I've ever done. I won the 3-meter springboard by 69 points.

I didn't win the platform event, though. I had been leading comfortably when it came to an arm-stand dive. I balked on the arm-stand, which cost me two points from each judge. That was just enough of a demotion that I dropped back to second place. The diver who won beat me by one or two points and went on to win the World University Games that year. So, he wasn't a slouch. He was good, and I'd had a couple bad dives. But I did well, considering I hadn't dived much at all over the previous year or so.

It was just another encouragement to return to Japan as often as possible over the years. That sentiment has had a very tangible manifestation since I took part in that first All-Japan championship in 1961. That's when I was awarded a beautiful geisha doll with a parasol—a most unusual prize and something far more meaningful than an ordinary medal.

The geisha stands about a foot tall and is coifed perfectly, dressed in a yellow silk kimono with red trim. Her pink parasol is open, propped casually on one shoulder as she casts a coquettish look over her other shoulder. Her pose suggests she's been caught in mid-stroll in a tranquil garden. Perhaps she's enroute to a tea ceremony.

That doll now stands in a clear museum box to prevent dust and the elements from draining her beauty. She casts her cheerful gaze over my office from atop the credenza, a beneficent artifact of a time well spent and a meaningful memento of a beautiful place that I've returned to over and over. She serves as a reminder of a fascinating culture and the amazingly friendly people I've been lucky enough to build a real connection with.

Chapter Six: The American Dream

"Pilots are a rare kind of human. They leave the ordinary surface of the world, to purify their soul in the sky, and they come down to earth, only after receiving the communion of the infinite."

– *Jose Maria Velasco Ibarra*

Positioned just to the side of the 1-meter springboard at a sparkling Miami hotel pool rose a narrow scaffolding tower about 80 feet tall. In high diving events, the announcers almost always tell the audience it's 100 feet above the water, but honestly, I think this one was a little less. Still, looking up from the edge of the pool to the tiny platform at the top of the tower where I would soon be standing, it seemed so small. Like the platform—and me atop it—could be swallowed up by a passing cloud at any moment.

As I contemplated climbing up, I realized that no matter what the exact height was, there was no denying I'd have a long distance to travel before hitting the water on my way back down. My brain flashed to some equation I'd learned in high school about terminal velocity, and I shook my head to stop the click of cognition. Best not to focus on that just now.

As I climbed hand-over-hand up, up, up the rungs of this narrow ladder to heaven, I felt like I was leaving Earth in some strange way. Once I was standing in relative safety on the petite platform, I glanced down and noticed that the 1-meter board looked like it was directly in the way of the water. How on earth I would be able to dive without hitting it, I wasn't quite sure.

I knew it was possible—I'd seen another diver do it just moments before—but from so far up, the angles skewed, and it looked like certain disaster awaited me if I were to step off this little ledge in any direction. I worried if my hand was even the slightest bit wide of where it needed to be as I neared the water, I'd surely smack the springboard and break every bone in my arm.

But, as I have come to know so well, what goes up must come down.

I paused and took a deep breath to steady my nerves. I set my shoulders, lengthened my spine, and looked straight ahead. From 80 feet above Miami, I could see far out across the ocean. And there, just above the beach, I spied a plane pulling an advertising banner.

I swear, I was looking right into the cockpit. I think I saw the pilot nod to me as he cruised past. I nodded back.

Realistically, I don't see how I could have actually been at eye level with him, but I will forever believe we shared a look that day as I waited for the slight breeze to quiet.

Finally, I exhaled, and burst off the platform, floating for a moment high above Miami.

Soaring.

For an instant, I was utterly free of all earthly bonds.

✳ ✳ ✳

When I left active military service in March 1967 after completing my 15-month tour in Southeast Asia, I immediately began interviewing with commercial airlines. I was lucky to land several interviews straight away, which was good because I didn't have much in the way of savings and needed to start earning a living as soon as possible. I got offers from Northwest, Pan-Am, and Continental, but all had start dates a few months up the road. I would need to enter their training programs, and I would have to wait for the next session to begin later in the summer. I wasn't quite sure how I'd make ends meet in the meanwhile.

I was going to talk with American when I ran into a friend who suggested I interview with Braniff Airlines, a small operation that had been launched in 1928 in Tulsa, Oklahoma, and was by then based in Texas. They had immediate openings in their flight engineer training program.

I went in there on a Friday afternoon and was scheduled to start the following Monday. Done deal.

I spent four months in flight engineer training with Braniff in Dallas. When I completed that training in late July 1967, I was told that it would probably be a few months before I could actually start flying because the company didn't have enough airplanes.

I caught wind that National Airlines, which was based in Miami—a place I really wanted to live—was hiring pilots to go right into the copilot seat rather than starting as a flight engineer. There were about 40 of us who'd gone through the training at Braniff who escaped to Miami to take a co-pilot's job with National Airlines. If I hadn't done that, I would have been sitting on the ground, waiting to be called up by Braniff, where I then would've had to work my way up through the flight engineer seniority list before I could become a copilot. I was concerned about how I'd support myself and my family in the interim, and I didn't want to be away from flying for so long.

A normal routine back then for most airlines was to hire new pilots to start out as flight engineers then move up to first officer, then copilot. After several more years of experience, they could work their way into the left seat as captain.

But National was one of the top six airlines in the country at the time. It was the smallest, but still among the top. They hired professional flight engineers—people who would not seek to advance to the copilot seats. These men were more mechanically oriented and well-suited to the role. They had to have a mechanic's license and be able to perform minor maintenance on the plane.

For the pilot jobs, they wanted a different sort of person. And that was just another instance of lucky timing for me.

Jumping at the National Airlines opportunity turned out to be the best move I ever made. I never spent one single flight behind a flight engineer's panel. I went directly into the right seat of a brand-new Boeing 727; these planes were just coming off the assembly line for National Airlines. A few years later when Pan-Am and National merged, I was higher on the seniority list. And again, when I transitioned to Delta Airlines for the last 8 or 9 years of my career, I was in a prime position to be a top earner and fly the routes I wanted to fly. I was able to go much further in my career as a captain because of that early decision to fly for National. It all worked out perfectly and, not to mention, I was excited to move to Miami.

Starting out with National, I probably flew about 14 days out of the month, which meant I had 16 days off. The pay was very low starting out as a pilot, so I also flew as an Air Force Reserve pilot in a C-124 outfit at the Air Force base in nearby Homestead, Florida.

It was a good deal to remain a reservist with the Air Force. I was paid for all my flights, so with a little effort, I could end up with 10 or 12 days of active reserve flying each month. That greatly helped supplement my small starting salary with National Airlines for the first year or two.

I was also quite grateful to be a reservist when National Airlines' ground service personnel went on strike in 1970. National shut down completely for four months while the negotiations went on, and we pilots were furloughed during that time. It wasn't an unusual occurrence back then—the late '60s and early '70s were a roiling era for workers and labor unions. But I was relieved to have my reserve job to bridge the gap.

As a reservist, I did some interesting flying, going to Trinidad, Bermuda, and the Bahamas. A couple times, I got a week off from work at National so I could fly longer missions to Germany, the Azores, or Madrid.

Most of my flights as a reserve pilot were uneventful, but there were a few interesting excursions. I flew one trip to Bangkok and another that was supposed to go to Saigon to bring back a piece of equipment, so we were going over mostly empty.

We made stops at Travis Air Force Base in California and carried some cargo to Hickam Air Force Base in Hawaii. From there, we went to Wake Island for another stop before heading to Guam. From Guam, we planned to make one more hop to Saigon. We never did make it to Saigon, though, thanks to engine trouble enroute to Guam.

We had gotten to the point of no return between Wake Island and Guam when one of the engine generators failed. We had to shut the engine down, which left us flying on just three engines. Luckily, we were light enough that we could stay up at about 10,000 feet.

The next thing we knew, we lost oil on another engine. We'd been doing OK on three engines, but then we were down to just two. If we'd had a full load, we would have certainly ditched. But because we were mostly empty, I was able to hold the plane at about 4,000-feet altitude. It was still a bad situation, though. I knew that if we had any additional problems, we'd be swimming for sure.

I called ahead to the tower in Guam to let them know what was happening, and an Air Force rescue plane came out and escorted us into Guam.

As with several of the runways I'd faced down in Vietnam, this particular runway was at the top of a steep cliff. It was a bit of a nail-biter, making that landing with just two engines, but we managed to put the plane down without major heartache.

Once we were safely back on the ground, it became clear we'd be stuck for a while. The only way we could leave again would be to have the failed engines repaired or if they could fly another engine out from the States for this old reserve airplane. It wasn't exactly a top priority. So, we waited.

I spent about a week in Guam with some of the other reservists who were getting nervous and complaining that they needed to get back to their day jobs. I was less stressed, though, since National was still on strike. I wasn't in a huge hurry, and in fact, found the down time in Guam to be quite pleasant.

Finally, the Air Force authorized us to fly home on a commercial flight. I really wish I could have stayed longer, though. It was truly a beautiful island paradise.

✶ ✶ ✶

Between 1967 and about 1971, when I wasn't flying, I could be found doing water shows on Miami Beach. My daughter Tracey arrived in 1968 to much joy and fanfare. I was beyond thrilled to add a beautiful baby girl to our growing family. Joyce had again done a stellar job in bringing a perfect being into the world.

But money was still tight. Supporting Joyce and the two kids meant that I needed to sometimes get a little creative in making ends meet. My skills as a diver—and the prevalence of water shows all around the Miami area that would pay me to perform—certainly came in handy.

These shows were often staged by beach clubs and hotels that wanted to show off the glamor of their pool and hotel accommodations as a means of building business. It was a good marketing ploy for them because people loved the shows. And it was a fun way for me to keep diving while earning some cash.

It was at one of these shows in 1970 where I was first approached by a promoter with a proposition that was truly intriguing. He asked me if I'd like to dive in the World Professional High Diving Championships in Montreal. By this, he meant those really tall ladders erected over a pool or natural body of water just deep enough to keep you from killing yourself on the bottom. These were the kind of stunt high diving towers that could be found along the Atlantic City boardwalk and would sometimes have horses going off them. Really crazy stuff, and something I hadn't much thought of doing before.

These ladders reached straight up—truly a type of skyscraper—and at the very top, was a tiny square platform, about 1 foot by 1 foot. You'd get up there, and dive down 80 or 90 or 100 feet into the water below—definitely not for the faint of heart.

I was indeed interested, but I wasn't sure I was up to the challenge.

The promoter suggested we go down to a hotel in Miami Beach where another diver had set up a tower for his exhibitions. That's where I met Barney Cipriani, a renowned acrobat and one of the best high divers the sport has ever known. He didn't let his rumored fear of heights hold him back from tackling dives from towers more than 100 feet tall.

Barney gave me some pointers—such as always climbing up the ladder on the pool side of the scaffold just in case you slip. Landing in the water instead of on concrete or rocks in such an event would mean you'd still get hurt, but you'd have a chance at survival.

After some small talk and orientation around the concept, it was time to give it a try. Looking up at that tower was a bit like the grown-up version of being that small 7-year-old attempting the dive from the 20-foot board at the pool in Dayton more than two decades before. I felt the same tingling invitation, the almost-physical pull of the challenge, mixed with a little bit of trepidation and a whole lot of curiosity.

No way to find out without doing, I told myself. So, I grasped the rails and started climbing. I figured I could always just jump feet-first if it seemed too intense from up there.

I started at about 65 feet. Not so very much higher than some of the dives I'd done in Monaco, and that seemed to go OK. Bit by bit, I edged farther and farther away from the water until I was able to make confident dives from more than 90 feet above the pool. I was so high up, I fancy I could start to see the curve of the earth's horizon from that vantage point.

I told the promoter that with a little bit of practice, I was willing to take part in the championships in Montreal.

To be able to compete there, I needed to complete four dives. One from 70 feet. Another from 80 feet. One more from 90 feet. And the finale from 100 feet. It didn't matter which exact skills divers chose to show off, the degree of difficulty was based solely on the height from which you dived.

Scores for each dive were multiplied by the number of feet. So, if I got a 10 on a dive from 70 feet, I'd get 70 points. And if I did a dive from 80 that was scored a 9, it'd be multiplied by that height, and I'd get 72 points. Even if your dive wasn't quite as clean from the higher platform, the fact that you dived from there earned you some extra points. The aim of this scoring protocol was to incentivize divers to launch from as high up as they could because that meant a better show for spectators.

High diving is a very particular discipline. It's as much like flying as a human being can ever hope to achieve without artificial assistance. Time slows down during one of these colossal dives, and it's the most in tune you can ever fully be with your body, hurtling as it is through the air at about 50 miles per hour. Being off by as little as 5 degrees upon entry can spell disaster. And high divers must always land feet first—that's to avoid breaking your skull and the delicate bones of the neck and spine.

I did a lot of practice dives from 70 feet, but only did the 80-, 90-, and 100-foot dives a handful of times in competition. It was far too easy to get hurt at those higher altitudes, so best to save them for when it would count. And in Montreal it would count alright—more than $10,000 in prize money was at stake. I was highly motivated to do well as I arrived there, still a little green but ready to give this new venture a try.

There were actually two competitions happening—the high diving event and a target diving category—a quirky offshoot of high diving where we'd dive from 70 or 80 feet aiming for a specific point in the water below, which in this case was the middle of a 6-foot ring of balloons on the surface. You'd be scored on the dive, but in order to get full credit, you had to land within the circle of balloons. Sometimes a breeze would push the target in mid-dive, and lining anything up that precisely from 70 or 80 feet up was a supreme challenge.

As in so many other areas of my life, I was well rewarded for having the gumption to give it a go. Even though this championship was my first time competing from above 65 feet, I won both the high diving and the target-diving titles. Barney Cipriani, the Miami diver and acrobat who'd been so gracious helping me find my feet in this discipline, placed fifth.

I took home about $4,000 in prize money, which replaced nearly four months of pay I'd lost to the National Airlines strike. Between my work as a reservist and my pro high diving prize, I came out of that strike having netted more money than I would have had I just been working as a commercial pilot.

In 1971, I, of course, had to return to defend my title, and was again the top athlete in attendance in the high dive. I didn't retain the target title however, as the wind had its way with that flimsy circle of balloons. I had the highest scores on the dive, but I completely missed the target and thus lost points.

No matter, the event was again broadcast on ABC's *Wide World of Sports,* and I again took home a tidy prize. That *Wide World of Sports* broadcast came on just after the University of Miami played Florida State, so it gained a huge viewership in the Miami area. In a short period of time, I got way more attention for this one high diving championship than I ever had for any other championship or even my Olympic bronze medal. It was astounding, and frankly a little embarrassing. But nevertheless, it was an important lesson in the power of television to tell a compelling story.

Even though I got some attention after that event, I figured I was pretty much done with high diving. But I should have known that I was far from through with any aspect of this sport.

A few days after the championship, the same promoter who originally recruited me for the 1970 championship came to me and said, "Tom, we're taking the top six high divers from this world championship to Mexico to compete with the Mexican cliff divers in Acapulco. You're obligated to go because you're the champion, and it's something you should really do."

My first response was negative. "I don't want to do it," I told him. By then, I had started coaching at the University of Miami and was back to flying full-time. I was way, way too busy.

"And number two, I don't know that National Airlines is really gonna like the idea of one of their pilots jumping off the cliffs of Acapulco," I told him.

He sweetened the deal.

"The divers who participate will come down for a week before the cliff diving contest, and we're doing a TV special called the *Aquacade in Acapulco.* It'll be held at the grand opening of the Princess Hotel in Acapulco."

OK, I was listening.

He continued. "In addition to diving in the water show and being paid to be there, I want to rent a couple of your diving boards and a trampoline." The boards I had installed at my lakeside home in Miami were well-known, and I did occasionally rent them out for events. The promoter explained that the hotel in Mexico didn't have the right equipment, "so we'll need to ship yours down and get things organized."

Hmmm. The more he talked, the more I started seeing an ideal, paid vacation.

"So, come down for the Aquacade. You don't have to commit to the cliff diving portion right now. Come down, see what it's all about. But just promise me that you'll think about participating. As the reigning champ in high dive, it just won't be the same if you don't join us on the cliffs," he said.

This guy knew how to close a deal. His pitch was just enough enticement for me to take Joyce for a vacation in Acapulco.

I came to find out that the show's commentators would be Ed McMahon and Tony Randall. McMahon was the announcer for *The Tonight Show Starring Johnny Carson*, and Randall was a highly recognizable movie star. Some of the skits were written and directed by Mel Brooks, the famous Hollywood producer and actor who wrote a lot of hugely popular comic movies like *Blazing Saddles* and *Young Frankenstein*. The famous comedy duo Jerry Stiller and Anne Meara who performed as *Stiller and Meara*, were going to do a couple of comedy skits around the pool, too.

These were big names headlining this show. It was quite a cast and quite a production to be involved with.

Joyce and I turned up in Acapulco and checked into a beautiful room at the hotel. For two or three days, we videotaped some fancy diving and comedy diving segments. It was all very Hollywood with beautiful girls in swimsuits lying on surfboards in a ring near where we were diving.

Some of the skits were hilarious. Mel Brooks wrote a takeoff on a famous Timex ad ("it takes a licking but keeps on ticking") and had a diver launch himself off the third-floor balcony of the hotel into a pool in the lobby bar that had goldfish in it. The trick was the pool was only about 14 inches deep.

This is a very specific and dangerous skill to master in diving, and you have to do a very shallow swan dive in order not to break any bones when doing something as outrageous as this. It's been done a few times by various stunt divers, but the gag here was that when this diver landed, Mel ran over and screamed, "Is it still ticking?"

The diver looked at his watch and says, "Yes. It's still ticking."

"Not that, you fool! Your heart!" Mel would cry to the guffaws of the audience.

It was typical slapstick fare for Mel, and it was silly and exciting to be around all that comedic energy.

But bubbling along in the background of all this fun in the sun with glamourous people was the decision I was going to have to make, and soon, about whether I'd participate in the cliff diving contest. I had certainly done the height before, that wasn't the problem. The part that worried me was the depth of the water.

The lagoon we'd be diving into was rimmed by steep, ochre cliffs. The sea surged in and out of this narrow chasm between two scraggy strands of rocks with each swell. We divers had to very carefully time our take-offs to hit the water when it was highest, so as not to hit the rocky bottom. When a wave rushed in, the landing area was roughly 10 feet deep. When the swell receded, however, it was probably 6 feet or shallower. Not exactly a big margin of error— timing and entry angle had to be just right to avoid catastrophe.

A cohort of local divers knew the cliffs and the water below very well, diving there nearly every day. And they taught me that once the top of the swell passed a certain rock, you had three or four seconds to land in the deepest water. Piece of cake, right? Well, maybe. I was still apprehensive that I would hit the bottom.

Ultimately, I decided to not let fear win outright. I would dive, but not from the ledge most of the divers went from. Instead, I chose to dive from a different spot that seemed a little safer to me because the water beneath was a touch deeper. Most of the local divers didn't like that ledge as much because you'd have to dive farther out to clear the rocks below. It was all about the angle of the cliff's slope in that section. But I was happy to trade a wider leap for an extra 10 feet of water to catch me.

I climbed up to the ledge. Looking down from there, I was reminded of the view from atop that very first high dive I climbed at that pool in Miami. There, the springboard looked to be immediately beneath me and unavoidable. Here, the rocks lining both sides of the lagoon seemed certain to nab me no matter what I did.

Intellectually, I knew there was enough distance between the two sides of this chasm for me to fit into the narrow gap. But optically, it seemed there wasn't enough space for me. Talk about a catch-22; if I pushed out too far, I'd hit the other side. If I jumped too conservatively, I'd hit the rocks immediately below. In either scenario, one slip, and I'd be doomed.

I swallowed hard and watched the water. When the swell hit a spot that seemed right, I pushed off and executed a double somersault with a half twist. I landed cleanly in the deep water. It had been a superlative dive, and I just hoped I could put together the same energy during the actual contest the next day.

But it wasn't to be. There were delays on the morning of the contest, and when I finally got my turn, I didn't quite hit the take-off the way I had the day before. As I was rapidly descending, I felt like I was just a little too close to the cliff. Concerned I'd hit the rocks below, I pulled up short. I avoided injury—despite the fact that I felt like I'd been hit in the rear with a two-by-four from the impact of the water on my backside. The dive wasn't good enough to win the contest, but I was so relived to not have found any jutting rocks or the bottom. I didn't care about the results. I was just glad it was over. I had survived.

That was the sum total of my cliff diving experience. It was an extreme adventure—definitely not for the timid. I'm glad I did it, but I'm also glad I don't ever have to do it again.

As I soon learned though, the television exposure that came from programs like that cliff diving show could open doors for me I hadn't even conceptualized I might want to walk through someday. The expansion of television throughout the '70s brought an ever-bigger audience and appetite for sports commentary and competition. Diving, and in particular some of the more exotic diving events I took part in, filled the growing enthusiasm for engaging programming.

Not long after I returned from the cliffs of Acapulco, I got a call from a production group in New York that wanted my help in creating a 30-minute TV show to promote sensational sporting events. At the time, they had already done one on kiteboarding, and they asked me if I'd put together a show for diving. They wanted to call it *Daredevil Divers*, and it, like others in the docu-series, would be hosted by Julius Boros, a golf star who'd won a number of majors in his career.

I was game for that.

I started out by writing a script where I would take Julius through the University of Miami and explain our diving program and how we worked. I'd show him our training tools and then we'd do some dives from a 10-meter platform. I'd invited a couple high divers I knew from the Miami Beach water show circuit to come demonstrate some dives that I could commentate for the camera. All very well and good—informative and beautiful diving. But it wasn't quite "daredevil" enough to really warrant the title.

So, we went off-roading, amping up the spectacle and the danger quotient.

We headed out to the Julia Tuttle Causeway, a 4.4-mile bridge spanning Biscayne Bay in Miami. It's a major thoroughfare that carries thousands upon thousands of vehicles around the region each day. Trucks, buses, and cars zoomed by as our divers stood on the railing, the breeze created by passing vehicles ruffling their hair. A picture of serene focus under pressure, they each dived cleanly into the water below. Dramatic? Check! Safe? Not entirely, but no one got hurt.

From there, we headed to the Yankee Clipper Pool in Fort Lauderdale for some additional fun. Shaped like a cruise ship, hence the name, the Yankee Clipper has a small pool that reminded me of that hotel in Bangkok where I dived off the top balcony to win a bet. The proximity of the Yankee Clipper's pool to the hotel balconies made it a prime location to put the "daredevil" in *Daredevil Divers.*

The Yankee Clipper pool had the added advantage of an underwater window beneath the bar where the television crew could get footage of the divers as they ripped through the surface and came screeching to a halt before meeting the concrete bottom with their faces.

Several of the divers climbed up to the roof of the building overlooking the pool deck, and the video crew got into position to get a variety of angles to show the full fear-factor involved with jumping from a height of about 50 feet into a pool that's just 10 feet or so deep. It was really quite sensational and what a lark for the divers.

We still weren't finished, though. The final segment of the program had us going back to Acapulco for more cliff diving. It took a while to get the filming date organized around Julius' golfing schedule. But he was slated to be in Acapulco finally, so I flew down and met him at the golf course to travel together with the cameramen to where the local divers congregate.

Cliff diving in Acapulco is traditionally done in front of the El Mirador Hotel, a hotel bar and restaurant built right into the cliffs. We checked in and took video of the divers performing a night show that evening. It's a regular feature to entertain folks in the restaurant, and it's stunning. The divers hold flaming torches as they leap into the inky water below and the overall impression is just breathtaking.

We hadn't bothered to tell anyone we were filming that night, but the next day, we contacted the divers and told them we wanted to capture them doing their thing. But this presented a problem, as they were a somewhat unionized group. They wanted a great deal of money to dive for the television show.

Furthermore, they recognized me from the contest the year before. They knew I could dive from the cliffs, so they added the stipulation that I not do the dives instead of them as a means of bypassing their demands for payment. An unexpected roadblock, for sure.

Undeterred, the producer contacted the Acapulco Tourist Bureau and explained that he was making this astonishing video of Acapulco that was going to show all the features of the beach and the hotels. He expressed how much he wanted to include the cliff divers and his disappointment that they were refusing to participate unless they got an exorbitant amount of money that well exceeded his budget. He was in a bind and needed some help.

Well, we didn't know it at the time, but the Acapulco Tourist Board sponsored the cliff divers, so they had the authority to compel them to perform. And that's exactly what they did. They told the cliff divers they had to do one or two dives for the show for the good of Acapulco and tourism. The board offered them some compensation to smooth the waters.

These guys were usually diving for coins and donations, and I think we ended up paying them about $1,000 for a couple dives.

That was manageable in the budget and a good deal for them, so it worked out in the end. We got some great footage of them plunging.

We had originally intended that I would close out the cliff scene with a dive of my own, as icing on the cake that the "expert" tapped to guide the audience on this journey in flight would seal the deal by participating himself. But because the Acapulco divers specifically stipulated that I not do it in their agreement to be filmed, we had to rework the final scene to cut that out.

As you might expect, I wasn't terribly disappointed to avoid those cliffs. It's a harrowing way to dive. But the production wrapped without further incident, and the 30-minute show aired on a Sunday on national television to good reviews.

That experience and the fact that the show got made at all showed me there was an audience eager to watch diving and an appetite among those viewers for the more extreme diving that I was dabbling in. That planted a seed for me—one I would nurture in coming years as my relationship with diving evolved at the highest level.

As I kid, I was part of an acrobatic tumbling troupe called the "Trampoleteers" that performed a 5-minute routine on national television for a program called Contest Carnival. *The show featured four circus-like acts competing for a shot at a $500, week-long engagement at Atlantic City's Steel Pier. The audience got to select the winner. I was probably 13 years old at the time, and we advanced to the semi-finals but didn't win. We wouldn't have been able to accept the prize, anyway, as it would have terminated our amateur status.*

My high-flying trampoline antics continued throughout high school with various clowning and stunt routines, in addition to competitive trampolining. I found that I loved to perform almost as much as I loved to fly. This photo was taken at the Dayton YMCA during an annual open house exhibition in 1956 or 1957. I was probably 16 or 17 years old.

During my sophomore year of high school, I was on the cover of the school newspaper showing off some early flying skills. This image is from January 8, 1956.

1959-61 Tom Gompf

DIVING/
GYMNASTICS
1959-61
Inducted:1999

Tom Gompf was a true two-sport star for the Buckeyes, winning All-America honors in both diving and gymnastics. A three-time All-America in both, he was runner-up on the three-meter board at the 1959 NCAA Swimming and Diving Championships and National Champion on the trampoline at the NCAA Gymnastics Championships in 1961.

THOMAS GOMPF

I attended The Ohio State University where I was a member of the diving and gymnastics team. I graduated in 1961, and in 1999, I was inducted into their athletics Hall of Fame.

THE OHIO STATE LANTERN

Monday, February 15, 1960

GLIDING GOMPF—Tom Gompf might find some of his flying ability handy in scurrying back and forth from the swimming pool to
the gymnastic court. He doubles for the gymnastic squad and Mike
Peppe's swimmers.
—Dept. of Photography Photo.

I often found myself in The Ohio State Lantern
newspaper after diving and gymnastics meets.

*After graduating from OSU, I served in the Air Force as a pilot, leveraging
my love of flying for service to my country. This photo, taken in 1963, is
about the only photo I have of myself from my time with the USAF.*

When I was stationed in Tennessee with the Air Force, I would sometimes drive to the University of the South in Sewanee to practice diving. Here, I'm diving from the brand new Duraflex springboard that Raymond Rude had just installed, as he and another diver look on.

Bernie Wrightson, a fantastic diver who would go on to earn the gold medal in the 3-meter springboard at the 1968 Olympics in Mexico City, and I share a laugh with our coach, Dick Smith.

This photo was taken in New York just after Lou Vitucci (far left) and I (far right) qualified to represent the United States in diving at the 1964 Tokyo Olympics. In between us are our amazing coaches Ron O'Brien (left) and Mike Peppe (right).

U.S. MENS DIVING 1964 TOKYO
TOM GUMPF, LOU VITTUCCI, BOB WEBSTER, DICK KIMBALL, FRANK GORMAN
KEN SITZBURGER, LARRY ANDRESON

The U.S. Men's Diving Team headed to the 1964 Olympic Games in Tokyo. From left to right: me, Lou Vitucci, Bob Webster, Dick Kimball, Frank Gorman, Ken Sitzberger and Larry Andreasen. We would take home five of the six medals on offer in men's diving at that Olympiad.

This is the only photo I have of myself competing at the 1964 Olympic Games in Tokyo. I earned the bronze medal in the men's 10-meter platform diving event.

During our European exhibition tour in 1965, a few of us divers decided to get a little wild by diving from the deck of a cliff-side restaurant in Monte Carlo. Micki King is alongside me and two other divers as we perform an almost-synchronized cliff dive into the Mediterranean.

During that tour, I also got to meet Princess Grace, who took my picture and offered me ice cream. These are some of the only "glamour photos" I have of myself!

In 1970, I won the World Professional High Diving Championship, held in Montreal. This image was taken as I dived from 70 feet, but I also dived from a height of 100 feet to take first place in the high dive event. I also won the target diving competition.

In 1993, I staged the first World Diving Coaches Clinic in Greece.
My coach, Dick Smith, came to help.

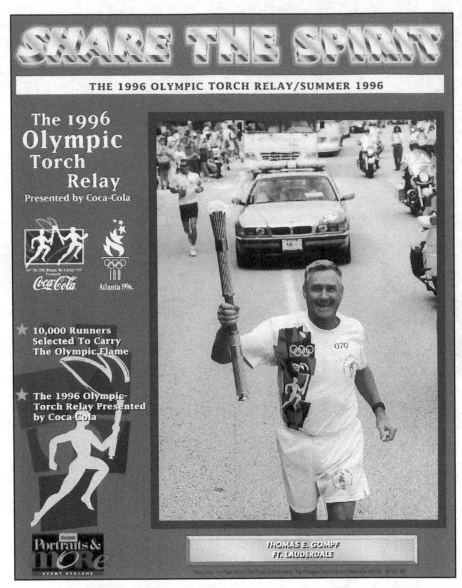

It was a huge honor to be invited to run a leg of the Olympic torch relay in 1996 leading up to the Atlanta Games.

In 2000, after years of lobbying for its inclusion, synchronized diving finally made its Olympic debut in Sydney. Here, I'm walking with the president of FINA and medal bearers to give out the first set of Olympic medals awarded in the sport of synchronized diving.

At the 2004 Olympics in Athens, I led the diving judges out for one of the sessions. Steve McFarland is the taller man standing in the third position behind me.

*Joyce and I enjoyed the competition and
atmosphere in Athens at the 2004 Olympics.*

*In 2010, I was awarded the George Steinbrenner Sports
Leadership Award from the U.S. Olympic Endowment. George's
daughter, Jennifer Steinbrenner-Swindal, made the presentation,
as George had recently passed away. Scott Blackmun, then the
executive director for the U.S. Olympic Committee, is on the right.*

Here are two photos taken about 50 years apart of me and my dear friend Masamitsu Ogihara. We first met in 1961 at the Japanese National Championships and became best friends. The second photo was taken of us in 2010. We both ended up being involved with diving for our entire lives, and hardly a year has gone by since 1961 when we haven't visited. Our sons are now close friends, too.

This is one of my favorite photos of me with my diving family, which was taken at the 2012 London Games. Immediately to my left is my lovely wife, Fran, and next to her is Rosalind Wong and Sammy Lee. Eldon Godfrey and his wife, Carlie-Jean, complete the first row. Behind us are several members of the FINA Technical Diving Committee.

After the diving events concluded, Sammy Lee and I attended a party with the U.S. Diving Team. Here, David Boudia shows off the gold medal he won in the 10-meter platform event, the same event that Sammy won 64 years prior, also in London, during the 1948 Olympic Games.

This image, shot at the 2017 FINA World Championships in Budapest, shows just how tall the high diving towers are. The 10-meter platform doesn't even come up to the halfway point of the tower, jutting out just below the screen and the American flag. The next platform up is the 20-meter platform that female high divers launch from, and above that is the men's 27-meter platform. That's nearly 90 feet in the air!

This photo from summer 2021 shows off the Olympic rings that American divers who qualify for the Olympics get at the end of Trials. Krysta Palmer (right) earned bronze in the women's 3-meter springboard event at the 2020 Tokyo Games. Jian Li You (second from left) was the first women's Olympic diving coach for the U.S., so she got a ring, too. On the far left is Sam Dorman, a University of Miami graduate and silver medalist in the men's synchronized 3-meter springboard event in Rio in 2016. Chris Askin of the Community Foundation of Western Nevada stands between me and Jian Li.

Me with Steve McFarland and Gary Myers—the first two divers I coached at the University of Miami. Here we are in 2021, in front of the 27-meter tower at the International Swimming Hall of Fame pool in Frt Lauderdale, Florida. This is the first permanant 27-meter concrete diving structure in the United States.

Me at the International Swimming Hall of Fame in my
airline uniform, with my Olympic medal behind me.

Chapter Seven: Building a Juggernaut

*"I look back now and realize what a huge thing it was—
that I didn't realize as an 18-year-old—getting scholarship
money. It was very exciting to be part of that as a pioneer,
and it was a really fantastic experience."*

*– Melissa Briley on being the first female to receive a diving
scholarship, awarded in 1974 at the University of Miami*

After my success at the World Professional High Diving Championships in 1970 and 1971, I was suddenly well known in Miami as a diver. As such, it's probably not a surprise that the University of Miami's swimming coach, Bill Diaz, reached out for help in building the program there.

Diaz, who could barely swim a stroke himself but had an extraordinary understanding of swimming mechanics and how to make good athletes faster, had been hired the year before to help revive the floundering aquatics program at the college. Prior to that, the only diving happening at the college had been in the swim team's meet points.

I was delighted to oblige, even though I knew it meant I'd probably have to give up my Air Force reserve flying—and the extra pay it brought—because this would be a volunteer gig. I don't regret that decision at all, because being part of that UM team and working with those divers was one of the happiest and most satisfying periods of my life. Giving back gave me opportunities that opened a whole bunch more doors.

I owe a lot to Bill because he cooperated in every way with me. Often, swimming coaches at other institutions could be territorial about their scholarships, reserving them for the swimmers and being stingy when it came to the divers. But Bill wasn't like that. He wanted the diving program to flourish, and thus gave me the tools and the scholarship money I needed to attract some of the best and brightest divers on the scene. As long as I could make a convincing argument that a certain diver would be able to contribute to the overall success of the program, Bill was happy to let me work.

Early on, I was fortunate to recruit several really wonderful divers, and before I knew it, the University of Miami diving team was chock-full of champions who would go on to great things in the sport and life.

The very first diver I ever recruited was Gary Myers. He wasn't at the top of most college recruiters' lists, but I knew his background, and I was sure he had real talent.

Gary was from Ohio, and there, he had often been outshined by a handful of divers coached by Ron O'Brien. Gary was often overlooked because he was rarely at the top of the podium, but he had a ton of potential; I knew I was getting a superior diver who just wasn't well enough recognized. In Gary's first year of competing, he set our school record for number of points in UM swimming and diving competition, and he held it for some time. He lived up to all my expectations.

One of the most remarkable recruits I brought aboard was Melissa Briley, whose last name is now Mieras. She arrived in the fall of 1974 and was the first female diver to receive an athletic scholarship from any institution in the entire country. UM had anticipated the enactment of Title IX in 1972, which prohibits sex-based discrimination at educational institutions. The university was eager to provide scholarship opportunities to women in sports, and I was thrilled to be able to make an offer that Melissa accepted.

Melissa was perhaps the most acrobatic female diver in the country at the time, and she used that innate athleticism to become a four-time All-American and win four national championships in the 10-meter platform event. She was all but destined to be an Olympian—she was one of the best female platform divers in the world, and in 1976 she dived at the Montreal Games. She absolutely had the talent to win, but it didn't work out for her on that day, and she finished in 7th place. But her beautiful diving skill, acrobatic style, and just generally joyful presence really helped set the tone for the program I was trying to build.

Julie Capps, now Julie Ahlering, was another outstanding recruit to the UM diving program. She placed second at nationals and was a four-year All-American. For two summers before she enrolled at UM, Julie actually stayed at my house in Miami so she could continue training with me. She shared a room with my daughter, Tracey. She's just a lovely person, and she became like a daughter to me.

Greg Garlich arrived from St. Louis in 1973. I had seen him dive in a high school meet and recognized he had exactly what I was looking for in a recruit. Naturally talented, he was just a super diver and probably the best springboard diver I ever coached. He just missed winning a national championship his senior year—he was edged out by one or two points at the very end of the contest. But, he became an All-American at the University of Miami, and in his senior year, he was second in the NCAA 3-meter championship. He was an all-around consistent performer. We could count on him to place in just about every event across all three disciplines, the 1- and 3-meter springboard and the 10-meter platform. I really enjoyed having Greg on my team.

I also recruited Greg Louganis to the University of Miami in 1978. I'd worked with him in 1976 at the Olympics, but he was still in high school at the time. I didn't work as closely with him as some of the other recruits because he came aboard as I was starting to transition out of my head coach role and began focusing more on administrative tasks at other levels of the sport. But he was so enormously talented and a real boon to the UM team. He would soon transcend the sport and become an outright celebrity who brought so much attention to diving with his sheer dominance on the international stage in the 1980s.

Perhaps the most consequential recruit I brought onto the UM squad was Steve McFarland. Steve was a promising young diver who'd gotten his start at Dick Smith's Swim Gym. I remember him as a small kid, just starting out. He was an excellent trampolinist, too, but because the NCAA dropped the sport, he pursued his athletic passions in diving instead. He enrolled at the University of Texas, but I was able to woo him to come to the University of Miami after two years. It was a fortuitous "get."

Steve quickly got to work and won the National AAU 10-meter Championship in 1973. He won it again the following year. He also won bronze at the World University Games in 1974 in the springboard and platform events. He just missed making the Olympic team in 1976.

Steve was an extremely talented diver, but even better, he understood the sport in ways many athletes just don't. He soon began assisting me with coaching the other divers. His calm demeanor and insightful analysis of a diver's strengths and where to make impactful changes really helped deepen our bench of talent. I relied on him heavily to keep things running smoothly when my day job as a pilot prevented me from being poolside.

Steve and so many of the other divers I worked with at the University of Miami became close friends. When you're working that hard together for so many hours over the course of several seasons, you really get to know each other. These athletes sometimes become your best friends. I'm blessed to be able to call so many divers I worked with at UM close friends still to this day. The coach-athlete relationship is a special thing, and one that can last forever with a little tending.

At the University of Miami, we were really just starting out in building the diving program and didn't have much disposable cash to finance fancy equipment or gear. Bill provided as much money as he could out of the coffers, but funds were limited, and we had to get creative in developing solutions to improve our training capacity and quality.

One of the things I really wanted to offer my divers was a foam pit for dry diving. This sort of thing had been used for tumbling and gymnastics, and it's good for helping divers learn new moves—single or double somersaults—with feet-first entries.

The "pit" itself is a thick crash pad that replaces the sand pits of old for dryland practice. It's used with an overhead harness system that prevents divers from landing too hard and getting injured. Divers strap into the harness and a coach or another diver counterweights them as they spin and turn without gravity's interference. The mat is there to soften the feet-first landing. It's an ingenious system that allows divers to build the muscle memory they need for new moves, with no need to dry off, either.

Sometime after I'd graduated from college, Hobie Billingsley and Dick Kimball teamed up to develop the Port-a-Pit, a modular take on the foam pit and overhead safety belt system that would be easy to set up just about anywhere. Dick promoted the Port-a-Pit system quite a bit, and even got at least one decidedly non-diver to try it out very publicly.

In 1972 after Micki King won the gold medal in Munich, she and Dick went on *The Johnny Carson Show* to do an interview about her amazing win. Dick brought the Port-a-Pit on the show, and they strapped Johnny Carson into the harness. With Dick kipping him, they helped him do a back double somersault right on stage. (Kipping is a technique in which a coach guides the athlete to feel the rotation of a new trick.)

If Johnny could be turned into a "diver" right there on stage in a couple minutes, anyone, it seemed, could get the hang of it with the assistance of these clever devices and a little practice.

Both tools really helped the sport of diving advance, and quickly, into a more acrobatic discipline while cutting the risk of injuries. It's not hard to imagine spraining an ankle or worse when practicing dives into a sand pit. But the foam pit and the harness kipping system made it all much, much safer. And frankly, they were a lot of fun, too.

I wanted to get this equipment for my divers, but we just didn't have the budget for it. So, I made my own.

I installed a dryland diving board and a huge canvas bag—bigger than a queen-sized mattress. I filled the bag with foam rubber from old airline seat cushions from my day job. It was way cheaper than buying the manufactured Port-a-Pit. We installed a harness rig so divers could do head-first dives and be suspended so as not to land on their noggins. We used that for several years until we could afford a proper Port-a-Pit.

I also built a trampoline. We found an old frame and built a stanchion to hold that up and had a trampoline and this pit as our dryland training devices long before most coaches had that capacity. It was strictly Hobie, Dick, and Ron O'Brien who had this kind of equipment at that time. Now they're the standard for most programs, and in some places, they've all but replaced water-based workouts. I could take you to a dryland training center in China that has 20 of them in one facility. Here, virtually every university diving program has these dryland training tools on deck now to help divers learn new tricks safely.

With our do-it-yourself version, my divers at UM were able to learn the ropes—or is that harnesses?—of new dives that would help them succeed in the pool and beyond.

My coaching also opened additional Olympic doors for me, in a different capacity than I'd already experienced as an athlete competing in the Games. In 1972, I served as a judge for the diving competition in Munich. There, I was assigned to room with a Russian judge, and we became friends.

But I noticed every day their diving manager and team leader would assemble with their judge and go over all the dives that he was going to see performed in the competition. They had a game plan for their judging—score a little high on the important dives with their divers and a little low with the competitors that would be in contention for medals. Basically, they were plotting to win by finessing the judging.

During the Olympics it became obvious that there was a pattern emerging. This was still the era of "built-in bias," where judges would favor competitors from their own country. And there were people who could be extremely biased in their judging. They would always downgrade their closest rivals and upgrade their own competitors.

I saw this in action again in a major event in Minsk, then part of the Soviet Union and now the capital of Belarus, in March of 1976. The contest was a run up to the Olympics, and all the judges in attendance were on the short list to be judges at the Montreal Games in a few months' time. A lot of strange things happened during that week in Minsk, thanks to the Soviet team's unscrupulous practices.

Individual judges were selected and taken out to be wined and dined with lots of vodka. It wasn't entirely clear what was happening, but I sure was suspicious of some of the dinner invitations I saw being doled out to specific judges.

I soon found out for myself exactly what was going on shortly before we were supposed to go home. I was invited to a meeting. My interpreter said we were going to speak with event organizers about transportation arrangements.

But when I got to the appointed hotel room, there were two gentlemen. One of them was Anatoliy Lariushkin, a Soviet judge who'd been involved with the competition. I didn't know the other man, but I assumed he was a KGB officer. This was a tense period of the Cold War, and I knew the whole time we were in the USSR for the competition, we'd been heavily monitored.

They had caviar, vodka, champagne, and every other Russian specialty laid out as though to receive a king to supper.

Anatoliy welcomed me into the room. "Before you go home, we'd like to have a nice talk and a good social time together," he said.

I sat down and accepted a glass of vodka.

Anatoliy sat down as well and began reminiscing about what a great time he'd had when he'd visited the United States and all the things he saw and did there when he'd visited for a diving event recently. "I hope you've had a similarly great time here. We've tried to accommodate you as best as possible."

He raised his glass to me and took a long swig.

We had a nice chat about the event and Minsk. After a few drinks, Anatoliy asked, "Do you mind if I speak frankly with you?"

"Sure, we're friends," I said. "Go right ahead."

"How do you think the '76 Olympics in Montreal will come out in the diving event?"

"Well, I think Ulrika Knape of Sweden is going to win the women's 10-meter platform event. She's diving very well. And Klaus Dibiasi of Italy won the 1968 and 1972 men's 10-meter platform. He's looking strong, and I think he'll win it again," I replied.

Anatoliy nodded.

"And Phil Boggs won the 1973 and 1975 World Championships, so he's the odds-on favorite to win the 3-meter springboard."

I considered the female contenders in the 3-meter for a moment. "We have a young girl named Jennifer Chandler who's been making great strides and has an excellent chance to win the women's springboard," I added.

Again, Anatoliy nodded.

"Now I will speak frankly," he said in his accented English.

"I think you are correct that Ulrika Knape and Klaus Dibiasi will win. And I think Phil Boggs will have a good chance on the men's 3-meter springboard. But Irina Kalinina should surely win the women's 3-meter springboard. She's by far the best diver in the world today, and she should win the women's 3-meter springboard."

He paused and took another slug of vodka.

"If you will help me assure that she wins the women's 3-meter, I will help you ensure that Phil Boggs wins the men's 3-meter."

I was astounded by the boldness of the request.

"Anatoliy," I said, "I think it's impossible to affect the outcome of the event. Things will happen the way they happen because the FINA Technical Diving Committee will ensure that the best judges will be picked," I explained.

He shook his head. "I think things can be changed."

I was intensely uncomfortable with the turn the conversation had taken and just wanted to get out of there. "I can't even talk about this now," I said, standing up to leave.

"Well, when you want to talk about it, name the time and the place and I'll be there with champagne, vodka, and caviar, and we'll go into further discussion," Anatoliy extended his hand and said goodbye.

I left the room and mulled over what had just happened. I'd been outright asked to fix a diving event. I felt quietly outraged—rigging the event would mean replacing an individual's skill and effort with cynical, nationalistic interest. No, absolutely not. I would not be part of that.

I soon learned that several other judges from Canada, Belgium, Italy, and Sweden had similar encounters with the Soviet team. They were likewise buttered up with the VIP treatment and, I suspected, offered very similar deals.

I reported the conversation to the FINA Technical Diving Committee. They found out the same meeting had occurred with the Canadian judge. Other officials had also made rumblings about how the Soviets were approaching them to build support for Irina Kalinina. The committee assured me they had the issue well in hand and would take care of it. So, I didn't worry too much more about it and got back to coaching my team.

Because of how well my divers were doing at UM, and the fact that I was available for a 30-day summer training camp before the Olympics, I was chosen to be the Olympic team manager for the 1976 Olympic Games in Montreal. Because we only had two official coaches and one manager slot, the manager also assisted as a coach. So, I had managerial and coaching responsibilities at the 1976 Games, and I was pleased to be able to serve in both capacities.

Melissa Briley was poised to do well, and I was keen to support her and to take part in the Games. The '76 Games seemed even more important than usual—we all felt a duty to help reclaim that intangible Olympic spirit that had been brutalized by the terrorist incident at the 1972 Games in Munich. Naturally, security in Montreal had been stepped up, and I think it's safe to say that everyone was eager to have a safe event to help restore faith in the original intent of the Games: to bring the whole world and disparate nations together in a festival celebrating human potential was our goal.

For the most part we succeeded, but there were some problems in 1976, too. Perhaps the best known of these was the doping scandal that emerged out of East Germany.

Later, it was discovered that a state-run, systematic program had created a generation of athletes who were cheating—in many cases without the athletes' knowledge or consent. East Germany, so under the USSR's sway, wanted to win at all costs, and thus had juiced all its athletes. With this steroid-fueled edge, many of them dishonorably topped the podium in many sports—most infamously the women's swim team. The female swimmers looked noticeably masculine as they dominated the pool and cheated clean swimmers like Shirley Babashoff out of multiple gold medals.

It wasn't just substances, though, that were at work. And that conversation I'd had in Minsk would come back to haunt me in Montreal.

The first diving event was the women's 3-meter springboard. Jennifer Chandler won the gold medal for the U.S., which took Kalinina out of the mix straight away. Phil Boggs won the men's 3-meter, and America was off to an excellent start in the diving competition.

It was clear by this outcome that despite the Russians' attempts to fix the judging, none of the other judges had taken the bait. The Soviet attempts at cheating had not been successful, at least for those two events.

Nevertheless, word of the backroom dealings swirled, amid several other improprieties at those Games. Chief among these was a scandal involving pentathlete Boris Onishenko. Turned out, he had wired his épée for the fencing portion of the event to register hits he hadn't actually made on his opponent. There was also some strange stuff going on with the water polo competition and the Russians threatening to pull out when it became clear they weren't going to finish in the top six.

Given all this cheating chatter, an Associated Press writer approached me for comment about the diving competition. The events were already over, so I told him, "There was no fix. We won the events fair and square."

"But I heard they approached you," he pressed.

"Well, I'm not really at liberty to say," I told him. "But I can assure you there was no hanky-panky in the judging. And it came out the way it was supposed to. No fix took place."

"But you're not answering my question," he continued. "Did they approach you about a fix?"

"I'm just telling you what I can," I said.

It was my position that it would be unseemly to complain about the judging after we'd just won both gold medals.

Well, he went off and wrote the story he wanted to write. In it, he reported that I wouldn't agree to the fix but that I had been approached by the Soviets and that they were trying to rig the event. The headlines were all about the cheating scandal rocking the Olympics or something to that effect.

This was a huge embarrassment for me. We'd already won the event. There was no fix, and the judging panel was made up of seven very good judges who were all acquaintances or friends of mine. I worried how they would look at me after that story came out.

I continued to deny that there was a fix in the event because there simply wasn't. But I was also very aware of the fact that the Russians had in fact unsuccessfully tried to tip the scales. I was suspicious of them all along after I watched how they judged the events in Munich and other international competitions over the years.

I wasn't alone in that distrust of the Soviets' desire to win at all costs. Hobie Billingsley once told me a story about making friends with a Russian judge and asking him why he cheated. The judge's response was "How dare you ask me that? I've been to your house, and I've seen how you live. Because I'm a judge in Russia, I live in an apartment with my family that doesn't have to share a bathroom and kitchen with other families. I would have to give all that up if I didn't cooperate. You're asking me to give up my way of life."

It was a strange answer, but that's the truth. Life was rough in the Soviet Union back then. Despite the propaganda, they lacked so much. It didn't make a difference if you were an athlete or a coach, the only way you got ahead was to participate in a corrupt system. They all did what they could to get that edge to get by as comfortably as possible.

This sad story has been borne out in many, many ways over the years as Russia has opened up and people have left and come to the West. And, there's been plenty of ongoing cheating scandals in Russia. Just recently, Russia was banned from international competition for several years for its continued subterfuge that has cheated many hard-working athletes across so many sports.

The news of the Russians' attempted fix landed during the Games in Montreal, and it was in all the papers. Ken Sitzberger and Howard Cosell were doing commentary for ABC's *Wide World of Sports* and asked me to come on the program to address what I'd said and what my position was. I told them I would go on, but I wasn't going to complain about the judging. Ken said that was no problem, they just wanted me to make a statement. So, I went on the program, and Ken asked me about whether the Russians fixed the competition.

"There was no fix," I said. "The results came out the way they were supposed to."

A moment later, Howard Cosell chimed in and said, "Well, he sure has changed his tune from what he said to the press the other day!"

The story had legs, and I even took flak from reporters in Miami who complained that they hadn't gotten an exclusive. Given that they had covered what was happening at the University of Miami and my own diving career for so long, they felt I should have given them the opportunity to break the story. They were really mad at me!

I couldn't win. I also got a little worried there might be repercussions from the Soviets. *Was I safe? Was my family?* It was hard to know for certain just how high emotions might run amid this brouhaha and who all had been involved and in what capacity.

I was relieved that the scandal blew over soon enough, and life went on.

Despite this unpleasantness, being named team manager for the U.S Olympic Diving team in 1976 was a real highlight for me. I've always loved being involved with the Olympics.

✳ ✳ ✳

Another opportunity to give back to the sport of diving would present itself sooner than I realized. Just after the Montreal Olympics, I attended the National Convention where I was nominated by AAU Swimming to be a representative to the board of directors of the U.S. Olympic Committee. My purview was to represent aquatics, and in particular diving, to this esteemed team.

It was a big job, with a lot of responsibility. Before too long, it became obvious to me that I was not going to have the time for coaching I'd had previously. Not only was I doing administrative tasks attending U.S. Olympic Committee meetings, but I was also being promoted to captain with National Airlines. I'd previously had a lot of seniority as a copilot and had a lot of control over my schedule, but once I moved up a rung on the ladder, I had to start over. I found myself working a lot of weekends and holidays as the new captain on the block. What time I did have available, I was working on administrative tasks for the USOC. It got more and more difficult for me to arrange my time to accommodate my coaching duties.

So, we worked it out with Bill Diaz and the athletics department that Steve McFarland and I would flip roles. I had mentored him as well as I could; it was his turn to fly.

He took over for me as the head diving coach at the University of Miami, and I stepped back into an assistant role. Steve was much more available to take care of the team on a day-to-day basis, and frankly, he did a better job as coach than I ever did. He was more available, and he had a real finesse when working with the divers. Under his care, Greg Louganis really blossomed, and the Hurricanes became a major powerhouse in collegiate diving, right up there with the University of Michigan and Ohio State.

I'd launched the program, but under Steve's watch, it became truly outstanding. To this very day, it's one of the most successful diving teams in the country, and I think Steve must be credited with a great deal of that success.

In addition to my getting to participate in growing the sport of diving at a higher level as a coach and through service to the USOC, I also found my expertise in diving was occasionally called on in other situations. One of the more interesting episodes of being tapped as an expert came in the early 1970s, when I received a phone call from a man named Dick Stone. He was a researcher for the Arthur D. Little

Company in Amherst, Massachusetts, and they were investigating the relative safety of diving in pools.

Throughout the 1960s and '70s, the concept of liability and suing for damages after an accident had begun to gain traction, and diving board companies frequently found themselves on the hook for damages. This trend accelerated after a highly publicized 1971 accident in which a teenager named Thomas Hooks became paralyzed at a hotel pool in Washington, D.C.

Hooks was a tall, thin kid who did a dive off the 3-meter board. He didn't have his hands in front of him and hit the bottom. He was left a quadriplegic, and the resulting lawsuit awarded him $7 million, which was quite possibly the largest personal injury award that had been made to an individual at that time.

That set a precedent for other liability lawsuits, and pressure grew for pool owners and diving board companies to improve safety.

It also caused the Sheraton Hotel chain to remove virtually all its diving boards from pools on its properties, which was a real shame. Many an Olympic diver had gotten his start on a hotel diving board, especially in the Miami Beach area. Marshall Wayne is just one example. He won the gold in the Berlin Olympics in 1936 and had used a hotel board for training. Reduced accessibility would be bad for developing American diving talent in the future.

In researching for another diving accident lawsuit, Dick Stone and his team were looking to better understand the forces and effects of bodies in water and how various pool environments might impact the outcome. Dick and his team had conducted a number of studies using photography and expert divers to measure the physics of what we do—the acceleration and forces unleashed in diving from various heights in a variety of scenarios and aquatic environments.

I was certainly interested in helping and had a lot of experience diving from various heights and types of boards, platforms, and ledges into pools of different depths. I'd engaged with all sorts of daredevil stunts that might help them shed light on the physics of making diving safer. And it was just fascinating stuff, so I gladly agreed to work with them.

I didn't know all the details upfront about the case they were working on, but Stone and his team wanted me to be available to testify in support of the defense team prepping for a trial in Boston. The suit involved a first-year medical student at Harvard who'd had a serious diving accident at a hotel pool in Cambridge, Massachusetts.

Apparently, the young man had dived from a half-meter diving board into the pool and hit the bottom where it slopes toward the shallow end. To have landed where he did, he must have done a running dive as far off the end of the board as he could go. When he entered the water, he clearly didn't have his hands up to protect his head as he sped toward the bottom. The impact rendered him a paraplegic, and his family sued the hotel and the diving board manufacturer, citing a faulty pool design as part of the problem.

I went to Boston and sat around at the courthouse in case I'd be called upon to talk about diving and what experiences I'd had in learning to do dives safely and in teaching others to do the same. But I didn't end up testifying; the case was settled just before the trial began. So, I went back to Miami where I continued to assist Dick and his team with conducting additional studies into diving and swimming pool safety.

From those studies came a lot of facts that would go on to be very helpful later, when I was president of USA Diving in the late '80s and early '90s. We used information gleaned during those studies to print a diving safety document that aimed to help protect pool operators and their diving equipment from accidents and the lawsuits that seemed inevitably to follow.

In our studies, we found that bodies actually accelerate upon first entering the water, which seems counterintuitive, but the data bears this out. However, doing just a couple of simple things—such as arching your back, flattening your feet, and turning your hands—can help you tap the brakes and decelerate quickly.

We also found that a diver entering the water at the worst-case angle has to extend at least one third of his body height into the water before water resistance or buoyancy even begins to slow him down. In other words, if a diver dives into the shallow end at a bad angle and doesn't take steps to slow himself, it's almost impossible to avoid hitting the bottom at a dangerous rate of speed.

We also proved definitively that signage—while certainly a useful tool—is often completely overlooked by pool users. Signage alone isn't going to prevent accidents because hardly anyone actually reads the signs or heeds their warnings.

As our work indicated, despite the common perception—and its somewhat daredevil reputation—diving is much safer than a lot of other sports. The risk of a concussion is much lower in diving than in other popular sports, like football, for instance. The recent discovery of traumatic brain injuries and their lasting repercussions in so many football players far outstrips anything we've ever come close to seeing in diving.

What's more, we learned that the very formula insurance companies had long used to determine what to charge for insurance for a board and pool environment was faulty. They lumped a lot of diving accidents into their statistics. They included diving in open water environments—off piers and bridges and the like, which is a lot different than diving into a pool with clear water and a visible bottom. Naturally, diving into murky water is more likely to result in injury and isn't a fair representation of the situation at the vast majority of pools.

In studying all these diving accidents, we found that over 85 percent of the diving accidents transpired outside of a competitive diving environment; it turns out trained competitive divers are at even less risk of an accident than kids playing around on a board because they've been trained how to use the equipment properly. Plus, our studies of the accidents that did occur in the swimming pool showed that 85 percent of those happened in the shallow end, not in the diving well where the boards are located.

With all this research, it became clear that the relative safety and danger of diving in the competitive pool environment with the specifications we recommended was much lower than the insurance companies would have you believe. These findings were significant for USA Diving, which has often struggled to grow access to the sport in the face of continually losing boards after accidents and rising insurance rates making it too expensive for facilities to keep the equipment. We found that there wasn't actually a correlation between competitive diving programming and a higher rate of accidents.

To this day, we still use a lot of the information gleaned from these studies to provide recommendations for diving equipment and how it should be installed. It was important work that I was glad to be able to contribute to, as it helped exonerate diving, which had been laboring under this gathering cloud of liability suspicion that was actually unwarranted.

And that young man who was hurt in that diving accident in the early 1970s? He made it out the other side fairly well, I came to find out later. Turned out, the young man at the center of the Boston trial that started me down this path to better understanding of diving safety was none other than Charles Krauthammer, who became quite famous despite his injuries.

After his accident, Krauthammer completed medical school and became a psychiatrist. He took a job with the Carter administration in the late 1970s and that put him on the road to politics. He became a speechwriter to Walter Mondale and, later, a political pundit who earned a Pulitzer Prize for his column in *The Washington Post*. I had no idea when I was called on to testify in that trial that eventually, that injured young man would become one of my favorite political commentators. But I was glad his accident didn't end up holding him back from achieving great things.

Chapter Eight: All for the Sport

*"Volunteerism is important to any amateur sport,
and I cannot think of anyone who has been a better
volunteer and servant to the sport of diving than Tom."*

– *Todd Smith, president of the USA Diving Foundation, Inc.*

As elite athletes all over America slept peacefully in the early hours of Christmas Eve 1979, a very different scene was unfolding halfway around the world. After more than a year of political upheaval and fighting in Afghanistan, a cohort of some 30,000 Soviet soldiers crossed the border into the war-torn country. When they reached Kabul, they promptly staged a coup that installed a regime loyal to the USSR.

In retaliation for this alarming action, a variety of Western nations demanded that the Soviets pull out of Afghanistan. Sanctions and embargos ensued, and the notion of boycotting the 1980 Olympic Games, slated to be held in Moscow in July and August, began gaining traction.

Those slumbering athletes stateside would soon be caught up in the struggle too, no matter what their political leanings or ideals might have been. Instead of the ascendant dreams of standing on the Olympic podium representing the USA while being crowned the best in the world, a goal they had worked so hard for over the previous three years or a lifetime—that single, far-away military maneuver would turn out to be a nightmare for so many of America's best athletes. They suddenly found themselves pawns in a wholly different sort of global game—a bit of political theater they should never have been involved in.

The Soviets would eventually expend nine years and thousands of lives fighting in the hills and sands of Afghanistan in support of communism, before being forced out in 1989 as their own coalition of states faltered. Many referred to the Soviet occupation of Afghanistan as a quagmire, the USSR's version of the Vietnam War. It likely contributed to the breakup of the previously invincible Soviet Union.

American athletes with Olympic potential in 1979 and early 1980 would also become casualties of this war; President Jimmy Carter's response to the invasion was to boycott the Games in protest. This was a departure from the whole spirit of the ancient Games; history states that the Greeks took a pause during wars to conduct the Olympic Games.

What's more, the U.S. had previously criticized other nations that had boycotted other Games. In 1976, 20 African nations boycotted the Montreal Games because the New Zealand rugby team had played a match in apartheid South Africa. Our delegates berated those African nations for that action, citing the historical ideal of the Olympic movement holding itself far above petty politics. To so soon thereafter be urging our own boycott smacked of a double standard for sure.

What's more, this certainly wasn't the first time that the Soviets had made trouble on the international stage—we had been embroiled in a simmering Cold War for decades, after all. In 1956, the Russians invaded Hungary, but that didn't stop anyone from participating in the Melbourne Olympics. As it turned out, roughly half of the Hungarian squad remained in Australia after the close of those Games, and many of the athletes eventually defected to the United States.

In 1968, the Soviets rolled into Prague to crack down on a budding revolution there, but the Mexico City Games went ahead as scheduled. Several Czechoslovakian athletes who competed there also defected, but despite that, it wasn't the business of the Olympics to intermingle sports and politics.

When Russia invaded Afghanistan, the Carter administration scrambled to find a diplomatic means of hitting back, rather than unleashing a military response. Instead of sending in troops, which Carter knew could well tip off World War III, he instead aimed to hurt the Soviets financially and internationally. Boycotting the Olympics and removing about 25 percent of the athletes from the Games, he reasoned, would result in a financial strain on the event hosts that might help bring them to heel. At least, that was their thinking.

As terrible an idea as it was, the push to boycott gained steam. You can imagine the dissention within the various committees and among the athletes that took place as the boycott talk burgeoned.

During a December USOC board of directors meeting about the plan to boycott, I had to state my case. I stood up and told the adviser, Lloyd Cutler, who was representing the Carter administration, that we had received a poll conducted by NBC that said Olympic athletes—amateur athletes—were held in higher regard than professional athletes. I also pointed out that the Olympics was a wonderful organization that puts ideals before politics. To boycott would be to put all those high principles in jeopardy.

"They hold the USOC in very high regard, and now you're asking us to boycott. How's it going to look to the public if we boycott the Olympics because of something occurring in Afghanistan?" I asked.

"We'll face that when the time comes," was the reply.

There was a lot of political jockeying between that December meeting and the Winter Games in Lake Placid in mid-February 1980. We fully expected the Russian team to come to Lake Placid, and they did. In fact, our hockey team beat theirs in one of the most spectacular games ever played.

Leading up to the Winter Games, members of the White House staff came to Lake Placid and spent weeks soliciting the International Olympic Committee to move the Summer Olympics from Moscow. Some members of the administration used less-than aboveboard tactics, threatening committee members who didn't vote to move the Games from Moscow. But it was too late. Readying a city to host an Olympics is always a multi-year, sometimes decade-long endeavor. The scant few months between those conversations and the July commencement of the Games meant there just wasn't time to relocate the festival to another host city.

In mid-January, President Carter publicly floated the idea of establishing a permanent Olympic site for both the Summer and Winter Games to eliminate any future geopolitical entanglements, but the IOC didn't go for that idea, either. Part of the magic of the Games is how every country has the opportunity to bid to host a

Games. Moving from city to city each time helps involve the whole world in the proceedings.

The 1980 Games were set for Moscow, and there would be no moving them. Thus, political pressure shifted to enforcing an American boycott.

Additionally, some White House folks began threatening Olympic sponsors, including Sears. These companies were told not to sponsor the U.S. Olympic Committee. They were told that supporting us attending the Games in Moscow could have serious repercussions for them commercially. What exactly would happen was never really articulated, but it would certainly not be anything good; the Feds assured the sponsors of that.

Not long after the Winter Games in Lake Placid closed, we had a USOC House of Delegates meeting where we took a vote about whether we would honor the proposed boycott. The U.S. National Governing Bodies convened as a caucus at a meeting in Colorado Springs on the Friday afternoon before the scheduled vote with the rest of the House of Delegates on Saturday. We wanted to review our position and how we were going to vote.

The guest speaker at that Friday meeting was none other than Vice President Walter Mondale. Ours was the largest group that would be participating in the vote the next day and Mondale wanted to make sure we fully understood the administration's preferred course of action.

He came in with the attitude that *you are going to boycott*. He gave a lengthy speech persuading the delegates to vote in favor of the U.S. boycott. Of the many things he said, one section of the speech really stood out:

> *A heavy burden lies on your shoulders. We recognize the enormous price we are asking our athletes to pay. We recognize the tremendous sacrifice we are asking of sports officials. But on behalf of the President of the United States, I assure you that our nation will do everything within its power to ensure the success of the Los Angeles Games; to help the Olympic Committee restore its finances; to provide even greater assistance to the development of amateur sport; and, above all, to recognize the true heroism of our athletes who do not go to Moscow.*

Also astonishing was how Mondale conveyed that the administration saw this boycott as a chance to undo the wrongs of 1936 when the committee had voted to attend Hitler's Olympics in Berlin on the eve of World War II. It was Mondale's position that because the world attended those Games, Hitler was only encouraged to continue down his path toward war.

In fact, historians have often suggested that our attendance of and extraordinary success at the 1936 Games was a highly impactful means of protesting Hitler's hegemony. Consider how Jesse Owens' four gold medals was a very obvious thumbing of the American nose in the Nazis' faces. So much for Hitler's notion of the supremacy of his Aryan race.

And consider as well that there was literally no one in that House of Delegates meeting that day in 1980 who had been involved with the vote in 1936, anyway. It was another time and a previous generation of leadership. That was a different conflict and another era.

Linking this boycott to the 1936 Games and Hitler didn't sit well with some of us. Bud Greenspan—the renowned documentarian who made a slew of films about Olympic athletes, including several divers—stood up in the meeting after Mondale had left. Bud said he couldn't buy what Mondale had said. To me, that was pretty ironic. Here's a Jewish guy who's part of the community that lost the most in World War II and he's saying Mondale's full of it.

Mondale's speech was high-minded and solidly constructed, but there was a fundamental flaw to the administration's stance—a political boycott goes against the Olympic charter. We could be kicked out of the Olympic movement or penalized if we used the term "boycott."

And there was another defect in their argument: the administration couldn't say for certain whether our boycotting the Games would result in even a single life being saved. There was simply no evidence that this action would have any meaningful impact.

Still, Mondale was not swayed. He suggested the White House had the means to prevent our departure to Russia by confiscating passports or cancelling visas—similar to how travel to Cuba was prohibited at the time.

The message was unmistakable: there were a lot of ways the federal government could prevent us from going to the Olympics. But for the optics of it, they wanted us to buy into a boycott and support this proposal.

I was shocked that the vice president of the United States would approach an athletic governing body in such a way the night before our vote on the matter. But I also had to consider the personal repercussions that could stem from this situation. For me as a pilot, I was wholly dependent on having a usable passport. There was just no way around it—to earn my living, I had to have valid credentials to travel.

I was in a tough spot, and I know I wasn't the only one in the room who felt conflicted about what to do. On one hand, as a military veteran, I felt I should follow the orders of the supreme commander of the military. But on the other, I felt I needed to uphold the values of the Olympic movement that I was now obligated to as a member of the USOC's House of Delegates and not mix sports and politics.

After the vice president spoke, the overwhelming sense we had was that it wouldn't matter how we voted, anyway—it was clear the administration was going to prevent us from going in either case.

I was heartsick over this. I'd never been more depressed in my life. It was just an awful, awful situation.

✳ ✳ ✳

As the vote commenced the next morning, I found myself sitting next to my friend Micki King, an astonishing diver who knew well the heartbreak of an Olympic near miss. She'd been leading in the 1968 Games when she hit the board on her second to last dive. The slip cost her the podium and broke her arm. She rallied in 1972 to win gold, but what would have happened if there'd been a boycott that year and she hadn't had the chance to compete? It was an idea that certainly hit home for her and resonated with so many other athletes in attendance.

Micki was head of the Athletes' Advisory Council for the USOC, and they'd come up with a potential solution. Naturally, the athletes wanted to go to Moscow, but they understood the value of standing up to this unsettling move by the Soviets. So, the committee of athletes suggested that they only compete on the condition that the athletes wouldn't stay in Moscow. The idea was they would shuttle in and out from another location, perhaps Frankfurt in West Germany, to compete in their events.

The kicker was the athletes wouldn't stay for the award ceremony—rather they would compete and leave. Imagine an awards ceremony where the top step on the podium was empty—while the America flag rises to the accompaniment of the American national anthem reverberating throughout the natatorium—because the athlete wouldn't endorse the host's politics. It would draw a lot of attention to the issue while still affording athletes the opportunity to compete in the event they had worked so hard to qualify for. The whole world would see that we didn't honor the Soviets by standing on their awards platforms. But it would also show the world that we honored the hard work and sacrifices of our own athletes.

What's more, our athletes wouldn't be spending any money in Russia, which would support the Carter administration's interest in hitting the Soviets financially. We'd be able to shine a spotlight on what Russia was doing, but we wouldn't be penalizing our athletes for something they had nothing to do with and no control over.

The athletes were pretty much 100 percent in support of attending the Olympics, and this plan offered a path to doing so in a way that was compatible with moral authority. To me, this idea seemed like the perfect way to thread the needle.

But the option was never put on the table. The vote was a simple "yea" or "nay" about attending the Games or boycotting them entirely. A group of athletes led by rower Anita DeFrantz even brought suit to assert their right to compete, but the case was dismissed.

Still, when it came time to vote, Micki and I looked at each other and nodded. We were both going to vote to send American athletes to Moscow for the 1980 Games. Neither of us saw any wisdom in punishing American athletes for the Soviet military's bad deeds.

As much as I was concerned about potential blowback that I might suffer from the vote and the conceivable impact to my ability to work given the threats that had been suggested, I had to vote my conscience.

So did Micki, who was in an even more precarious position than me by going against the wishes of the supreme commander. As an Air Force officer, Micki's duty was to follow orders, and any request by the president is typically viewed to be a direct order. Except this one made no sense, was punitive against the wrong group of people, and would not have the intended result. It wasn't the right thing to do, and Micki had to do what she knew to be right. Sadly, she suffered career repercussions for many years because of how she voted.

We delegates voted. Of the 10 aquatic votes that were counted, three of us in total voted against the boycott. Burt Shaw, who was a representative from water polo, also voted against the boycott.

When all the votes were tallied across all the Olympic sports, about 75 percent of the delegates had voted in favor of not attending the Olympic Games. We did not want to say boycott—we knew that was a word that shouldn't be used. But the House of Delegates voted to forgo attending the 1980 Olympic Games in Moscow.

After the count had been announced, U.S. Olympic Committee President Bill Simon said, "OK, the majority says we're not going to go. We can do a recount and give those people who voted to go the opportunity to change their votes so we can show 100 percent support of the president of the United States."

That struck me and a few other people in the room as a stunning statement.

Immediately, Burt Shaw ran to the microphone, and said very gruffly, "I don't care if it's a thousand to one. I'll never change my vote."

We almost all stood up and applauded! Or, at least Micki and I wanted to. It really showed me that Burt Shaw was a man of honor who understood the ethics of doing the right thing. I was glad that he spoke up to stop the revote, because if we'd been coerced to fall in line, that would mean we'd all go home with the shame of having sold out. At least 25 percent of the votes showed that there were some people who thought better of the boycott.

In the end, the die had been cast and 466 American athletes who qualified to compete in the 1980 Moscow Games were denied the opportunity to participate. Some 220 of them never got the chance to compete in an Olympics at all, as they missed qualifying for the 1984 Games for any number of reasons and hadn't made the team in 1976.

The quadrennial cycle of the Games is relentless and sometimes out of sync with an athlete's peak. This cruel fact of time and nature was made even more painful by the leveraging of these athletes' dreams for a high-minded ideal that shouldn't have been negotiated in this forum.

The anguished stories of coming within a fingernail's width of qualifying are far too common among the members of the 1980 U.S. Olympic team, and my heart aches for the lost opportunities those Moscow Games represent.

In the end, the boycott was all for nothing, anyway. As we had suspected, it had no impact on the situation in Afghanistan. Today, even the U.S. State Department acknowledges that the Olympic boycott was a misguided resolution that did absolutely nothing to support the cause of peace. Worse than nothing, it robbed nearly 500 American athletes of their opportunity to shine in international competition. It was a failed endeavor, and it made for a difficult time to be in the mix at the USOC. In retaliation to our boycott of their Games, the Soviet team did not attend our Games in Los Angeles in 1984. The USSR chose revenge against us at the expense of their athletes.

✴ ✴ ✴

The U.S. lost face because of the 1980 boycott, and our representation on the committees that held elections at the Games also suffered because we simply weren't there. We had very little leadership in Olympic sports after the 1980 Games as a direct result of the boycott.

It took a lot of hard work to rebuild our standing in the international sporting community leading up to the 1984 Games in

Los Angeles. We had a tall mountain to climb and not a lot of time to make that course correction. It's amazing how quickly the interim between Olympic festivals can go.

During that period, I continued to serve as a USOC delegate and had a lot of administrative tasks on my plate. I was also again chosen by USA Diving to be the team manager, which was probably one of the most enjoyable experiences in my entire aquatic life.

All of us involved with that Olympic event had our work cut out for us in trying to salvage our esteem in the world of sport, but we figured the best way to do that was by hosting a really great Olympics.

We also faced a financial challenge in preparing for the 1984 Games. Though the city of Los Angeles had voted to host the Games, worries arose about costs. In 1972 and 1976, both Munich and Montreal had experienced considerable cost overruns. And in fact, Denver had won its bid to host the Winter Olympics in 1976 but gave it back because of concerns over costs. If LA were to experience the same types of financial pitfalls other cities had faced in recent quadrennia, it could be ruinous for the city. Thus, a movement grew to renege on the commitment.

But the LA Olympic Organizing Committee, a group of businessmen chaired by Peter Ueberroth, a savvy, LA-based sports executive, stepped in to move things along. This group had connections and convinced some West Coast oil companies to fund the stadium renovation. They got McDonald's to sponsor construction of the Olympic pool. The convenience store chain 7-11 funded construction of the velodrome. Arrangements were made with the University of California Los Angeles, and the University of Southern California to use their dormitories as an Olympic Village, which saved millions in expenses. And a clever commemorative coin marketing campaign netted a heap of revenue, too.

Still, we didn't know how it was all going to play out as the opening ceremonies loomed. I remember very clearly Bill Simon, president of the USOC, standing up during a board of directors meeting just prior to the Games and saying that we might make $30 million. Or we might lose $30 million. With the Soviet-led boycott in full effect, we were poised to either have a sweeping triumph or a crushing defeat with these Games. Such was the uncertainty of how things were going to go.

The LA Olympic Organizing Committee had done a yeoman's job bringing sponsors on board and getting various expenses covered, but ticket sales had been lagging. Ticket sales were expected to contribute a significant portion of the profits projected to be realized by the Games. The eve of the Games was a make-or-break moment. And there was nothing left to do but move forward and find out.

After much negotiation, it was decided that the profits, if there were any, would get divvied up on a percentage basis. The U.S. Olympic Committee and the LA Olympic Organizing Committee decided they would retain 60 percent of any profits to create the LA Olympic Foundation. Anita DeFrantz would become president of that organization.

The remaining 40 percent of profits would go to the USOC, and 20 percent of that split would then be distributed to the national governing bodies. We just had to figure out how we would share that windfall among ourselves, should there be any profit at the end.

Bill Simon appointed a committee to meet during lunch to figure out the split. I was appointed as a member of that committee, and was made the unofficial chairman of the group, which included seven other representatives of other sports' national governing bodies. We went to lunch and discussed the fairest way to distribute any funds, which at the time we expected would be paltry anyway.

The folks representing track and field, of course, felt they should get most of any profit because they're the big guy in town. They got this big stadium, and because they and gymnastics are super popular sports, they'd have more ticket sales. It made sense that those two sports felt like they should take the lion's share of the profits.

There were other suggestions about divvying up the profits based on the number of members each national governing body had, which also made sense. But that formula could get complicated quickly and would leave small sports like diving with little to show for our efforts.

What's more, I had talked with a television producer who told me that diving was always in the top five and sometimes first or second in terms of the number of hours on television. That was likely in part because of the way the prelims and finals played out over several days, but there was no denying that diving was a popular spectator sport that brought people into watching the Games, where they might stick around to see archery, water polo, or another of the less popular sports. The viewers liked it, so shouldn't we get more of the money?

Figuring out how to divvy up this still-uncertain profit was something of a Solomon's dilemma. All sides made good arguments, and there wasn't an obvious right answer—unless you thought about unity and fairness.

It seemed to me that perhaps the best way to split this baby was equally.

"Look," I said to the group. "We're not talking about a great deal of money, and we may even be looking at a loss of $30 million and no profit, anyway. I think we should show that we're united as Olympic sports," especially in light of the Soviet boycott and the nastiness around the 1980 Games.

"What if, rather than creating some complex formula based on membership numbers or viewership hours, we decide that all participating Olympic sports get an equal share of anything that comes down to the NGBs?"

It got quiet around the table for a moment as the other representatives thought over what I was saying.

Straight away, the smaller sports saw the appeal. Handball and synchronized swimming, for example, were thrilled with this plan that would give them an equal share of any earnings as the larger, more powerful sports. The bigger sports like track and field and gymnastics were understandably somewhat less enthusiastic but couldn't deny that there was a certain elegant simplicity to the idea. Establishing the notion that we were in fact the United States of Sports appealed to most of the reps.

Soon, we smaller sports had persuaded the bigger sports to adopt the idea. It wasn't a universally loved idea, but we had enough support to get the plan accepted.

With our profit plan—should there be a profit—in place, it was time to open the Games.

Initially, ticket sales had been lackluster, and we had lingering concerns over how many tickets were left. But once the Games opened, an extraordinary thing happened—local people got swept up in the excitement and the spectacle of the event. It became a huge happening, and suddenly, they started selling out all sorts of events, even the obscure ones like soccer games between two countries that had nothing to do with the United States. It became impossible to get a seat to any event in town.

During nearly all of the events, there wasn't a single empty seat. It was an Olympic happening and by golly, people wanted to go to whatever event they could get into. LA broke every attendance record and certainly showed the world how to host an Olympic Games. I've been to just about every Olympics since LA, and I don't think any of them have reached the high point that LA did.

One of the reasons it was so successful was because we actually addressed the traffic problems that LA is famous for. We created special lanes designated for Olympic traffic and encouraged locals to schedule vacations to create space for the athletes and spectators to move around. And it worked. I could get from Orange County to the Coliseum in 20 or 30 minutes when it might normally take an hour or an hour and a half. I could go from downtown to the pool in a matter of minutes. It was just amazing how well people cooperated to help make the Games run smoothly.

We hosted the most successful Olympic Games in 1984, and it's still held up as the ideal, the model for how a Games should go.

Financially, the Games were also a run-away success, and our gamble about how to share out proceeds ended up being an excellent one for USA Diving. When all was said and done, the Olympics earned a surplus of more than $225 million. Of that total, roughly $30 million was made available to the sports through an arrangement between the LA Organizing Committee and the USOC. This meant that each sport got $1.25 million, which at the time was a huge sum. For us smaller sports, that money meant the world and would help propel us into the next millennium.

As with some other sports, diving created a foundation, the USA Diving Foundation. That seed money has since grown to about $5 million over the past 40 years or so, and helps fund programming, equipment, the national team's expenses, and many other costs related to building the next generation of great American divers. It was really gratifying for me to have been able to set in motion the funding for the foundation.

Those 1984 Los Angeles Games were also a huge triumph for me both personally and professionally. Not only did the Games come off without a hitch, but my whole family was there to support me during it and were able to enjoy the rush of Olympic fever in '84. They had a great time and were able to see a bunch of events. And I had the pride of being able to tell them I had something to do with this amazing festival of human potential and talent that dazzled like gems before us. I stayed in the Olympic Village, but Joyce, Tim, and Tracey stayed in a nearby rented fraternity house with other swimming and diving families who had relatives involved with the Games. Everyone was there, and my kids got to meet top athletes and their families from all over.

Those Los Angeles Games represented a real comeback for the U.S. Olympic movement after the body blow we'd been dealt with the 1980 boycott. We'd made a jubilant pronouncement that despite politics, we knew how to host a stellar Games that truly welcomed the world—in fact, nearly $7 million of the profits were paid out to visiting teams to help defray their expenses.

I still have a full set of the official Olympic International Flag Pin Series that was so popular in that era. Each lapel pin features the mascot of the Games, Sam the Eagle, holding a flag from each nation represented at the Games. It's a collector's item for sure, and a colorful reminder of a welcoming, world-class undertaking that hangs proudly on my office wall.

At every Olympics, the major international governing bodies for sports have their conventions. The international body that oversees the aquatics sports of swimming, diving, artistic swimming and water polo is no different. Fédération Internationale de Natation, better known as simply FINA, also holds elections for the next quadrennial and appoints committee members for various needs at every Games.

Leading up to the 1984 Games, R. Jackson Smith, a former Dartmouth graduate and diver and chairman of the Amateur Athletic Union diving committee, took me under his wing and showed me the ropes in international competition and how FINA operated. He paved the way for me to replace him on the FINA Technical Diving Committee, and during the 1984 Games, I was appointed by the president of FINA to be a member.

That twelve-member group is responsible for all the rules, regulations, judging, and so on for all international competitions— all Olympic and World Championship events. I became a junior member of the committee.

Where diving had given me an identity, diving administration gave me a voice. In 1986, I was elected president of USA Diving. As I progressed deeper into the administration of the sport at these national and international levels, I found ways to raise my voice to advance the sport on several fronts.

First among these was a push to improve how diving was conducted in international competitions. As much fun as I'd had on my many international diving excursions over the years, one stark and unpleasant fact had become increasingly apparent the more competitions I participated in, both as an athlete and a judge.

Judging wasn't always a fair affair.

As I'd experienced during the 1964 Olympics, the final standings in these various international competitions weren't 100 percent down to how well an athlete performed. I saw bribery attempts and blatant bias in many settings.

At one all-Asia competition I attended, for example, there were judges from Japan, Korea, Malaysia, and other Asian countries. The Japanese were by far the best divers in the competition, but the Koreans had a couple of good divers. And when the Korean judge gave a score to a Korean diver that wasn't the highest score, the team manager ran over with a rolled-up newspaper, climbed the judge's chair, and beat him over the head with the newspaper. I couldn't believe it! They were outright expecting the judge to cheat. He gave what he thought was the correct score, and he got clubbed for his integrity!

It was par for the course for that time but something I now held some power to help correct.

Judging can be complicated. There's more to it than just a subjective assessment of how pretty a dive is. Athletes have to show that they're capable of a number of specific skills—that they're adept at the approach and starting position, the takeoff from the platform or springboard, and that they can hold a clean line while in the air and enter the water with minimal splash—if they're going to earn top points. It's a lot to keep track of in the scant few seconds between a diver launching the dive and surfacing after completion.

Keeping track of all this as a judge can be challenging, but over the years, systems have been developed and judges become seasoned in being able to quickly sort the superlative dives from the mediocre ones in ways the average non-diver watching a competition simply can't.

The 1964 Tokyo Games was the first time I'd been exposed to computerized judging analysis. We still do the same type of analysis now—it's the standard required at all events. But it was eye-opening for me then.

After the event, our official showed me the judges' analysis of the 10-meter platform event. Two judges in their combined scores had me in first place. But at the same time, two judges had me dead last out of the top 8. Those two judges hailed from Russia and Mexico. Perhaps not surprisingly, their divers were just behind me in the standings.

The bias seemed so very obvious, and it seemed absurd to me that the scores could be so all over the place when each judge had witnessed the same dive. And the competition ended much closer in points than we felt it really should have been.

The way the judging was handled at the time, there could always be a biased score in the computation; it sure looked like if you had enough friends on the judging panel, you had a better shot at winning. Learning how scores could be tweaked through favor or fortune was a revelation that would galvanize my interest in helping correct some of the inherent bias in the sport when I became part of FINA and the Olympic committee later.

I attended my first meeting as a junior member of the FINA Technical Diving Committee, and luckily I was familiar with all the other members. I'd met them at various world championships and other events they'd attended over the years. I didn't feel like a stranger, and I'd soon be able to call many of them close friends.

But before all that, I had to survive my first meeting as a member of the committee. And there, I made my first move to help standardize and improve how diving is judged at the Olympic level.

I proposed that we write an officials manual, a guidebook essentially, for how to interpret and apply rules and regulations. It would also include a consensus on the important aspects of judging dives. It's still hard for me to believe that no such resource previously existed. But what I was suggesting would be the first officials handbook to give the judges a road map.

Much to my satisfaction, the proposal I made at that first meeting got the green light. Everyone seemed to think it was a sensible idea and a good use of the committee's time to generate this resource. We doled out assignments to various committee members to write pieces of the manual. Because it was my idea, I ended up being in charge, a de facto editor-in-chief, even though we had an official secretary. But the committee wasn't made up of the most technically qualified people to do this kind of work, so I happily shouldered the responsibility of guiding the project and bringing this manual into existence.

Over the next several years, we met regularly and hammered out the specifics. To me, this was so very important. My own Olympic experience had been somewhat marred by the fact that the officiating, judging, and the rules had been questionable. None of these elements were in sync with the sport at the time, and developing this manual was my first attempt to address this systemic problem that was holding the sport back.

That officials manual is still being published by FINA today with very few alterations. There had been some additions as new events have been added over the years, but the baseline product was solid and has stood the test of time—a fact of which I'm very proud.

By the time the 1988 Olympics in Seoul and the FINA Convention rolled around, I was very experienced in the ways of the Technical Diving Committee. I'd shown the sort of leadership qualities needed to head the committee over the previous quadrennial. However, I was still junior, and another member was expected to be appointed chairman, so I was floored when I received the nod.

I didn't campaign for the job—which put me in charge of all World Championships and Olympic Games events—and I really thought that other gentleman would be selected. But in 1986, I'd been elected president of USA Diving, and that gave me some extra stature heading into the '88 Olympics. At the time, we were still top in the world, with Greg Louganis and a lot of other diving stars still competing.

I was excited to have the opportunity, and after that convention, I was well positioned to work on some of my longer-term goals— namely, opening up the books and allowing more complex dives into international competition.

Since my own days competing, I'd been itching to allow more creative dives in Olympic competition. These were the dives I most excelled at, and it was to my detriment when I was coming up as an athlete that the sport was so focused on the staid and clean-line dives that harkened back to an earlier time for the sport. The rules and awards in terms of degree of difficulty just weren't open to creativity in the way trampoline had been.

Those were the rules, but it seemed to me that the rules needed updating. Now that I was leading the Technical Diving Committee, I was able to push the adoption of thoughtful changes to the rules that would support the evolution of diving into a more athletic and entertaining sport.

Up to that point, there was still a pervasive attitude that the basic dives should constitute 50 percent of the points in competition for championships. Divers needed to demonstrate that they had the basic competencies and could perform the simple, elegant dives of old. But there was a very real problem with this approach—crowd apathy. In Seoul, we had about 50 male divers in the preliminaries just doing the simple dives. Spectators began leaving after about an hour and a half. You can only watch so many of the same dive over and over, even if Greg Louganis is in the mix. It got monotonous, and the audience couldn't take it.

By the time we'd advanced to the semi-finals where the far more difficult and more interesting dives start happening, there was hardly anyone left in their seats. They'd been gone for hours. We had to make a change. We had to speed up the boring parts and cut to the more exciting dives as quickly as possible.

It seemed to me the best way to do that was by using the rule book to incentivize more difficult dives. And this could be accomplished by changing the formula by which degree of difficulty was calculated and eliminating the basic dives from the requirement. Instead, let the cream rise to the top by tossing out those boring dives and let divers take on the most complex and challenging stunts they were willing to risk in competition.

Previously, dives had to be pre-approved to be permitted in Olympic competition. But my proposal would allow divers to stage new dives using a simple formula to calculate degree of difficulty, rather than having to usher a particular dive through a lengthy approval process.

I was borrowing from the world of trampoline when I proposed that each additional half somersault and each half twist would add fractions of points to the degree of difficulty. It became an uncomplicated matter of just adding it all up.

With this simple table in hand, a judge could take a list of dives submitted by a diver and quickly calculate the degree of difficulty for each proposed dive. It was a straightforward change that seemed so obvious and utterly necessary to me if the sport of diving were to retain any relevance at all as we hurtled toward the end of the 20th century.

Prior to those changes, a 3.0 degree of difficulty dive was considered the top of the charts. But with this new formula, divers have been able to exceed a 4.0 degree of difficulty on several dives. Daring athletes continue to innovate and break barriers that were once unimaginable, much less attainable.

Similarly, I worked to make arm-stand dives more common occurrences. Prior to my chairmanship of the Technical Diving Committee, arm stand dives were relatively rare. Now, if you want to win a gold medal, you're going to have to get comfortable with leaving the platform from a handstand position at least once during the competition.

However, my push to "open the books" and usher in this greater level of creativity in the sport met with some resistance. About half the members of the Technical Diving Committee hailed from European nations that lagged behind the rest of the world in dominance of diving. As such, they were reluctant to add new dives or allow the degree of difficulty to rise, apparently because they were afraid their own divers wouldn't be competitive. In time, they came around to the notion that advancing the sport would, in the end, be good for everyone. But I have some of my friends and supporters from the Technical Diving Committee to thank for that turnabout.

There are so many people I should name, but two of the committee members I worked with very closely during my time on the FINA Technical Diving Committee in particular really supported my efforts and backed my suggestions. Eldon Godfrey of Canada and Toivo Öhman of Sweden really helped me push through several proposals.

Toivo competed at the 1952 and 1960 Olympics in the 10-meter platform event, and like me, after he concluded his career as an athlete, he moved into administration. An attorney by training, Toivo served as chairman for diving in the European Swimming Federation and as honorary secretary for diving in FINA. He served as my secretary for eight of the years I served on the FINA Technical Diving Committee. He was not only my right-hand man but also became a very dear friend.

In contrast, Eldon was not a diver himself. But his daughter, Allison, was very good. The further she went into the sport, the more her father followed. Eldon had been a football coach and was a competitive golfer, and before long he was coaching, judging, and otherwise assisting the local diving program in Canada. Eventually, he began working with Canada Diving, and as these things do, one volunteer gig led to another, and he wound up serving as my secretary on the Technical Diving Committee for at least four years. He, too, became a very good friend to me.

Both men were instrumental in helping me push through reforms and improvements I hoped to make to the sport of diving. Between the three of us, we came up with a lot of big ideas, but it took the entire 12-member committee to bring about their execution. I'm forever indebted to Eldon, Toivo, and so many other very dedicated committee members I've worked with over the years. Without their support we wouldn't have accomplished much at all. And without their enduring friendships, my life would be far less rich.

Together, we were able to push through a few simple changes to the rules and usher in a new era of innovation and creativity in the sport at the Olympic level.

In addition to leading the FINA Technical Diving Committee and USA Diving, I was also frequently asked to judge diving competitions all around the world, following on from my first major appointment in 1972 as a judge at the Munich Games.

Fast forward to the 1988 Seoul Games. I was sitting in the judge's chair poolside when the unimaginable happened. Greg Louganis began one of his most challenging dives, a reverse two-and-a-half pike off the 3-meter board. But he botched the take off—his hips were too far back as he hurdled at the end of the board, and he didn't get enough thrust away from the edge to fully clear it. As the crown of his head struck the last inch or so of the board, I almost did a back flip right out of my chair.

Anybody's natural urge would be to run over to see if he was OK, but as a judge, I had to stand back and let the drama play out. Ronnie O'Brien, Greg's coach, rushed in. Greg had surfaced straight away and gotten himself out of the pool, and while he had a good cut, it seemed he was going to be OK. He needed three or four stitches to close the wound, but the doctors were able to finish their work in enough time that he could complete his last dive of that preliminary round.

About 30 minutes after the accident, he was back on the board and executed a very good last dive, qualifying him for the finals. He scored well enough to make up for the low scores he got on the previous dive and was in third position heading into the finals.

The next day, he came back and performed magnificently, winning the 3-meter event and gold. Two or three days later, he also won the 10-meter platform event, earning him his fourth gold medal, a most extraordinary result from arguably the best diver the sport has ever known.

As much as I was deeply involved in the administration of diving at the national and international level, I was still flying full time for Pan-Am.[2] Airline travel was changing. And though I was integral to diving's advancement, the evolution of airline travel was totally beyond my control.

When I first started out as a commercial airline pilot, that was still during the glamor era of air travel. Travelers dressed up for their flights, and you got served a nice meal in flight. You'd have cocktails, and it was a special experience. The overhead bins that are now overstuffed with roller-boards were originally designed as coat racks. Flight attendants would come along and neatly fold your jacket or raincoat and stash it overhead.

But things started to change quickly in those early days as costs rose and airlines consolidated. Air travel became less of a luxury and more of a necessity as the world got smaller, and one of the primary issues we pilots had to worry about was potential skyjackings, which became far too common in the late 1960s and early '70s. Often, the hijacker wanted to go to Cuba. Sometimes they wanted to hold the crew for ransom. In either case, it felt like a pervasive and persistent threat.

We pilots had to be ready for that possibility, and security measures adapted to cope with the problem. There was no metal detection until 1973—and it was only instated then because of the all the skyjackings. Crew weren't subject to these checks, though,

2   National Airlines merged with Pan-Am in 1980.

so a few carried guns on board for much of their careers. But our training procedures were to basically do whatever the hijacker wanted unless it was an impossibility, too dangerous, or life-threatening. It was this very training that worked against the crews during 9/11—there was a formula for how to resist nonviolently, and the terrorists exploited their knowledge of that philosophy to horrible ends.

Part of being ready for a possible hijacking meant we pilots were always thinking about places where we could put a plane down in an emergency. For those of us who flew in and out of New York with any regularity, we'd all considered the Hudson River might have to be an option, as Capt. Chesley Sullenberger so famously brought to the world's attention with his own miracle on the Hudson in 2009.

In fact, on one of my first flights out of LaGuardia, during my take off, the captain I was flying with said, "If ever you lose power shortly after takeoff or need to put the plane down right away because you know you're not going to be able to maintain flight, there's only one place you can land. And that's the Hudson River." That stuck with me my whole career, especially when I started flying into and out of New York as my regular route.

I'd been based in Miami from 1967 through about 1985. At that point, for me to move up in pay, prestige, and position, I had to take an assignment to John F. Kennedy Airport in New York where I'd be flying mostly European flights. So, I did.

After taking the New York gig, I frequently flew to Nice in the summer, which was lovely. We had a wonderful hotel right on the ocean, and there were great restaurants and gorgeous weather. The topless approach to sunbathing was not something I had any issue with, either!

I also flew often to Stockholm, Berlin, and Vienna. Some of these flights got further extended to places like India, Pakistan, Kenya, Saudi Arabia, and so forth. It was all very interesting flying to beautiful destinations. I hadn't done a lot of international flying since my days in the military, so it was fun to be back on that long-haul circuit.

Being based in New York didn't necessarily mean that the pilots or flight attendants lived there. Some 90 percent of us were commuters. You'd commute on one of your company's airplanes when you had flights scheduled. As such, I and many of the other New York-based pilots and flight attendants needed temporary quarters in New York—commuter pads, if you will—houses or apartments rented in the New York area and used by more than one crew member.

Sometimes, I'd arrive the night before and stay over if I had an early flight the next day or stay over the night after a flight to be able to catch another flight home the next morning. And if I were flying reserve, I might need to be in New York and on call for four or five days at a time. In all these instances, the house was a great way to get the rest I needed while also getting to spend some time out of the airport and airplane with these other pilot friends.

The group of pilots I chipped in with secured a really nice house in Forest Hills, Queens, which was located conveniently right between LaGuardia Airport and JFK—it was a very easy ride from the house to either airport, and it was also quite close to Flushing Meadows Park where the Olympic Trials had been held in 1964.

There were about 20 of us who shared this home base in New York. We were all older pilots—we'd been on the job for more than 20 years—and we were all ex-military. We were good friends from our National Airlines days and now were flying for Pan-Am.

There was plenty of space for everyone, and we each had our own area. We even had a "honeymoon suite" for pilots whose wives or families joined them in town for one reason or another. We had a fully stocked refrigerator, and a big television and a stereo in the living room—a couple of computers. The dining room was enormous and could seat 10 or 12 people. This all made what would otherwise have been a lot of boring layovers in New York into a throwback to the fraternity houses we'd all lived in during our college days.

Though there were 20 of us on the lease, it was rare that you'd have more than four or five pilots there at a time, because we'd shuttle back to our actual homes in between flights. So it wasn't always wild; there were times when I was there all by myself—just me rattling around in this enormous house.

But sometimes it was a zoo with 10 other pilots hanging out. That's when we would earn our reputation as being the fun house on the block.

When we had more than four or five of us in the house at the same time, we'd appoint somebody to be the head cook. Each one of us had our specialties. One of the pilots made a mean Texas chili. Sometimes we'd have lobsters flown in from Boston on a shuttle flight. We had a barbecue on the deck and could make steaks or chicken or whatever else we fancied.

There were other commuter houses in the neighborhood, too, where crew members from other airlines had similar arrangements. One nearby called the Oddly House had about 20 pilots in it, and a few flight attendants from various airlines had houses in the area. Sometimes when we had several of us in the house, we'd put the word out to these other airline folks that dinner was served at our place, and we might end up with 10 or 12 people for dinner. After the meal, a party would sometimes erupt. That's how our place acquired the nickname the "Animal House."

Well, the house got to be fairly famous. It got to the point where I could hop in a cab at JFK or LaGuardia and tell the driver to take me to the Animal House and he'd know exactly where to go. Our antics even caught the attention of a Hollywood script writer who'd worked on the popular show *Cheers*. He was interested in turning our stories and adventures into a sitcom. But the idea died on the vine. Too bad. I would have liked to have seen what they would have done with my character.

I hope it's obvious that I loved every second of my airline career and was very happy with the path I chose all those years prior in deciding to enter the Air Force and then going on to become a commercial airline pilot.

Across the thousands upon thousands of flights I've piloted over the years, I never resented taking a single one, and the rhythm of travel gave a shape and meaning to my life. It gave me the opportunity to see the world and visit the friends I'd acquired across many years. I cannot imagine a better lifetime occupation.

And in respect to my service to diving, being able to travel cheaply meant I was able to fulfill my duties no matter where on the globe I was required to be. A meeting in Stockholm? No problem. A championship in Sydney? Easy. A clinic in Beijing? See ya there tomorrow.

Even better, I often arrived with family members in tow. I've taken the kids to Vienna and Paris, Guatemala, London, Rio, and Stockholm. I've taken my whole family to Japan, Hong Kong, and Hawaii. I could go on listing various exotic locations, but suffice it to say, we've been everywhere. Together. All thanks to a lifelong love affair with flying that allowed me to have the best career I could possibly imagine for myself.

Chapter Nine: All for the Audience

"After a great career as a diver, he figured out how to become an important international official, which is not an easy thing to do. He's politically skilled and just an absolutely terrific person, always with the best interests of the athletes at heart."

– Peter Diamond, former executive vice president, Olympic programming at NBC

It has been the love of my life to fly, whether up in a jet or down off a diving board. There's just something magnetic about the pull of leaving gravity's authoritative grip and soaring high above the clouds. Turning and twisting, climbing, and swooping. There are many words that can describe the feeling of flight, but few that fully contain my mesmeric drive to fly, whether under my own power or inside an airplane.

I think in some ways, the freedom offered by flight helped me transcend the myriad disappointments we're subject to on the ground.

Growing up, pilots were my heroes. It seemed anyone cool was connected to flight, and I was enthralled with the idea of one day joining the Air Force.

I got my first taste of flying alongside my grandfather, who was a traveling salesman. He had a plane and flew into Dayton to visit my family one day when I was about 9 years old. He took my mother, my brother George, and me in the airplane for a couple hours' ride. It was thrilling, and I thought it was the greatest thing ever. I just couldn't wait to get back into the sky.

Now that I am almost perennially grounded, apart from the odd vacation flight or to attend a diving event, I have found I'm still able to get that sense of gratification from helping others learn to fly and become the best divers they can be. Through revising the rule book to permit more complex dives, championing new events, and working with luminaries in the sport to expand the reach and influence of diving, I have enjoyed the ability to feed my need to fly though service to others.

From 1988 onward, NBC acquired exclusive rights to broadcast the summer Olympic Games. It was an innovative deal that reduced the risk to the network by tying the price paid for broadcasting rights to the income from advertising deals. It was the first time a network had come up with such a formula, which had been devised to help offset Korea's 14-hour time difference from America's East Coast, which cut into the ability of the network to carry events live. There also remained a lingering concern about another boycott that could impact attendance or proceedings in Korea.

But as it worked out, the 1988 Seoul Olympics was a success, and NBC has been home to the summer Olympics ever since. NBC would go on to develop its unique mix of Olympic coverage that really showcases a wide variety of sports to maximum effect for the audience.

As their coverage developed and expanded, it was clear we could do more for diving's home viewers. As I'd learned from Peter Ueberroth during the 1984 Games, diving always was a fan favorite during the Olympics, and it was relatively easy to televise. Unlike some sports that cover great distances or can seem boring or confusing, with diving, there are brief bursts of speed, excitement, and daring that can make for great television if you're able to harness the right camera angles and storylines.

As head of the FINA Technical Diving Committee from 1988 onward, it fell to me to work with Peter Diamond—the lead programming executive at NBC tasked with bringing the Olympics to the world via television—to develop their coverage of our sport. In the lead-up to the 1992 Games, we collaborated to best leverage diving's innate beauty and fear factor to elevate the profile of the sport. The viewer value is tremendous for diving, and Peter knew this. The key was finding the right places to put the cameras to capture the best elements of each dive and diver's process.

I always advocated that the primary angle for television cameras should be the same as what the judges see. Rather than giving audiences a front or aerial view that might clearly show the diver and his work, it made more sense to me to allow viewers to sit in the judge's chair and see what they saw. That's the only way viewers would ever be able to appreciate how the scores came out.

This really became apparent in Munich where the broadcasters set up a front-quartering view of the divers and the commentators' critiques of the dives were based on these views. But this was not the same as what the judges were seeing. It put judges under unnecessary pressure and opened them up to criticism that wasn't warranted. A commentator might muse, *I wonder why the judge didn't see that split in his tuck,* which would have been so obvious from the broadcaster and television audience's point of view, but completely invisible from where the judges sat.

We had to get the camera angles right, and I worked closely with NBC and Peter to make sure to deliver that and help the commentators put each dive in context while showing the extreme talent of the athletes at the very top of their game.

The Barcelona Games provided the proving ground for finding the right balance of camera angles and approach to televising diving in a viewer-pleasing way. But it wasn't without challenges.

In Barcelona, there were three 3-meter boards positioned side by side, and having all three in use for the competition would make for lousy home viewing. It took some figuring, but ultimately, we designated one of the 3-meter boards for training only and the other two were for competition. To this day, that's the approach used whenever there are three diving boards side by side.

Another issue was that the placement of the 10-meter tower also blocked the preferred angle for positioning the camera for filming divers on the 3-meter board from the judges' angle. The way that pool was configured, placing a television camera and crew in the best position would interfere with proceedings and potentially block the judges' view. So, we had to find another way to give the audience at home a prime window to see the action. With a little creativity and a few false starts, we finally found just the right spots to place cameras in that venue.

In finding the most television-friendly angles and views, we not only made the 1992 Games a visually stunning success, but we also learned how to best showcase diving for future venues.

As anyone who watched the 1992 Games on television will probably concur, we really nailed it in photographing the divers at the Barcelona Games. We had the venue itself to thank for some of this, as the pool overlooked the city and divers standing on the 10-meter platform executed their craft with a stunning vista of a beautiful city on full display behind them.

✷ ✷ ✷

A few weeks after the Barcelona Games closed, Hurricane Andrew barreled through Florida, leaving a wide swath of destruction in its wake. I barely made it home from a trip to Helsinki, Finland, before the storm hit. I landed in Orlando around midnight and headed south to my home in Miami. I never saw another car driving southbound for 200 miles—everyone was headed away from the storm.

The tempest made landfall just a couple hours after I'd arrived home, at about 5 a.m. on Monday, August 24, 1992. By then it had ballooned to a Category 5 hurricane, and it tore through the southern part of Miami where my house was located. I don't think I'll ever forget the clamor of that ferocious wind. Like most people who've ridden out a hurricane say, it's a haunting sound that stays with you forever.

The next morning, there were trees down all over the neighborhood. I had to drive through a lime grove to get out to another road where I could find passable streets. Once I was out, I took movies of cars flipped upside down and huge concrete poles broken like strands of spaghetti. Whole trailer parks had been wiped out, leaving nothing but concrete stubs where the mobile homes' foundations had been. Every streetlamp and traffic light was down, and there were wires everywhere. The area was unrecognizable.

Miami hadn't had a hurricane for about 25 years prior to Andrew, and all the unimpeded growth of vegetation that had occurred over those two and a half decades had been leveled to stumps in just a few hours. The way the trees fell made it look like a bomb had gone off.

My house withstood the assault fairly well, except the wind peeled the roofing off so I suffered some water damage. It wrecked the swimming pool and destroyed a stable I had in the backyard. It was pretty bad. But mercifully, we didn't lose everything. Again, it seemed I was in Luck's good books.

Within a week, we'd moved to a house in Fort Lauderdale, and I dealt with the damage from there. The insurance paid out well enough, and we moved on. We actually ended up building a house in Fort Lauderdale in 1993, and I never did move back to Miami after Hurricane Andrew.

I've read that many people who were living in South Florida at the time have since divided the way they think about their lives into the "before Andrew" and "after Andrew" periods. And when you lose everything like that, it's truly unimaginable. You have to live through the experience to truly understand it. We were lucky that our losses weren't as devastating as some of our neighbors'. But the storm forced change on us all the same, and we had to adapt.

In that difficult period, my diving family came to my aid. I went to a FINA Technical Diving Committee meeting in Egypt in the fall of 1992 and there, the Japanese representative handed me an envelope full of money. The Japanese diving community had collected a sizeable sum to help me out after the storm. I really didn't need the money, but they insisted I take it. I just couldn't believe that my friends from Japan were so kind to contribute those funds to me and my family. It was amazingly thoughtful, and I was awed and humbled by their generosity.

✱ ✱ ✱

Over the past several decades, the world has become an ever more visually-driven place, with imagery permeating all aspects of everyday life in ways I couldn't even have imagined as a child. I can remember the impact that one photograph—the Marines raising the flag at Iwo Jima had—because a skilled cameraman was in the right place at just the right moment. Today, it seems that virtually every last person has a very good camera in their pocket, and the proliferation of photos has grown alongside that ubiquity.

The escalation in demand for more visual presentations of sports and the advent of social media platforms means that the Olympics—the pinnacle of athletic achievement—has to have the best visuals, period. NBC has understood this from the beginning of its coverage of the Olympics, and Peter Diamond and his team have placed the utmost emphasis on disseminating the stories of the Games while leveraging the ever-evolving cutting edge of visual technology.

Once NBC became the primary home of the Olympics, they have only improved and expanded their ability to showcase the raw and beautiful athletic prowess on display at each Olympics and many other international competitions. I was proud to have played a small part in making diving a more viewer-friendly sport.

When we were preparing for the 1992 Games, I attended a worldwide TV consortium in Barcelona to discuss the best way of presenting all the Olympic events. Everybody was there—all the vice presidents and the heads of sports departments of all the networks—ESPN, NBC, ABC and so on. There were representatives from the sports, too, and I was there on behalf of diving. During the meeting, we discussed the best ways to show diving and whether there were any developments that would help aid us in televising the Games.

That conversation would become an ongoing one, and in advance of the Atlanta Games in 1996, a new technology really expanded the ability of television cameras to put viewers in the action, by literally bringing them along for the dive.

In the past, the camera had been mounted on a stable platform or affixed to the diving tower somehow. This was often done in such a way that you'd get basic photography where the viewers would be able to see different elements of the dive—a view from the board, a side shot as the diver twisted and turned, and possibly a finishing image with the diver half in and half out of the water. But as we'd discussed in that Barcelona meeting, if there were a way to follow the diver along the whole dive and even down into the water to see what they do after breaking the surface, that would be phenomenal.

As it turned out, Garrett Brown, a filmmaker and inventor, was also in attendance and was listening intently to our discussion. He had recently invented a miniature camera that he could pull on cables along the bottom of the pool to watch the swimmers from underwater, an innovation that offered a whole new viewpoint on aquatic events. Being able to watch swimmers race from a fish's perspective made for much more exciting and instructional viewing for the audience. We got to talking and decided there had to be a way to adapt this new technology for diving.

He took my advice about the best angles to see divers from and adapted his camera system to our needs, creating a device called the DiveCam. It's a small camera slipped inside a hollow, glass tube. A camera operator pulls the camera up before the diver launches, and then drops it down to follow the diver all the way into the water.

He brought that camera rig to Atlanta in 1996, but because the ceiling in the natatorium there was 120 feet high, the camera system couldn't be installed the way we'd envisioned. To operate it in such a big space, we'd need to have a cameraman manually operating the drop, and he'd be standing right in the way of the judges' line of sight. So while it was the greatest idea going, it simply wasn't going to fly.

We had to come up with another plan.

With a little more thought and looking around at the set-up in Atlanta, we finally settled on installing the tube at the back of the 7.5-meter platform, which isn't used in competition. That's a platform used in training to help divers transition from the 3-meter springboard to the 10-meter platform, and during an international competition, it would remain empty. This offered the camera operator a place to stand where he wouldn't be seen by the judges or the divers but could still get killer shots of all the action.

When the diver was getting ready for the dive, he could draw the camera up to get a good face shot. Other cameras could splice in other angles to show the diver from front and back readying to dive. And when the diver took off, the DiveCam would follow him right up into the air, then zip down and into the water right on pace with the diver so the audience can see every detail of the dive in action. The final product wasn't exactly what I was hoping for, but nevertheless, it was nothing short of groundbreaking. This innovative solution brought viewers closer to the sport than they'd ever been before.

When this technology debuted at the Atlanta Games, the viewers loved it. So did the National Academy of Television Arts & Sciences. NBC received an Emmy Award for the innovative camera work during its coverage of diving at the Atlanta Olympics in 1996.

For my efforts in assisting them, I got a letter from NBC thanking me. Garrett Brown deserves the bulk of the credit, however, for inventing the technology to get these pioneering shots. I was glad he was able to adapt it with my input, and the acknowledgements were nice. But really, I was most excited about the fact that viewers were finally getting a chance to see the sport in a way that could put them right into the action.

It's so difficult to convey what it feels like to fly as you soar, turn, twist, and hurtle in that pause between breaths. From your feet leaving the platform to your hands hitting the water, there's that suspended moment in time, full of grace and muscle tension that had been so elusive to share with viewers. Finally, the television audience was along for the ride in a more tangible way, and since that advance, coverage of diving at the Games has only continued to improve.

Chapter Ten: In Sync

"He sees what is invisible to others and then has the ability to translate that vision into reality. He's like a great chess player. He's always a couple of moves ahead."

– Todd Smith on Tom's vision for adding synchronized diving and establishing the USA Diving Foundation to fund the sport in perpetuity with profit shares from the 1984 Los Angeles Games

In the fall of 1988, I boarded an Eastern Airlines plane in Tampa bound for Philadelphia. As per the typical courtesy when a pilot flies on another captain's plane, I introduced myself when I boarded. The flight wasn't overly full, and the captain invited me to have a seat in first class. He told me to check with one of the flight attendants about where I should sit.

I went back to the flight attendant and introduced myself. "I'm a pilot with Pan-Am, and the captain has invited me to sit in first class. Where do you want to put me?" I asked, in as affable and charming a way as I could manage.

The flight attendant looked perturbed by my presence. She sighed heavily.

"OK. So. I know he told you that. And you can sit in first class. But I need you to know that we have a super VIP coming on board. He's a very, very important person who does not like to be bothered. So, I want you to sit there, and shut up, and not interfere with this passenger," the attendant told me.

That struck me as a little strange, but I just nodded and said, "No problem." I had no idea who she was talking about or why it needed to be stated that specifically. And frankly, I didn't really care. I just wanted to get to Philly. I wasn't planning on messing with anyone anyway, and I was happy to keep to myself. I sat down and got comfortable.

A moment later, a couple of Eastern employees came abroad escorting the VIP. Would you believe, it was George Steinbrenner?

George Steinbrenner was the archetypal irascible, New York character. The former owner of the New York Yankees, he always took a lot of flak from the press. He was outspoken, but he was a shrewd businessman. And in 1988, he was invited to become a member of the U.S. Olympic Committee to represent the interests of the public sector. I figured he was on that flight for the same reason I was, heading to the USOC meeting in Philadelphia.

As he boarded the plane, George was friendly enough, greeting everyone as he found his way to his aisle seat. He sat down right across from where I had already settled.

The flight attendant gave me the evil eye. I could all but hear her scolding me not to say a word, wagging an imaginary index finger in my face.

I did as instructed and said nothing.

As soon as we were underway, George looked over and said, "Hey! Where are you going?"

"I think I'm going the same place you are," I said.

George looked quizzically at me, as the flight attendant shot daggers at me with her eyes.

"Well, I'm going to a U.S. Olympic Committee Board of Directors meeting," George said with a smile.

"That's exactly where I'm going," I replied.

He smiled in stunned glee. "Get over here!" he motioned for me to join him. "I want to pick your brain because I've never been to one of these meetings."

He was excited to have made an insider connection before he'd even landed.

So, with the flight attendant telepathically sending me death threats, George moved over, and I sat down next to him.

"What's your position with the Olympic Committee?" he asked.

"I've been on the board of directors since 1977. I'm the representative for the sports of swimming and diving."

"Swimming and diving?!" he said. "Did you know Mike Peppe?"

"Know him? He was my coach at Ohio State!" I think I saw the flight attendant mouth a hex in my direction.

"I love that guy," George laughed. "He gave me an A when I was in the Air Force. I was based at Rickenbacker, and I took some graduate classes at Ohio State. He taught the swimming class I took, and I got to meet all the members of the team!" George started naming all these famous Olympians who'd been on the OSU swimming and diving team. Most of them had been there just a few years ahead of me.

As the flight progressed, George asked me to stick with him during the meeting, as he hadn't been to one before and he wanted some assistance in how to navigate the scene. He patted me on the back, and I caught a flash of fire coming from the flight attendant—I think she was really about to lose it. She probably had visions of having the opportunity to chat with him during the flight, and here I was, soaking up all his time and attention.

But that's how I met George Steinbrenner.

When we got to Philadelphia, we preceded to the Hershey Hotel. Some other members of the Olympic Committee, including the president, were already there in the lobby. Within moments of us walking in, these folks—all very important people in their own right—seemed to be orbiting around this bigger star, the super famous George Steinbrenner.

And George said, "You must know my good friend Tom here?" to all these muckety-mucks within the Olympic Committee. They reacted like I was their long-lost best friend. I don't know that I'd ever had a real conversation with any of them before, but they weren't going to let George know that.

At the board meeting, George had me sit next to him so I could guide him through the procedures and answer any questions he might have as we went along. It's amazing how all these people wanted to come by and meet the great George Steinbrenner. I thoroughly enjoyed acting as his right-hand man at his very first USOC meeting.

The quadrennial flow of the Olympic Games really gives an overarching rhythm to the life of those involved with the proceedings. And there were only two Games that I missed after winning bronze in 1964. The first of these was the 1968 Mexico Games, as my daughter Tracey arrived at about the same time the Games were happening. I also missed the Games in 2008, because Joyce was ill.

Each quadrennium has its own flavor for me personally, and I can mark the progress of my career as an athlete and administrator in tidy, four-year cycles. Behind the scenes, FINA and the various other governing bodies are hard at work during the years in between the Olympic Games reviewing proposals for new rules, making changes to how they administer the sport, and readying for and hosting world championships and other important events leading up to the next Olympics. There's a lot going on in those off years, and I loved being part of the bustle.

The period between the 1992 Barcelona Games and the 1996 Atlanta Games was an especially important interlude. After the vast television success we'd had with the Barcelona Games, I continued working with Peter Diamond and NBC to push the envelope on making diving the most-watched of all the Olympic sports.

During a discussion with him one day, he mentioned that he wished diving had a team event like gymnastics does, as that's a really appealing way to present the sport to audiences. In gymnastics, the top few athletes come back and do the same routines they did in individual competition, but in a team format. Their scores all add up to determine the best team in the world. As such, adding a team element can make an individual sport seem much more appealing to some folks, and I liked Peter's idea. But there was a flaw to the concept.

Most countries didn't have enough top-flight divers to make up a five-person team the way they do in gymnastics. Countries like France, the UK, Spain, and Italy might have two or three divers good enough for Olympic competition, but they couldn't put four men or four women together and compete with Russia, China, or the USA. Those would have been the same three countries going for the medals every time, just because of the depth of the programs in those bigger countries that didn't exist in smaller nations.

I told Peter I felt like I could get most of these countries to come up with two divers to dive together in a team format. But rather than have them repeat the routines they'd already shown in individual competition, why not make this a different animal all together and have them dive in tandem? It would be a totally different event with a different focus, where precision timing and athlete compatibility would drive the wins, not the depth of the country's program.

Suddenly, we were talking about synchronized diving, and the possibility of adding it as a new Olympic event.

Though in that context, synchronized diving was a "new" idea, there's actually a lengthy history of tandem performances that goes back to the earliest days of vaudeville. Synchronized diving first started cropping up in Europe in the 1890s, and by the 1930s, it was an integral part of virtually every water show and vaudeville performance that involved diving or trampolining. In fact, in 1936, there was a pairs diving exhibition at the Olympic trials. Around the same time, Harold Smith, the Olympic gold medalist in the 10-meter platform in 1932 and Farid Simaika, the Egyptian man who earned silver in the 10-meter platform in 1928, teamed up as synchronized divers on the various touring circuits. Together, they became as famous for their synchronized diving routine as anything they'd ever done individually.

In other words, as new-fangled as it might have seemed, synchronized diving actually had a long and illustrious history and was a known crowd-pleaser. I told Peter all about it and made a pitch on the spot for adding it to the program. Peter still liked the idea of a team event, but I was convinced that synchronized diving would be the better way to go. So, I began promoting the idea and working to build a coalition of support for adding this new event to the Olympic slate.

Adding any event to an Olympic program is a years-long process that requires a lot of buy-in from a lot of players all over the world. For a new event to be accepted, it must be widely practiced by men in at least 75 countries and on four continents and by women in no fewer than 40 countries and on three continents. The sport must also increase the "value and appeal" of the Games, while retaining and reflecting modern traditions. It's a tall order to check all those boxes, but since 1980 alone, almost 100 events have been added to the Olympic program.

Events can be added as a whole new sport, as a branch of an existing sport, or as a specific competition within an existing discipline. In the case of synchronized diving, we were looking to add synchro as a new branch of the existing sport of diving. To do that, we'd have to write new rules and a judging rubric for synchronized diving, so I got to work putting it all together as part of my advocacy for this new event.

We'd also have to convince the host nation for the Games where it would debut that it was a good addition. To be sure, the IOC had to give us approval to add these four events, but the bigger decision maker was Lynne Bates, the Sydney Aquatic Competition Director and a member of the FINA Bureau. We had to convince her that it was a good idea to add synchro for the Games she was helping plan for 2000 in Sydney. Before we got that far though, we had to arrange some exhibition and world championship events to show off the new events to help build interest and support for its inclusion.

We'd also have to develop a standard set of rules and judging rubrics. Judging and scoring for synchronized diving would naturally have to be a little different from the other two diving events already in the Games. With the 3-meter springboard and the 10-meter platform events, there are seven judges, and the two highest and two lowest scores are discarded on each dive. With synchronized diving, because there are two divers executing the same dive, there's a lot more for judges to watch and assess, but the time between the commencement of the dive and the divers hitting the water is the same. Therefore, it made sense to have additional judges watching—some with very specific areas of focus.

For synchronized diving, we originally decided a team of nine judges would best be able to handle the added duties. Four of the nine judges (two for each diver) look for the execution of the individual dives. Each judge watches just the diver they're supposed to be focused on and scores the dive the same way as would be done in individual competition.

The other five judges are concerned with the synchronization between the two athletes. They're looking to see clean lines, and when viewed from the side, there should only be one diver visible. The other diver should be in such perfect sync, he or she disappears behind the other diver.

Each dive is scored on a scale from zero to 10 in half-point increments. The high and low scores from both groups of judges get tossed, so there's only two execution scores and three synchronization scores that count. These scores are added together and multiplied by the degree of difficulty. The aim of the judging protocol is to see consistency in the synchronization and the skill level in all five or six dives across both divers.

At the FINA Congress in Rome in 1994, we finally got approval to add synchronized diving events to international competitions. The rules that I wrote were accepted and put into the rule book. Synchronized diving would be contested as a medal event at the World Cup in 1995 for the first time, and it was an exciting step along the path of adding the event to the Olympic roster. But there was still a lot of work to be done before that happened.

Part of what makes synchronized diving so appealing to non-divers is because it's very obvious whether the dive has been done well. Someone who doesn't know diving and what makes one dive harder than another can still see whether the two people have fallen out of sync.

In drafting the rules, I had stipulated that there would be two relatively easy dives that would really concentrate just on the synchronicity of the divers and the old-fashioned beauty of the dives. By 2000 we had gotten away from doing these simple dives in international competition because of the boredom factor, but in synchro, these dives take on a whole new significance; a lay audience can really appreciate just how difficult the discipline is—even with relatively simple dives—because if they're even a split second off in their timing, it becomes obvious.

This inclusion of simpler dives also allowed more teams to be competitive. Sure, China is probably going to blow you away every time; they have a real assembly line over there that keeps cranking out elite divers left and right. And Russia has always had a big program. But by requiring simpler dives, that allowed smaller programs, like those in many European and African nations, to stay in the competition up until dive three or four when you get to the more difficult dives.

I baked that in on purpose and assigned a degree of difficulty value on those first two dives of 2.0 (a relatively low degree of difficulty) to help level the playing field and increase the simple elegance and synchronicity of at least a few dives in the event. That philosophy of *can-you-perfect-the-basics-together?* is still in place today. After those two simpler dives, teams are welcome to execute three or four dives of unlimited degree of difficulty to show off their acrobatic skills.

In addition, at least one dive must be performed with both divers facing forward on the takeoff. Another must have them both facing backward. At least one dive must feature the two divers facing opposite directions. Beyond that, it's up to the skill and creativity of the pair to figure out what the specific dives will be.

The formula really worked, and the competitions were beautiful, skillful, and ultimately showed promise for this new event.

But still, it took a good deal of effort to get the discipline adopted. One of the toughest groups to convince was the American coaches. Most of our coaches are collegiate coaches. When I was in college, there were really only four schools that had diving programs of excellence—Ohio State, Michigan, Indiana, and Southern California. But now, because of the value of scholarships and the increased number of diving programs across the country, there are several hundred college programs and coaches with divers at many schools. Now, you could have an Olympic hopeful coming up in any number of college programs, not just the traditional diving powers of yore.

But these divers don't necessarily have a teammate who's at the same level as them to train with, and what we found was that you'd have to take a diver from Indiana and pair him or her up with a diver from Texas, for example. The only time they could get together would be in prep for a major championship or the Olympics. This didn't give them much time or opportunity to fine-tune their dives and synchronicity.

Another issue is that at most of these programs, there simply isn't the physical equipment needed to train for synchronized diving. Many pools don't have diving boards at all, and those that do typically have one each of a 1-meter, 3-meter, and 10-meter platform. What's more, for these collegiate coaches, their bread and butter and their salaries revolve around preparing divers for collegiate competition and perhaps the two traditional Olympic events—the 3-meter springboard and the 10-meter platform events. Adding this new wrinkle was seen as a big ask by many of them.

That meant some of these coaches were reluctant to share their divers for this new event. Some of them are very protective of their individual divers and didn't want them working with another coach, even if it meant that diver might then have a better shot at an Olympic berth or potentially lucrative endorsements. For some of these divers, it meant a lost opportunity all together, as one diver might be instructed by his coach to focus solely on the individual event and forego the synchro event, which means his partner wouldn't get a chance to go to the Games at all. Things tend to get complicated when there's multiple people and competing priorities involved in an endeavor.

So ironically, while we had originated the concept of synchronized diving in the United States, it took the home-grown programs years to catch up with those in other countries that adopted the sport faster.

I just wanted what's best for the United States in terms of medal count and providing opportunities for American divers to compete. I'm less concerned about what's best for Miami or Ohio State or any other individual college program. Don't get me wrong—at the USOC level, we're so grateful to the collegiate programs for providing coaches and facilities and training in so many ways. Without them, there would be no American Olympic divers at all. But it's important to understand that sometimes, there's been a little bit of conflict between the aims of college coaches and their programs and what's happening at the international level.

In recent years, we've had high performance directors who've tried to assemble a synchro camp where divers from various parts of the country could come and train and make a good match, so we can put forward the best possible team. Some coaches still don't want their divers to attend, but a lot of countries like Germany, Russia, Great Britain, Malaysia, Korea, and Japan have all really endorsed synchro and have special training sessions. At all levels, we're still working through that here, and just trying to provide the best opportunities for all divers to pursue their talent in the best context for them.

But before all that, we needed to get the event added to the Olympic program. And that meant staging exhibition events so various stakeholders could see what we were talking about and the potential for this new discipline.

In 1995, Atlanta held a pre-Olympic World Cup event, where the 4,000-seat venue sold out and everyone went crazy over synchronized diving, including several FINA directors. Getting those directors to see the event in Atlanta was key in getting synchronized diving added to the Olympic program. Looking back now, I think that meet was really the turning point in the quest to add synchro.

The following summer, to further build the argument for and excitement about synchronized diving, we planned an exhibition event for the 1996 Games in Atlanta. It too, went off without a hitch and was a crowd favorite.

The last hurdle left was convincing Lynne Bates, the director of aquatic sports for the upcoming Sydney Games, that adding synchro would be a good thing to do. And that took a little doing.

The primary concern that Lynne, who would later become just the third woman to be elected to the prestigious 22-member FINA Bureau, and some other administrators had was whether adding synchronized diving would increase the number of divers in attendance and thus increase the host's costs. Sydney was to be the first Olympic host to cover all the divers' room and board costs. From a financial perspective, there was a lot of pressure to keep the number of divers attending the Games to a reasonable level. I met with Lynne in Lausanne, Switzerland, at a FINA and IOC meeting and we struck a deal—if we could restrict eligibility to only qualified divers that were already coming for the 3-meter and 10-meter events, we could add synchronized diving.

So, I got to work coming up with a plan. We would run a prequalifying event at a World Cup event prior to the Games, and that would determine which countries would qualify for a synchronized diving slot in Sydney. We would permit only the top 8 teams to take part in a final-only event at the Sydney Games, and the teams would be made up of divers who were already there representing their country in the 3- or 10-meter events. This meant that the number of divers attending the Games would be the same whether synchronized diving was added or not. No added cost would be incurred by the host to add synchro, but it could officially debut as an Olympic event. It was good plan, and Lynne backed it. If she hadn't, I don't know where synchronized diving might have ended up.

Finally, in April 1999, after nearly 10 years of lobbying for its addition, synchronized diving was formally added to the Olympic program. The final decision came during an International Olympic Committee meeting in Sydney, and I was thrilled.

At the Games the following summer, also held in Sydney, synchronized diving made its Olympic competition debut to much fanfare. *The Boston Globe* produced a beautifully-illustrated, full-page explainer of the new sport that showcased my hard work in a way that audience members—who might be tuning into the Games and seeing this tandem-style diving for the first time— could understand. I have a reprint of that broadsheet framed in my office, a newspaper clipping I'm particularly proud of having been associated with, though the *Globe* gave me a bit more credit than I deserve in saying I "created" the sport in the early 1990s. I didn't actually create it, but I sure had invested a lot of energy into codifying a discipline that I knew the crowds would love, and I certainly helped bring it to a much larger audience.

At the 2000 Games, the divers performed spectacularly. There was one pair in particular whose performance was especially noteworthy, because they illustrated the future of this new sport and how divers might best work together in training specifically for it.

Vera Ilyina and Yuliya Pakhalina of Russia won the gold medal in the women's 3-meter springboard synchronized diving event, but both had trained at the University of Texas at Houston under head coach Jane Figueiredo. They'd done all their training in the U.S. at a U.S. institution, but the medal went to Russia! Nevertheless, all three did a great job. Jane, who hails from Zimbabwe, is now Great Britain's high-performance diving coach, working closely with the stellar Tom Daley. She's done great work building the UK team into a world power.

Because of Jane's attitude and approach to synchronized diving, we asked her to present a session at our United States Aquatic Sports convention after the Games about how she trained her Olympic divers to a gold medal. She told us the father of one of the women had been her individual diving coach, and he wanted to come in and comment on the synchro training sessions with her new partner. It made sense to many diving coaches that he would be involved in some capacity, as the young woman's primary coach.

But Jane wouldn't hear of it. She outright banned him from their workouts and told him that his contribution was welcome on the individual side, but when training the divers for synchro, she was in charge. Her only focus was on helping the two divers get in sync. She was looking to improve the team as a whole rather than tinkering with the little things that you might emphasize for an individual.

This is a wise approach, and Jane made a very good case for us in how to better train synchronized divers as teams rather than individual athletes. We filmed her talk and used that demonstration for years afterward at the now sadly defunct National Training Center.

For example, in 2008 we had a very good synchronized team—a boy from Florida and a boy from Georgia. They trained individually at their own venues and only got together about a week before the Games. They had dived well but just missed a medal on the 3-meter. Afterward, in the debrief, it became clear that both coaches, in trying to support their divers, had ended up working at cross proposes. Each had tried to adapt their athlete's movements to the other diver.

The one coach in Florida was trying to get his diver to twist earlier in the second somersault of a double twisting two-and-a-half. Meanwhile, the coach in Georgia was training his diver to twist later. Essentially, they were counterproductive and didn't meet in the middle. Instead, they sort of swapped styles. The result was they were still just enough out of sync—despite all that hard work executed individually—to be problematic for a podium finish as a pair.

As Jane had told us so early on, the sum is greater than its parts in synchronized diving. To truly be great in the sport, both divers must strive for perfection in relation to their partner, not just their own skills.

While diving programs around the country adapted to bringing the sport into the fold, at a viewership level, synchronized diving was a hit right off the bat.

Somewhere between when synchro debuted in 2000 and its second outing in 2004, Peter Diamond looked at the viewership data and came around whole-heartedly to the idea that synchronized diving would be an audience favorite. He became a real believer, and by 2004, Peter was asking me to organize proceedings so that we could have synchro events run in the first four days of the Olympics. Synchronized diving was so popular among television audiences, that NBC was promoting it as a major draw for their entire Olympic broadcast.

As far as individual countries and federations were concerned, adding synchronized diving to the Olympic program increased the opportunities for medals. Prior to synchro's debut, there were four diving events on the Olympic docket and a total of 12 diving medals up for grabs. Those included gold, silver, and bronze in the men's and women's 3-meter events (6 medals), along with gold, silver, and bronze in the men's and women's 10-meter events (the other 6 medals).

With the addition of synchro, we added a full slate of gold, silver, and bronze medal opportunities to both the men's and women's 3-meter and 10-meter events. To go from 12 potential medals to 24 potential medals opened all sorts of opportunities for a whole new generation of divers around the world. It also helped galvanize the attention—and purses—of aquatic federations around the world determined to go after more medals to improve their standing in the eyes of their national Olympic committees.

For individual divers, it meant that a new crop of divers—those who specialize in the precision timing and ability to mesh well with another diver—now had another avenue to pursue. Over time, as the sport of synchro has evolved, divers who might not have been able to nab an individual slot now potentially could compete in just the synchro events.

Instead of limiting eligibility for synchro to just those divers already participating in an individual event, now the rules stipulate that 136 divers in total can come to the Olympics, and a country can send no more than two divers per event. This means that some countries can bring a couple divers just for synchro, giving some athletes another chance to make the Olympic team that might have been out of reach with only the individual slots available. Adding synchronized diving was a win-win-win for everyone involved.

✳ ✳ ✳

At the 2004 Athens Games, diving celebrated 100 years of inclusion in the Olympics, and over that century of competition, the discipline had doubled in size. It was a special experience for me to be able to visit the original home of the Olympic movement and reflect on how far the sport of diving had come in the preceding century. I felt so lucky that I'd been able to contribute to that evolution and have loved every minute of my work in support of those goals.

It was fitting, too, that in 2004, Greek synchronized divers won big. Thomas Bimis and Nikolaos Siranidis won the men's 3-meter springboard synchro event. They were definitely underdogs going into it—it's probably not overstating it to say that their triumph was perhaps the biggest surprise ever in diving.

Greece had never even had a finalist in any of the individual diving events, and they'd only earned a berth in synchro for this event because they were the host country. But the Chinese and the American teams each botched a dive, and that left the door wide open for the quite capable Greek duo, who offered up a superlative performance. The next day, Greek postage stamps bore an image of that pair of divers, and they became instant national heroes. It was really something.

The following year, I retired from FINA at the World Championships in Montreal. It was time. I had contributed a lot over more than three decades, and it was time to step aside and let other contributors take the reins.

As I had so many years before at the University of Miami, I had mentored Steve McFarland to take my place on the Technical Diving Committee. Steve had been on the international diving scene for some time, having worked as a broadcast commentator in 1988 and 1992 for NBC. In 1996, he did the radio presentation—most people don't even know that the Olympics are broadcast on the radio. Steve has also contributed to ESPN, Turner Broadcasting, and has worked on several programs about cliff diving in Acapulco. He's held in very high regard in international diving circles and has also served as a judge at the 2000 and 2004 Olympics.

Though it wasn't assured that Steve would get the job, I did my best to promote him as my replacement. So, I was pleased that at the FINA congress in 2005, he was named to the committee.

Not long after I'd stepped down from the Technical Diving Committee, FINA asked me to put on judging clinics that had been requested by various federations. Many of the up-and-coming programs wanted to develop the skills of their potential judges, and taking part in a clinic hosted by the past chairman of the Technical Diving Committee was a good way for these organizations to show they were committed to high-quality judging.

I spent the next four or five years traveling the world, putting on clinics. I went to Madrid and returned to Japan, China, England, and Canada. I traveled to a few other countries, too and put on three-day seminars and clinics for better judging that always opened with a special video we'd created, because that would elicit a lot of questions. I was a traveling teacher, and before long, I realized that it was too much for one person.

I was approaching my 70th birthday and I felt it was time for the Technical Diving Committee to take over providing these clinics. They were agreeable to that proposal, and by 2010, the TDC had taken over running the clinics. To the best of my knowledge, they still use a lot of my materials and my approach.

From 2010 until 2012, I had a little time to relax. I'd been so busy for so many years, it was nice to have a little down time. But my retirement wouldn't last, as the sport that has meant so much to me over the years still had a few tricks up its sleeve.

Chapter Eleven: Life Marches On

Marriage—yes, it is the supreme felicity of life.
I concede it. And it is also the supreme tragedy of life.
The deeper the love the surer the tragedy.
And the more disconsolating when it comes.

– Mark Twain in a letter to Father Fitz-Simon, June 5, 1908

Luck has been a constant in my life, a veritable persona and character who pops up in some of the most unlikely places. I don't know why I was so often in Luck's good graces, but I feel very blessed for her constant assistance. And that sense of gratitude extends to the family I found in diving and with Joyce.

For someone like me who grew up with so little support from my own family, it was a real blessing and a source of power and comfort to me that I now had such a loving family that we'd built ourselves. Really, it's all I ever wanted when I was young, and while diving provided me with a wonderful extended family, it was really Joyce and my children—my own flesh and blood—who had the biggest hand in helping me become the man I am.

In trying to describe how proud I am of my family, I stumble in finding the right words. So, let me tell you a bit about their accomplishments, as that's one way to help quantify what they have meant to me without getting too sappy.

My son Tim was always a good kid who did well in school and worked hard. That diligence has paid off—he's now a well-respected pediatrician. In medical school, he met his beautiful wife, Sandra, who has since become a top infectious disease specialist. They live in Plant City and have three children, Juliana, Philip, and William.

My daughter Tracey is a marvel. A devoted Christian, she's beautiful, bright, and has too many talents to list. She's become an accomplished writer and speaker who works with women to tell their stories. She married Mark Russell, a successful businessman and wonderful husband and father. Together they have four children, Chase, Holt, Trey, and Faith Joyce.

These two loving children and their spouses have provided me the most important gift I've had during a lifetime steeped in good luck—my grandkids and the deeply rewarding experience of being part of a loving and devoted family.

When my children were young, we lived on a lake in Miami. I had a pair of diving boards installed on docks anchored in the water behind the house, and we could dive and play to our heart's content nearly year-round. I would also often conduct water safety sessions for my children's classmates, so that others might become water-safe and learn their way around a diving board. Sometimes, I'd harken back to my days as a comedy diver to put on little shows for the kids. I believe it was an idyllic way for my children to grow up, and I'm grateful I was able to provide them safe, regular access to the water and the joys it can bring.

As Tim and Tracey grew up and had their own children, I was gratified to see they both passed along a love for the water to their kids as well. My seven grandchildren have gotten into a wide variety of activities through the years, but they all know how to swim, and all have had the joy of a gleeful summer day by the lake.

But that serene family playtime scene that I treasure from when my kids were young would turn tragic many years later for Tim and Sandra.

Back in 2009, Tim's son, Philip, was just about to turn 10 years old. On a late summer Saturday, he was playing in Lake Arietta in Polk County, Florida, and probably trying not to think about school starting up again in a week or two. They'd spent a typical weekend summer day wakeboarding, tubing, and splashing about—a most innocent and near-sacred right of childhood.

But a threat lurked unseen in the water. The *Naegleria fowleri* amoeba, widely feared as the "brain-eating amoeba" lives in the silty bottoms of freshwater lakes, rivers, and springs in warm climates. It thrives in water ranging between 80 and 115 degrees and can easily be kicked up by shuffling feet at the water's edge.

Once it's freed from the bottom and floating in the water column, a simple splash is all it takes for the amoeba to come into contact with the nose. From there, it can travel to the brain where it sets up shop, attacking and destroying brain cells systematically. Once the infection is established—a quiet process with no outward symptoms—death approaches inexorably and completes its task within days of that initial transmission. It's an incredibly cruel microbe that's endemic to many of Florida's freshwater spots.

The good news is it's a rare infection—there's only been 148 known cases of the amoeba in the U.S. between 1962 and 2019. But it's nearly always deadly. Of those 148 cases, only four have survived.

As much as Luck has been a prominent force in my life, for Philip, Luck was not on his side that day in 2009. At some point during his frolic in the water, the amoeba gained access to his brain and began its vicious work. He died eight days later. A tragedy I can barely begin to describe, it has reverberated through our family ever since.

Every summer, Tim and Sandra take pains to raise awareness of the risk associated with warm, freshwater swimming spots. Because as deadly as the amoeba is, it's 100 percent preventable. Wearing a nose clip can stop the amoeba from getting into the nose and sinuses. It's as simple as that—or just opting to swim in a pool or ocean during the warmest months. Had we known of the risk, we might now be cheerfully watching Philip excel in college or whatever else he could have gotten up to, had he had the chance.

When Philip died, we were devastated—Joyce especially. It's difficult to put into words what it feels like to lose a grandchild, but it takes a little piece of your own soul when any loved one dies. Somehow, it's harder when it's a child who's just starting out in life, with nothing but promise ahead.

A few short months after Philip passed, Joyce's cancer returned.

Joyce was first diagnosed with a rare, but mercifully slow-growing form of cancer, a liposarcoma in her abdomen, in 1987. She had surgery and it seemed they'd gotten all of it, and we moved on with our lives. But over the course of the next two decades, she underwent an additional eight surgeries, as the tumor kept returning. Each time, they'd take it out, and we'd think we were in the clear. But a year or two later it would return.

Over the years, the cancer became an aspect of our lives, but a background element. We got on with life and enjoyed ourselves in spite of the lingering concern about the cancer's possible return. Still, we were always open to new possibilities of how to dispel the constant low murmur of worry. One such opportunity presented itself during a trip we took to China in 2000.

I had been invited to China for the grand opening of Xu Yiming's international diving school. He was the Chinese national coach and one of the winningest diving coaches to ever have been in the sport—he really built the Chinese program into a superpower. He invited me to the grand opening because I had written a letter to the bank in support of a loan for his school. He felt like he owed it to me to be a VIP at the grand opening, which was covered on television and graced by celebrities. It was quite a to-do.

We arrived in China about a week before the grand opening—Joyce came with me, and we made a brief vacation out of the visit. I wasn't terribly familiar with China, so I was glad to take recommendations about what to see and do. The team nutritionist acted as our guide as Joyce and I got a whistle-stop tour of all the popular tourist stops in China. We visited the terracotta warriors at Xi'an and took a boat tour in Qinling through those incredible mountains and caves. In Kunming, we visited a natural wonder called the stone forest. There, jagged stone cliffs stick up out of the ground, maybe 100 feet high. They're almost like a forest of trees but all made of stone.

While walking down a side street in Kunming one morning, I noticed an older, distinguished-looking gentleman. He approached me and asked if we were American.

"Oh, good, because I'd like to speak English. I don't get to speak much English since the days I was with the Flying Tigers," he said.

I had encountered the Flying Tigers a few times over the years, and it was always a big deal for me. Every pilot of my generation was enthralled with them and how they helped save China from Japanese occupation during World War II. I couldn't believe that, yet again, I was encountering someone affiliated with their illustrious history. That's the thing about living a long life—certain things come around again, and again, and again.

As it turned out, this man was a doctor of Chinese medicine and was well-versed in the ancient, Eastern ways of healing. He pulled out an album full of magazine articles and letters from people from all over the world thanking him for treating them. These letters claimed he'd cured everything from cancer to polio. I don't know whether any of it was real, but the album was about a foot thick, and it was clear that his patients certainly believed in his abilities.

Despite some skepticism, I was quite interested in what he had to say, given that Joyce had been dealing with this ongoing journey with cancer for more than a decade already. We were open to listening and possibly trying just about anything that seemed like it might solve the problem.

The elderly doctor invited us into his house, introduced us to his wife, and told us about his work with the Flying Tigers. They made tea for us, and he said he'd be glad to give Joyce the proper teas to treat her cancer. We took home a big bag of leaves and herbs that Joyce faithfully decocted and drank as directed for the rest of her life. I don't know that any of those remedies helped at all, but we tried anyway.

✳ ✳ ✳

For most of Joyce's life, she was able to work around the sarcoma, and it didn't slow her down too much. But there was sporadic pain and the frequent surgeries to deal with. I know it took a toll on us to have the constant threat of cancer lurking. I never quite knew when her time might come, so I had to prepare myself to lose her, as I knew I would someday. We'd been living in a borrowed moment—albeit one that lasted more than 20 years—since she was first diagnosed in 1987. So, we made the best of it.

Joyce was a positive person who put so much of her trust and faith in God and the miracles He can work. She bore up and stoically soldiered on despite her health issues.

Early in 2010, she had her ninth surgery. The surgery didn't go well, and she never recovered. She died a few days later on January 22.

Joyce passed away only 5 or 6 months after Philip died, and I believe in my bones that losing him influenced how she went through that final operation. She died not from the cancer itself, but from the operation. They couldn't stop the bleeding, and honestly, I think she was suffering a broken heart after losing Philip. I think that made it more difficult for her to come through that surgery the way she had so many others before.

The emotional tumult of the days that followed Joyce's passing are mostly a foggy recollection of sorrow punctuated by stray memories of specific conversations and other bittersweet reminders of our life together. Those glimmers of joy, and the support of my children and grandchildren, eased the pain of Joyce's passing.

As hard as it was to lose her, especially after such a long, drawn-out struggle, I treasure the lifetime we shared. I've always felt like I was the luckiest man alive to have had Joyce for my wife, and all my friends told me the same thing. I was one lucky son of a gun to have been married to her. I never would have achieved half of what I have in life without her support, encouragement, and steadfast belief in me.

I was also buoyed by the fact that while Joyce was beyond question the best thing that ever happened to me, she was the best thing that ever happened to our family, too. Joyce helped me create this family full of characters and love—children, grandchildren, and a connected community that surrounded us. She was a very family-oriented person, and her life was complete when she finally had a son and a daughter.

But when the kids went off to college in the 1980s, that was hard for her. She had a little bit of empty nest syndrome. But by 1995, both Tim and Tracey had gotten married, settled down in central Florida, and started growing their own families. It didn't take long for Joyce and me to decide that it made no sense for us to be in South Florida, so far away from Joyce's primary source of joy.

Instead of taking long weekend trips to see the grandkids, we moved to the middle of the state to be closer all the time. Tim had landed in Plant City, and Tracey was in Lakeland. So, Joyce and I found a beautiful home on a golf course in Plant City. That meant we were in the same neighborhood as Tim and only a 20-minute drive from where Tracey lived.

This was just a wonderful period in our lives. Being close to our kids and grandkids was a truly special thing for both of us. It's difficult to describe the relationships between grandparent and grandchild, but it's elemental and all encompassing. Where Joyce and I had once felt complete in having our own children, the arrival of grandchildren showed us there was so much more love to be had—and to give—that we hadn't even conceptualized.

The first grandchild to arrive was Tracey's son Chase. He's turned out to be such a joy, and I brag about him all the time because he's a very talented athlete who's good at everything he tries. He's a competitive kiteboarder. In fact, the whole Russell family is into kiteboarding. A few years ago, they took a 50-mile kiteboard trip from Miami to Islamorada in support of an orphanage in Tanzania that now has a library that bears Joyce's name.

Then Sandra and Tim had Juliana, who is a beautiful and talented artist and just a joy to be around.

Next came Philip, who was becoming a really delightful young boy when he passed on.

Next, Tracey had Holt, who is kind, devoted, intelligent, and caring.

Not long after Holt arrived, Tracy had Trey. He's turned out to be a brilliant young man with a great sense of humor.

Tim and Sandra had one more son named Wil, another bright child with an excellent sense of humor.

Tracey always wanted four children, and she finally had a girl, named Faith, to complete her brood. Faith is beautiful, intelligent, and easy to love. She'll go far in whatever direction she takes.

Indeed, all these kids have extraordinary futures ahead of them, and if I had to summarize them in a single phrase, I'd say they're all incredibly bright. They're truly a joy to behold. Each one has a unique personality, traits, talents, and interests, and it's been just the delight of my life to see what they get into and how they have excelled. They have given us so much joy.

While 2009 and 2010 crushed me in the loss of Philip and Joyce, there were a few real high points that followed soon after. That's the thing about life. As difficult as it can be sometimes, if you can hang in there a while longer, it usually gets better.

The first of these happy things that happened was receiving the award I'm most proud of. I've been honored to receive so many meaningful awards over the years—from my Olympic bronze medal and my commendation medal from the Air Force to induction into the International Swimming Hall of Fame. But the award I'm most proud of having received was the 2010 George Steinbrenner Award.

Though George Steinbrenner is often remembered, at least in New York, for his hard nose for business and his often-gruff persona and frequent feuds with Yankees players and other notable people, he actually was an enormously charitable person. One example that's really stuck with me is his response to the tragic death of swimmer Ron Karnaugh's father. Ron was poised to win gold at the 1992 Olympic Games in Barcelona when his father suddenly passed away of a heart attack during the opening ceremonies. George stepped in to look after the Karnaugh family, and he went on to pay for Ron to go to medical school. That was the sort of generous thing George regularly did.

Here in the greater Tampa Bay area, we have many reminders of the charitable works George has done, with roads and schools he's funded named after him. You can't find a bad word about him in Tampa, and that's true in other communities, too.

I'd worked with George on the USOC Board of Directors, but I'd retired. I'd also retired from the U.S. Diving Board of Directors. I was sort of just floating along, a bit untethered after Joyce's death, and trying to figure out what comes next in the wake of so many years of flying hard as a full-time pilot and working tirelessly to further diving.

In one of those rare spells of leisure, I went golfing one day with Ron O'Brien. While we were out on the course, my phone rang. It was Bill Hybl. He'd been president of the U.S. Olympic Committee, and he was calling to congratulate me for being named the recipient of the George Steinbrenner Sports Leadership Award.

The annual award is supported by the United States Olympic Endowment. It aims to honor a member of the U.S. Olympic and Paralympic family who has made outstanding contributions to sport through management, sport organization endeavors, or the enhancement of competitive opportunities. Coaches, administrators, boundary-breaking athletes, even whole teams have earned the nod in various years.

When you look at the list of people who've received the Steinbrenner award—all of whom are engraved on a large crystal sculpture housed at the U.S. Olympic and Paralympic Committee headquarters in Colorado Springs—it's pretty much a who's-who of sports. And sometimes, I can't believe that my name appears among them.

The 2010 award ceremony was held at Club 21 in New York City, and everybody who was anybody at the time was there, including Henry Kissinger—yes, that Henry Kissinger—and Peter Diamond from NBC. It was quite an event.

I brought an entourage of about 25 people with me, including Tim's and Tracey's families. Every past executive director of USA Diving attended, too. To this day, I think I have the record for bringing the most people to attend the ceremony. It wasn't cheap, but it was worth it!

To be so richly recognized for many, many years of hard work while surrounded by family and friends was truly a day to remember. It was a culmination of a life spent building family, both my own and a wider diving family, and I was humbled to be praised for only having done what seemed natural and necessary for all those years.

I was floored to have been selected for this particular award. From all the athletes and coaches and administrators across all the Olympic sports—that they decided to bestow upon me this meaningful accolade named for a man I respected and had enjoyed working with on the USOC was just incredible. To say it was an honor is a vast understatement, and the beautiful crystal award they gave me fills the most prominent place of pride on the credenza of artifacts in my office.

The real prize, though, is the lasting friendships I've earned through the service that earned this nod and the larger glass statute that resides in Colorado where anyone can see it and reflect upon what it means to truly love a sport.

Toward the end of 2010, another miraculous thing happened. I met Fran Munson. And I have my daughter, Tracey, to thank for the introduction.

Tracey was doing some charitable work in Lakeland and met Fran on a committee. They became fast friends, and Tracey learned that Fran was divorced. I'd lost Joyce about 11 months prior, and Tracey didn't like seeing me on my own, so she suggested that Fran and I meet.

Fran, being Fran, wasn't all that interested at first. She's fiercely independent and had carved out a happy life for herself in the several years she'd been on her own. She didn't need to go on another blind date. "I've met a lot of fathers," she told Tracey.

But Tracey was certain that Fran and I would make a good match, and she persisted.

"Maybe you should Google him before you say no," Tracey told Fran.

Maybe that advice would have been better directed at me! Fran was quite accomplished herself, and I came to find out she had been the executive director of the Community Foundation of Greater Lakeland. In that position, she raised over $70 million during her time helming the organization between 1997 and 2005. She left in 2005 to pursue her passion for interior decorating and set up a business.

At first, I was primarily interested in picking her brain about the work she had done with the Lakeland Foundation. At the time, we were in the process of switching the Raymond C. Rude Foundation, that I'd helped found in 2005 from a private to a public foundation. It wasn't a straightforward process, and I wanted to learn more about the work Fran had done in Lakeland and how it might help me figure out our situation. I told Tracey I was game to meet Fran, and eventually, Tracey convinced Fran to give me the time of day.

So, Tracey set up a group dinner—definitely not a double date. Tracey and her husband and Fran and I went out. The woman who was running that charitable group where Fran and Tracey met also came with us. It was a nice group and a pleasant dinner.

Fran and I hit it off, and by the beginning of 2011, we began having regular dinner dates. We discovered that we had a lot in common, and she's so much fun. She has this cracking wit and a devilish sense of humor. She's kind and generous and afraid of nothing. She's a small spitfire—gregarious and charming and gorgeous to boot. Everyone who meets Fran falls in love straight away, and so had I. Tracey's instincts had been spot on, and I'm forever grateful she made this introduction.

Fran fit immediately with the rest of the family, too. After Joyce passed on and I found happiness with Fran, she became the substitute grandmother for our grandkids. As I write this, she's preparing Easter baskets for each of the grandchildren, and whenever Fran's around, they flock to her as much as they ever came to me. They've just adopted her as "Franny Granny."

I know the power of that relationship goes both ways. Fran has no grandchildren of her own but has thrown herself into doting on these kids. And their lives have helped enrich hers so thoroughly, too.

It's been an extraordinary thing for me to watch this take place. The grandkids certainly remember Joyce and treasure fond memories of their time with her. That will never change. But Fran has done a magnificent job stepping into that role without erasing Joyce. She has taken up the responsibility of giving these wonderful kids the grandmother that cancer took from them, with grace and aplomb.

After dating for three years, Fran and I finally decided to get married. We didn't want to make a big fuss. We'd both been there and done that. The plan was for the wedding to be just us and two of Fran's cousins to act as officiant and witness. We planned the wedding to be held in the clubhouse at our condo complex in Placida, right on the Intercoastal Waterway.

As we were coming down the steps to the clubhouse to start the wedding, Fran's son John appeared. He and Fran are very close, and she couldn't keep the wedding a secret from him. So, he was there to walk her down the aisle.

I worried that Tracey and Tim and their families might feel hurt or left out that we hadn't told them about the wedding. Tracey in particular would be crushed that she didn't get invited, so about a month later, we had a second wedding, a small church ceremony that everyone could attend.

It was a small, low-key affair—just family—but it was perfect. I was so glad we made the decision to hold the second ceremony, and Tracey did a beautiful job organizing everything for our special day. It really was the ideal way for us to begin our new life together.

Shortly thereafter, Fran and I headed out for a honeymoon cruise in the Baltics. We ended that trip in Stockholm with a visit to my good friend Toivo Öhman, who was celebrating his 50th wedding anniversary and 80th birthday with a big party.

From there, we traveled onward to Barcelona so we could attend the World Aquatic Championships in Barcelona. That's where high diving, my current crusade, debuted as a FINA sport. And we sure weren't going to miss the big event.

Chapter Twelve: The Final Frontier

"Pearls don't lie on the seashore.
If you want one, you must dive for it."

– Chinese proverb

The annals of sports history record those brave, individuals who climb to great heights only to launch themselves from there to hurtle back to the earth. These few daredevils stand head and shoulders—or should that be nearly a hundred feet—above the rest.

High diving is a potentially dangerous, beautiful sport that requires nerves of steel and demands that practitioners understand physics and how to move their own bodies in ways that most people simply don't. Split-second reactions and alterations to the pitch of a hand or the tilt of the head can save a dive from becoming a tragedy.

There's a growing interest in high diving around the world—we have the efforts of energy drink–maker Red Bull to thank for that in recent years. As I've come toward the end of my career in service to diving, I've turned my attention to helping this fledgling sport really take off. To adapt a phrase from Red Bull's marketing team, it's my fervent hope that my efforts will "give wings" to the sport at the Olympic level.

At the USAS Convention in 2012, it was announced that FINA would be establishing a commission (not a full-fledged committee, because it wasn't an official part of the FINA program yet) to study the introduction of high diving as a new sport under the FINA umbrella.

They were requesting candidates for that commission, and everyone turned and looked at me. I was the only one in the room who had any qualifications of any kind with high diving, given my professional successes with the sport in the early 1970s. I also had plenty of recent experience ferrying synchronized diving through the labyrinth of steps to join the Olympic program. So, I guess it wasn't at all surprising that I was named a representative to that high diving commission.

I didn't intend to stick with the commission long-term. I hoped to help bring it to the stage where FINA adopted the sport and then step aside to let someone else lead the group after it formally became part of FINA. But that's not exactly how things went. I ended up being appointed chairman of the commission!

The commission met, and we came up with rules, a formula for facilities, and we hosted a couple FINA-sponsored events—a world cup in Cozumel, Mexico, another in the United Arab Emirates, and one in Kazan, Russia. At that Russian event, the riverbed was dredged to a depth of eight meters to allow enough clearance for the athletes to complete their dives safely.

At the Congress in Doha, Qatar, in 2014, I made a presentation to the entire FINA delegation to have FINA accept high diving as their sixth competitive sport and add a new star to the FINA logo. If they agreed, the commission would become a committee, and high diving would become an official discipline under the FINA umbrella.

Now, you may be wondering why high diving was being considered as a whole different sport rather than being added as a new event under diving, the way synchronized diving is. It's a good question—at first blush they seem quite similar, but they're actually very different.

High diving was initially proposed to become part of diving, but the feeling was that would be counterproductive to Olympic diving—high divers are going from a 27-meter-tall platform, often outdoors in natural environments, such as harbors and lakes. Olympic divers, on the other hand, top out at 10 meters and practice their craft mostly in indoor pools. Few natatoriums can accommodate the 90-foot tower and the sturdy stairwells to reach them; the rules stipulate that the rickety ladders of old are history.

In addition, high diving, as the name implies, is a higher-stakes endeavor than diving from a lower platform or a springboard. A lot of traditional coaches have had little experience with and tend to disparage high diving. Certainly, most of them enjoyed watching the

Red Bull events and the pro high diving circuit. But many coaches had never dived from a height above 10 meters themselves or had ever coached divers on how to do the same.

There's also a smaller margin for error in high diving than in springboard or platform diving, and that impacts how the sport works. There's a fundamental difference between diving from nearly three times as high at 27 meters than going from just 10 meters. In the 3-meter and 10-meter events, the dives always end with a clean, head-first entry. But the first rule we wrote for high diving was that high divers must enter the water feet first.

To many practitioners, feet-first versus head-first entries are apples to oranges, and some traditional divers look down on high diving as more of a circus act or stunt than a real athletic endeavor. High divers aren't always wholeheartedly welcomed in the traditional diving fold—often, they're seen as daredevils, stuntmen, or publicity seekers. After all, 27 meters is about 90 feet or the equivalent of diving from an 8-story building. Divers reach speeds in excess of 50 miles per hour when they hit the water.

Many coaches and administrators were more interested in coming up with a team event or mixed-gender diving than adding high diving. They didn't want any part of high diving, and they were happy that they didn't have to be burdened with it. In truth, high diving attracts a different kind of personality.

So instead of trying to become another branch of diving, we looked toward the Red Bull Cliff Diving circuit and the several professional events they run each year for inspiration in developing high diving as a distinct sport for inclusion in FINA events—the way swimming is a completely separate sport from artistic or synchronized swimming.

The Red Bull competitions usually take place in sometimes remote and always spectacular locations, drawing enormous crowds and playing extremely well on television. Those viewers are overwhelmingly young, and that's the audience we need to bring into the sport of diving for it to stay viable as older divers and administrators like me retire or pass on.

It soon became apparent to FINA that if we wanted to tap into even just a fraction of the tens of thousands of young spectators that

Red Bull draws to its events all around the world, we would need to cater to this X-Games-friendly crowd and put on a great show.

It makes sense that this more extreme iteration of diving would attract a lot of viewers—it's spectacular and breathtaking. And it's in no small way a fantastic example of athletic talent and strength. Being able to control your body when you launch yourself from 90 feet up in the air and arrive safely in the water below takes enormous skill, a heap of courage, and maybe just a little bit of madness.

I think it's safe to say that today, the average viewer probably knows more Red Bull divers than Olympic divers. That's in no small part because Red Bull Cliff Diving Championship events appear on television several times a year. Olympic events? They're once every four years, and even for world cup events that might be televised occasionally, you simply don't get the draw in viewership for that elite level of diving that you do with an outfit like Red Bull. They're all about marketing.

My interest is in harnessing some of the television viewership alchemy Red Bull has attained and sharing that onward to all types of diving under the FINA umbrella. I think that can be achieved by bringing high diving into the Olympic fold as a separate sport. When that happens, we can tell viewers, "Come for the death-defying high dives. Stay for the elegant and acrobatic springboard, platform, and synchronized diving events."

✳ ✳ ✳

In championing the addition of high diving as an international event under the FINA umbrella, we've used a similar approach to what I developed for synchronized diving in terms of scoring and how to set up the event. There are two dives in the beginning that are restricted in their degree of difficulty. After that, athletes present two dives of whatever degree of difficulty they want.

We've also had to develop our own separate facility rules that are different from what's used in more conventional diving contests. Meeting these requirements sure isn't cheap or easy because you have to host it in an environment where you can erect scaffolding that can accommodate a 3-meter, a 5-meter, a 7.5-meter, a 10-meter, a 20-meter, and a 27-meter platform, all on the same structure.

To date, FINA has held six high diving world cup events and four high diving world championships. I expect there will be many more in the future as acceptance of the new sport takes off.

It's been an honor for me to chair the FINA Technical High Diving Committee to help launch this sport. But chairing the Technical High Diving Committee has been a lot different than working as the chairman of the Technical Diving Committee. When I was leading the TDC, we had little or no support from the FINA Office. At the time, FINA was made up mostly of volunteers, and there was no professional staff in the headquarters to assist us. We took care of virtually all the committee's business ourselves.

However, in the past 20 years or so, FINA has really grown up as an international sports federation with millions of dollars in financial support. Thus, the organization has been able to add professional staff. It's grown by leaps and bounds since those early days.

Sometimes I feel now there's much less need for the work of the committees than there used to be. So many of the tasks we used to cover have been adopted by professional staff members. But the committees are still critical to conducting events. And to be able to make these happen, I've relied heavily on Melanie Beck, the committee's secretary.

Melanie's involvement with diving goes back to her childhood. Her dad, Jeff Cook, served as the president of the Amateur Swimming Association of Great Britain for 25 years. He started in diving administration in 1977 and organized many swimming and diving events across the UK until his retirement in 1993.

Starting in 2000, Jeff served on the FINA Technical Diving Committee with me and was a huge help. He and his wife, Jean, became great friends to Joyce and me. They often vacationed with us in Florida and abroad. I spoke at his funeral as did several other people from the diving community. A few years later, Jean and Melanie flew from England to attend Joyce's funeral. I so appreciated their coming such a long way to bid Joyce farewell.

After Jeff passed away, Melanie stepped in to fill her father's shoes in England's diving administration spheres. She has since become just as wonderful a leader as her father was, and more.

Melanie is a marketing genius and rose to become a member of the FINA Technical Diving Committee. She became, and still is, the marketing director for the FINA Diving World Series.

When she's not volunteering for FINA, Melanie works as the marketing director for the city of Milton Keynes in the UK and does marketing work for Duraflex. She's received a lot of awards over the years. Most recently, her work in Milton Keynes earned her a 2020 Commonwealth Honor. Presented by the Queen of England, the MBE award has been offered in gratitude for Melanie's efforts during the coronavirus pandemic. She helped get supplies and resources to those who needed them, and for that she gets to have tea with the Queen! I'm a little envious but also enormously proud and happy that she's getting some recognition for her talents, hard work, and big heart.

These days, Melanie serves as the secretary on the Technical High Diving Committee. She does all the heavy lifting in the administration of the THDC, and I wouldn't want to be on the committee without her. In fact, she's the reason I stuck around to serve a second term on the THDC. I only stayed on because she asked me to and because she promised she'd stay on the committee with me. Melanie is the same age as my son Tim and is almost like a daughter to me.

✳ ✳ ✳

Sometimes I think I could write a book just about all the incredible people that diving has brought into my life, from coaches and competitors to mentors and best friends. I've been lucky to cross paths with so many incredible people over the years, many of whom love diving just as much as I always have. And it's been my honor to be able to really get to know many of them.

One such special experience took place in 2012 at the London Olympic Games. That's when we made a big and quite necessary fuss over a very special diver who deserves all the many accolades he's earned over the years.

It all goes back to the 2008 Olympic Games, when Linda Paul, who was installed as the CEO of USA Diving in 2010, noticed that Sammy Lee, a pioneer of the sport, had seemed a little lonely in Beijing. She mentioned that she'd noticed that he didn't have great seats and wasn't being supported as well as she thought this legendary diver should have been. So, with Linda now in charge of USA Diving as we moved toward the 2012 Games, she was in a position to do something about it. She asked me if I'd help her make sure Sammy was better looked after in London. I was delighted that she asked and all too happy to help him get around and see the events.

The London Games were to be a homecoming of sorts for Sammy. It was in that same city 64 years prior that he'd made history as the first Asian-American man to win an Olympic gold medal, which he did with his performance from the men's 10-meter platform at the 1948 Games. His win happened just a couple days after Vicki Draves became the first Asian-American to win a gold medal, which she did in the 3-meter springboard event. Sammy would go on to win another gold medal four years later in Helsinki.

Even after Sammy retired from competition, he remained deeply involved in the sport, contributing as a coach—Bob Webster was one of his stellar protégés—and staunch supporter of all of America's divers in so many capacities throughout his whole life. He was one of these guys who came to every meet. Sammy was at every single championship I ever participated in, and I'm sure he was at many, many more I didn't attend. I was 10 years behind him in the competition, but he was always there and just a great contributor. He really lived and breathed diving.

And he broke barriers for Asian-Americans. His first Olympic title came shortly after World War II, when some Americans still felt a deep distrust of Asian people. Lee, a Korean kid from Southern California, had served in the U.S. Army Medical Corps and was 100 percent American. He went on to have a successful career as an ear, nose, and throat doctor. But in 1948, we weren't so far removed from the time when Asian people were rounded up and stuck in internment camps. His very visible success in diving helped change perceptions.

The greatest thing, though, about Sammy was his personality. Everyone loved him, and so in 2012, Fran and I took Sammy and his really wonderful wife Rosalind Wong to the London Olympic Games. It was Fran's first trip to an Olympics, and who knows how many for me and Sammy. But we spent our time in London with Sammy and Ros. We shared an apartment there, and Fran and I helped Sammy navigate the cobblestones of London in a wheelchair so he could revisit the glory he'd attained there more than six decades prior. Everyone fussed and fawned over Sammy and Ros, and we all had a delightful time.

That visit is perhaps my most favorite of all the trips I've taken. I will always treasure that experience and so many other memories that have been bubbling up to the surface lately as I've reflected on my life aloft and what it's all meant to me.

One of the most important friendships I've had over the years was with Ray Rude, the man who founded Duraflex and created the diving boards that would launch divers into the next century of the sport. We first met in California at a party Sammy hosted in the early 1960s, and we bonded over our love of diving and precision craftsmanship. The relationship grew over the years until Ray became a sort of surrogate father to me, indeed the closest thing I ever had to a true father figure.

While I was in pilot training in Phoenix in 1962, Ray and his wife came out for a diving event. We spent two or three days together and I showed him around the base and the Phoenix area, and we became firm friends. Our common bond was flight—after having spent so much of his life working around airplanes and their engineers, Ray was as impressed with the fact that I was a jet pilot as he was with my diving.

In the early 1960s whenever a big diving meet took place in California, Ray would invite me to his house, and we'd go out on his boat. There was one day in particular, in 1964, that really sticks in my memory and highlights the humor in Ray's character.

Joyce and I were visiting with Ray and his wife, Ina Mae. We went out from Long Beach to Catalina Island off the coast of Southern California. Ray had spent a few years in his late teens living and working on beautiful Catalina Island, so he knew the area well.

We were fishing and didn't want to dirty up the docks in Long Beach with our catch, so we cleaned the fish out at sea and tossed the refuse over the side of the boat. Before long, we found ourselves surrounded by sharks. I got caught up in throwing the chum out to the sharks and accidentally tossed back a fish that Ray thought I should have kept.

"Hey, I wanted that fish!" he said. He made a move toward the side of the boat like he was going to jump into the middle of the sharks to go after the fish.

"You can't do that, you're crazy!" I shouted.

"I dive with them all the time," he laughed. "They know me. They won't bother me!"

I obviously wouldn't let him into the water, and he was just teasing. But for a moment there, I really did think he might pitch himself overboard into this flurry of sharks. Despite my affinity for water, being from the landlocked Midwest, I'd had little experience with sharks and the sea. That's probably why I found the whole episode so highly memorable. This was just one of many shenanigans Ray and I enjoyed over the years as we traveled together for many diving events.

In the early days of Duraflex, when there were still other boards in the field, Ray insisted on travelling to major events to personally ensure that his boards were being used and installed correctly. It might sound like micro-management or eccentricity to do that, but it made good business sense that the installation be triple-checked every time. It's critical that the boards don't move side to side or bang against any metal on the fixtures, as that can cause the board to crack. I often helped him check boards and fix ones that weren't up to snuff.

In 1972, Ray and Ina Mae came to the Games in Munich where I would be acting as a judge for some of the proceedings. Ray was concerned about how the boards there had been installed, so the night before the diving events began, after the pool was closed, we went in and reinstalled the boards properly. It took us until well past midnight to get them adjusted just right, but we both wanted to make sure that the boards were up to the Olympic task they had the next day. They were.

After the diving events closed in Munich, Ray held a big party to celebrate the success of the Games. As the owner of Duraflex, he wanted to promote his boards and applaud the divers, so the whole diving community was invited. That became the standard operating procedure from then on, and Duraflex would host a post-Olympic party for all the divers and diving officials and coaches from all over the world. To this day, Duraflex still hosts parties after all the international diving events. I'm often involved in arranging these soirees. We've had many memorable social events after world championships and Olympic Games.

Through all this, Ray and I became very close. As my kids were growing up, I would take them to Reno to visit Ray, and we would borrow his snowmobiles or his all-terrain vehicles and have family vacations in the desert and nearby Sierra Nevada mountains. My kids thought of him as Uncle Ray.

As Ray neared retirement age, it started to become clear that he was considering leaving me the Duraflex company. In fact, he asked me to take over operation of the company, even though his daughter Janice had been doing a fine job running it for many years as his own day-to-day involvement had waned. Ray came from a generation and mindset that didn't countenance the idea of a woman running a company, and while I was flattered that he wanted me to take over, it didn't seem like the right choice for a few reasons. We had worked together so well over the years and had such a close relationship; I could understand why he might want me to take over the company. But I just didn't want to give up flying. I appreciatively declined the offer and supported Janice in assuming the role of CEO of the company.

But I would remain deeply involved with the organization—I still work as a consultant for Duraflex and have served on the board of the Raymond C. Rude Foundation for years, a foundation I helped establish and that has thrived with the seed funding that came from Ray's hard work in building the Duraflex company.

The aim of the foundation, which really got going in about the year 2000 or 2001, has always been to support diving programs, up-and-coming-divers, and other efforts related to the sport around the world. We decided at least 50 percent of all grants would be earmarked to support or promote the sport of diving.

Right from the beginning, the treasurer of the foundation, who was Ray's accountant and financial advisor, invested heavily in real estate. At the turn of the century, the real estate market was hot—especially in Nevada—and it made sound business sense to invest some of Ray's hard-earned resources into this thriving sector.

Over the course of the next several years, the foundation's nest egg grew robustly. Ray sadly wasn't able to see this success. A year or two before he died, he went back to North Dakota to his hometown and deteriorated quickly. He passed on in 2004 at the ripe old age of 88, and sadly never really got to see how the foundation functioned—our first grant was made in 2005 after he'd passed.

Still, Ray lived a long and productive life and was honored in business and in life many times over. I was pleased to be his friend and to have so richly benefited from his mentorship and guidance.

I'm also gratified that Ray was able to see that the Duraflex Company, which was still being run by his daughter, Janice, when he passed, was thriving.

The foundation that Ray had lent his name and funds to was also doing good work and increasing in value. By about 2007, the foundation had more than $9 million invested in local properties. This made me a little nervous. By 2007 I told the accountant we needed to diversify and get out of all this real estate and find some other investments.

Unfortunately, in 2008 and 2009, before we could agree to diversify, the bottom fell out of the market completely. That put the sustainability of the foundation into jeopardy. Nearly all the foundation's investments were tied up in Nevada real estate and spread out among two dozen properties. Quite simply, the Great Recession tanked their value. Ray had always done very well with the accountant and investor we were working with and had expressed his desire to stick with the game plan after he was gone. For a while, we honored that wish. But then the housing crisis hit, and the value of those investments eroded precipitously. It became obvious we had to make some changes, or the foundation might evaporate all together.

To make matters more challenging, it was difficult for our small board to manage the portfolio. I was the president of the foundation at the time, living in Florida, and the vice president was living in Minnesota. Steve McFarland was the secretary, and he was based in St. Louis. Micki King was involved, too, and she was living in Kentucky. There was just no way that we could deal with the multitude of problems we were having with the real estate investments in Nevada, given that none of us were based there.

So, we looked into joining forces with the Community Foundation of Western Nevada in Reno, where most of the investment properties were located. This would transition the private Ray Rude Foundation into a public, community foundation and provide much needed, on-the-ground support in Nevada. There was a lot of paperwork and legal maneuvering involved with that. I began meeting with leadership at the Community Foundation of Western Nevada in 2010 to see whether we could work together. Their expertise in the local market would be key to our future success, and they were amenable to figuring out how to combine the two organizations. It took about two years to fully transition and was not an easy process, but it was well worth the effort.

Today, the Raymond C. Rude Foundation is the supporting organization for the Community Foundation of Western Nevada, which makes grants and scholarships available for a variety of philanthropic programming needs related to western Nevada and diving. It's stipulated in our bylaws that at least 50 percent of our grants must support diving in some capacity, and to me, this is perhaps the most significant and lasting impact I will have on the sport.

To date, the Raymond C. Rude Supporting Foundation has donated several million dollars to the sport of diving. These funds are distributed via the USA Diving Foundation and other international sports federations. Many people don't realize where the money for their programs comes from. For instance, a large percentage of funding provided by the USA Diving Foundation comes from the Rude Foundation. Many programs and equipment grants awarded by international federations also come from the foundation.

This is a means of honoring Ray's significant contributions to the sport. It's only appropriate that everything that came from the Duraflex company goes back into the sport. Over the past 20 years or so, that's added up to millions of dollars in grants and disbursements in support of diving at various levels. From buying equipment to covering travel expenses, the foundation has been a major supporter of diving around the world.

Looking back on my career, I am proud to have improved scoring and judging of diving, standing up in support of athletes wanting to attend the 1980 Olympic Games, and my efforts to add synchronized diving and high diving to the Olympic program. However, I believe that the creation of the Raymond C. Rude Foundation and my work to financially support the Olympic sport of diving has been the most rewarding and personally significant thing I've done. And I hope it may be viewed as my lasting legacy and crowning achievement.

An autobiography is about the individual's life, sure, but it's also about the people who made so many of those things happen. None of us achieves anything worth noting without the assistance of others. And that's true of my work with the Ray Rude Foundation.

I would be terribly remiss if I didn't mention some of the people who've helped make the foundation the success it is, starting with big kudos to Ray's daughter, Janice Rude. Janice's able helming of Duraflex for many years as Ray got older and was less able to run the company was a big factor in our ability to establish the foundation. She's been very supportive of its mission right from the beginning.

It's also worth noting that while she was leading Duraflex, Janice did a magnificent job creating employee health and retirement programs and improvements to equipment and facilities—all those things that Ray had let slide as he got older and was less able to manage. Ray was an old-school businessman. He got his start during World War II with aircraft manufacturing, and Ray kind of ran his plant like we were in the middle of the war. Duraflex needed to be brought up into the 21st century when Jan took it over. And she accomplished that in marvelous fashion.

When Janice decided to retire from Duraflex, Steve McFarland stepped into the role of CEO and has continued the great work ever since. Steve was the first national champion I coached at the University of Miami. He did such a great job helping me run the program there that I turned it over to him in the late 1970s. He coached there for several years, building an extraordinary program that drew divers from around the world. He'd made a name for himself in diving and coaching in the early 1980s and was named the outstanding age group coach at the national age group championships in 1983.

That same year, he was jokingly called the U.N. diving coach because he was coaching divers from Japan, Australia, Great Britain, and Brazil, all at once. Several were Olympic contenders. Being at the University of Miami, so many divers passed through there because of great diving conditions and to be coached by Steve. He coached there until 1984, before heading off to pursue other business opportunities.

Steve has been such a great friend for so many years, and I hope to have been a good mentor to him. He followed right in my footsteps, eventually being named president of USA Diving in the mid-1990s. He held that position for four years, and later as we proceeded with the transition of the foundation after Ray died, we found a position on the Duraflex Board of Directors for Steve. He's been an integral component to the success of the business ever since.

When Duraflex needed some legal advice, they brought Todd Smith aboard. In any business that makes athletic equipment, there's always a need for legal consulting because of the potential for accidents and lawsuits. Todd has since become the president of Duraflex and has been a great help in modernizing its business practices.

Todd was an Ohio State diver and national champion who coached at Mission Viejo in California and the University of Tennessee. Along the way he earned a law degree and became the executive director of USA Diving, a position he held for 26 years. He was the glue that kept everything together there. He had the legal mind, the business mind, and he lived with a deep commitment to the sport of diving. He treated all the clubs and divers fairly and his guidance really put USA Diving as a national governing body on the map.

When I was president of USA Diving from 1986 through 1990, I was on the phone with Todd every day, and we established a really good working relationship. That close collaboration continued in my work as a representative to the board of directors of the U.S. Olympic Committee and during my tenure as chairman of the FINA Technical Diving Committee. It's hard to overstate just how much good Todd Smith has done for USA Diving over the years.

Having him join Duraflex in 2008 was a big get, and we were thrilled to have him join the team and round out our expertise. Steve is currently the CEO, and Todd Smith is the president of Duraflex, a dynamic duo and a fantastic and smart pairing if ever I saw one. To me, it's been a wonderful transition, and Duraflex has just blossomed into a fantastic organization. It's probably doing three times the business it did when Ray was running it, and the future looks bright for the company.

Similarly, the future looks good for the Raymond C. Rude Foundation, too, and I should note that Chris Askin, the executive director of the Community Foundation of Western Nevada, has had a lot to do with that. He's been an important figure in my life over the past decade or so. Without his help and guidance through the many legal and investment problems, and without the support to the CFWN, I don't know where we'd be as a foundation. Chris is now the treasurer of the Rude Foundation, and he works so hard to keep everything going. He's also become the biggest fan of diving and loves to go to the many diving events that we support. I love traveling with him.

Gail Humphreys, a banker who lives in Reno, is also a member of the board of the Community Foundation of Western Nevada. Chris recommended she join, and she's been a great addition. She only has another year or so on the committee before she moves on, and she'll be leaving big shoes to be filled by the next board member.

Bill Walker is another person who's been crucial to our ongoing success with the Foundation. He was a diver at the University of Miami before I got there and became a lawyer and a volunteer coach of several high school teams in the Tampa–St. Petersburg area. He doesn't take a dime for that coaching, but he's built dryland facilities and has gotten the schools where he coaches to buy the best equipment for his divers. Many of the kids he's coached have gone on to college on diving scholarships, and he has made substantial efforts to bring minorities and kids from underserved areas into the sport of diving.

In 1998, Bill became president of USA Diving where he made a big impact in helping transition the small, volunteer-driven organization into a much stronger professional business with a CEO and board of directors backing his work as president. His legal background has been enormously helpful to the foundation, and his love of diving is true. His heart has belonged to diving since day one, just like mine.

My gratitude to the many people who've supported me along the way extends well beyond the work I've done with the Rude Foundation. Indeed, as I think back along the arc of my life, I realize I had so much help and support at every turn.

In the beginning, my life was shaped by coaches and teachers who mentored me into the direction that I would take. I lived in an amateur world—the Olympics and all the sports that I was involved with were amateur sports. Our word for a nonprofessional athlete, *amateur* comes from the Latin *amātor*, which means love. This fits with my experience of the sports I pursued. We were all in these events for the sheer love, not the money.

That's been a through-line of my life—doing so much for diving because of my love for the sport and the people in it. (I love being aloft, so maybe I was an amateur pilot, too.) But in most of my diving and administration career, money just wasn't a factor. I never paid a penny to anyone for coaching. It was all done by volunteers. And if I did get coaching from a professional coach, you can bet he wasn't paid very much money and was providing his services for the love of the sport.

Even college coaches in my era were paid more like teachers than the multi-million-dollar contracts some of the top college coaches of today make. When I was in college, Woody Hayes, then the football coach, refused to be paid more than the university president. His salary topped out at $43,000 in 1978, even though he was one of the most famous coaches in the world. That, of course, meant that all the coaches below him in all the other sports had to stay under him on the pay scale, far below what we usually see today.

But that was the world I lived in, and no one really went into sports thinking they were going to have a big payday. If you go back over the history of Olympic gold medalists, you'll find that only one or two were really ever able to capitalize financially on their Olympic fame through much of the 20th century. But again, that's definitely not how the world works today.

We did it for love, pride, and the friends we made along the way.

I do look back on my life and career as a wonderful life. And I've had a very lucky life. Maybe it's because I was born on St. Patrick's Day and some of that luck of the Irish rubbed off on me. But the real reason that I feel so lucky every day to have lived this life circles back to the friends I've made throughout that lifetime.

Lou Vitucci is one such person whose friendship has meant so much to me over many years. We had the pleasure of traveling together quite a bit when we were younger. We were competitors, yes, and there were several events where Lou and I were first and second. But we always left the best of friends, no matter how the competition turned out. We weren't competing against each other. We were competing to perform for the judges.

Ron O'Brien is another person I've built a special and lasting friendship with that I treasure. He was at Ohio State for a year or two while I was competing. As with Lou, Ron and I were good friends but also competitors. In the 1961 National Championships, Ron was first, and I was second. We were on the phone just yesterday setting a time to get together and play golf again now that he's living in Fort Lauderdale.

Of course, the conversation drifted to talking about the old days and good times—we've enjoyed so many—and our shared Olympic experiences have spanned decades. Ron is probably the only living coach in the Olympic movement who's coached eight Olympic teams. He was recognized for that extraordinary record with an induction into the Olympic Hall of Fame in 2020, another honor to add to the long list of his other hall of fame inductions.

Bob Webster is another great diver I've been lucky to have in my life. He won the gold medal in 1964 in Tokyo when I took bronze, and we've remained very good friends over the years. He and Lou and I try to get together every year to play golf and catch up. There's hardly a day that goes by we don't email or call each other and check in. It's wonderful to have such good friends, and they're a big part of my life.

Dick Smith and Sammy Lee were also important forces in my life, and they were best friends to each other and so many other people in the diving community. I was lucky to be able to spend time with them throughout my career and to develop great, lasting relationships with these men whom I looked up to and who helped light the path I would follow in their wake.

Micki King has long been another special person in my life, ever since we took that trip to Europe in the late 1960s. Her influence has been significant in the sport of diving for decades, not just as a sensational athlete, but as a savvy advocate and member of the board of the Raymond C. Rude Foundation in recent years.

Micki's dry-side contributions began when she was elected to be the first chairperson of the Athletes' Advisory Council of the USOC in the 1970s, which contributed to the development of the Amateur Sports Act. That was an important piece of legislation that still governs all Olympic sports.

Throughout that process and in other capacities, we've always supported each other—I advised her to go into the Air Force after she graduated from the University of Michigan because I knew it would be a good place for her to continue her diving career. In turn, she supported me in representing athletes' wishes to attend the 1980 Olympic Games in Moscow. She's always been a big influence and presence in my life, and there's hardly a week that goes by, even today as I'm approaching 82 years old, that I don't call Micki and make sure she's doing well.

The list of exceptionally talented people I've worked with at various levels within the sport over the years is lengthy, and with each new step along my journey, I have been lucky to encounter many new and fantastic individuals who love the sport at least as much as I do, and quite possibly more.

Diving might be an individual sport, but you don't do everything on your own, and there have always been people within the sport who could lend a hand. One person who's often not given enough credit by the sport is Don Leas. He was the coach at Clarion University of Pennsylvania and had a real knack for finding young talent and developing those divers into Olympic potential. The divers usually then moved on to another coach and found that Olympic success under them, so Don doesn't always get the kudos he should. But he was an excellent coach with a sharp scouting eye.

Where he really shined was with his ability to draft rules and articulate nuances to build a comprehensive, logical, and eminently useable rule book. For years he wrote the USA Diving Rule Book, or edited it, and was chairman of the rules committee. Sometimes he was involved in laws and legislation, too. In all this work, Don made an enormous contribution, but so much of it took place behind the scenes. A lot of people don't know just how much he did for the sport from behind a desk.

I leaned on him quite often, particularly in drafting facility requirements, as he represented the Association of Pool & Spa Professionals. He was the go-to guy for how to put it all down in writing. He sadly passed away in 2019, and he'll be sorely missed.

In the 1980s, when I was chairman of the Olympic Diving Committee of USA Diving, I made sure that Don would attend the World University Games. At the very first one of these meets he attended, he was appointed to become the chairman of the World University Diving Committee. That's how impressive Don was.

During his time as chairman, he added new events, improved rules, and added team events and scoring. There's no way I could have functioned in my administrative roles without his support. He held that position from the early 1980s until he passed, and that's just an enormous credit to his talent and dedication.

In my international work with FINA as chairman of the TDC and THDC, I have worked closely with Cornel Marculescu for many years. Cornel got his start in international aquatics sport as a member of the Romanian water polo team that competed at the 1964 Olympics in Tokyo. He went on to serve as technical director of the Spanish Swimming Federation for about 10 years in the 1970s and '80s. He joined FINA as its executive director in 1986.

Cornel wasn't always the easiest guy to work with, and he has often courted controversy. But he was always a big supporter of my efforts to guide and improve competitive diving for the better part of 30 years. I am grateful for that support and his belief in helping diving evolve with the times.

After serving as executive director of FINA for 35 years, Cornel has only just recently announced his retirement in early 2021. He'd been with FINA since the beginning when it was a two-person operation. Now it's a much larger organization with specialists and departments for all the events. Cornel should certainly be congratulated and credited for all that growth and development.

In 2021, I'll also complete my service to FINA as chairman of the Technical High Diving Committee. I have thoroughly enjoyed my time in that role, but I look forward to passing the torch on to the next generation. I'm also looking forward to the Tokyo Olympics, which were postponed because of the coronavirus pandemic in 2020. I had hoped to be able to watch those Games in Japan, in my own sort of homecoming to the place where I found Olympic glory nearly 60 years ago.

Nevertheless, I'm optimistic that my recent efforts will lead to the addition of the exciting sport of high diving soon, as I think this represents an area of tremendous growth for the sport and the addition of an enthusiastic audience. It's that audience engagement that will drive so much of the future of Olympic sports across the board, as we travel through the second millennium of this ancient sporting tradition.

✶ ✶ ✶

Nearly every day, I wear a gold ring on my right hand. Though it's small, that golden ring has a big history.

At the 1968 Olympics, there was a Mexican official who was a timekeeper at the pool. He was also a jeweler and had cast a small, simple ring featuring the five interlocking circles of the Olympic emblem in silver. He was selling those rings for about $20 a pop. It was unique and different, and after seeing the ring, I thought, *Wow. I really like this.*

Many years later when I was the team manager for the 1984 Games, the idea of that ring reemerged, and I looked into getting similar rings made for the divers who qualified for LA. I footed the bill for making a set of silver rings for the American divers who'd made the Olympic team. You'd think I'd gifted them diamonds, given how coveted these rings became. They were the envy of every other U.S. Olympic squad.

In 1988, we made a big deal out of buying them for all the Olympic divers. I was able to work with a jeweler in Coconut Grove in the Miami area, and he gave me a great deal on the price. He made those rings for us for just the price of the gold, about $60 each. At the time, gold prices were fairly low, and USA Diving decided it was a good investment of some fairly petty cash to honor the Olympic team.

In 1992, we continued this tradition, and it has become the biggest thing to the divers. To some of these athletes, earning that ring was the real goal—they wanted that ring more than anything. It's awarded at the completion of the Olympic trials event, and for some, it's the one award across a whole career in diving they treasure the most.

Particularly for divers who don't stand much of a chance of earning an Olympic medal, the ring has become a mini-Olympic medal of sorts, and a very tangible, coveted signifier of their skill that they can show off forever.

Who knew that a simple ring could have such significance to so many people? But the Olympic rings, the instantly recognizable, multi-colored, interlocking emblem of sporting greatness the world over, carries so much significance for me as well as others.

I often absentmindedly twirl that ring around my finger when wearing it in day-to-day life. It's a touchstone and a wearable object that links me to the Olympics, its history and mine interlocked in the shining metal. Where some athletes carry the meaning of the rings with a tattoo on the body, others, like me, wear a golden version of them on our hands. It's another small reminder of what I've done, where I've been, and what I've accomplished, both as an athlete and an administrator.

Recently, I received several requests for autographs from people living far away. In some countries, like Germany, the practice of collecting autographs from Olympic medal winners from long ago is popular.

I gladly sign the photos or postcards they send and mail them back. I've learned there's a market for such items on eBay, but I'm just flattered that anyone still thinks of me and wants to have my autograph. I guess they, too, want to be able to display mementos in their office, just like I do.

To be able to glance around my office and see all these reminders of a rich life, and one I felt so lucky to lead, has been a blessing that's difficult to describe in words, but feels nearer when I reminisce over a photo or touch that ring.

The lessons of my Olympic journey, and indeed a life spent in service and flying, still carry so much weight, that they want to be shared.

First, it pays to be good to people. Folks don't always remember when they've been treated shabbily—indeed most of us are sadly well accustomed to the casual dismissal and disengagement that's part of modern life. We usually just ignore the slights and unhelpfulness of strangers day-to-day. But we all remember and treasure the person who did right by us and gave us a fair shot. I know I sure have, as I think back to some of the opportunities I've had over the years and how, without a helpful acquaintance or friend involved, I might have missed that chance all together.

I've tried to be good to others throughout my life in all things as a means of paying back all the wonderful people over the years who've helped me in so many ways. From the coaches who gave me nightly rides home from the Y in high school, to the various administrators who've put their trust in me to help advance the sport of diving more recently, I've had a lot of superlative help along the way.

Secondly, you have to hold true to your morals and uphold a level of ethics. "Cheat not lest ye be cheated" has been a guiding motto for me down the years. My efforts to push diving's evolution to become a fairer sport that celebrates sheer athleticism as much as clean, beautiful lines, is a legacy I'm proud to call mine.

I've also learned well just how much Luck favors the bold. It's a cliché, sure, but there's good reason for that—it's because it's also true. Lady Luck has been a strong character and presence throughout my life, and I think she's always rewarded me best when I've taken a risk. Setting up a dive that's right at the edge of your abilities and nailing it when the stakes are high is so much more exciting and rewarding than staying safe with the simple, rote routine that you know can't fail. *Where's the joy in that?*

I don't know what all I did right to wind up in some of the situations and relationships I have over my eight decades on Earth. But I do feel blessed, I've spent my time as a favored son of fortune.

But most importantly, I've learned that family doesn't have to mean a blood bond. The kinship I've shared with so many divers, tumblers, coaches, soldiers, pilots, volunteers, and friends over the years means that I've never felt like I've lacked in having the supportive family that helps anyone enjoy life and get the most out of it. We really do get by with a little help from our friends, and through diving, my friends list is long and full of wonderful people I count as family. They've been there with me during the many highs and lows of a life lived aloft.

But that said, I don't know where I'd be without my wonderful family. My son, Tim, has always been such an incredible source of pride for me. Growing up, he was a good kid who worked hard, and with our encouragement, he got through university and medical school and became a successful pediatrician. He leads a partnership in Lakeland, Florida, and I've heard often from the parents of kids he's treated what a wonderful physician he is.

Tim found his lovely wife Sandra at medical school. I'm so proud of her, too. She's in charge of the infectious diseases department of the VA Hospital in Tampa, one of the biggest hospitals in the area. I occasionally go to the VA for a checkup, and Sandy has an incredible reputation throughout that hospital community. Tim and Sandy and their children are just really wonderful sources of pride and support for me, and I feel truly blessed that they are my family.

I can happily say much the same for my daughter, Tracey. Tracey has been the joy of my life, and Joyce's life, since before she even arrived. Tracey did everything almost in the footsteps of Joyce, and she went on to become a high school cheerleader and homecoming queen. She's just beautiful and did all those things that make a father proud.

She's also proven herself to be an incredible mother and family maker, and now that she's got a little more free time with only one child still at home, she's taken on some writing and church work. She's been publishing her writing nationally and has established a guidance program for women on how to tell their stories. She recently wrote about my niece Marianne and sent me the essay. I couldn't keep from crying while reading it, it was so beautifully written. I'm so proud of her and love the wonderful husband, Mark, who she chose for herself and the beautiful children they have together. They all enrich my life so profoundly.

And I'm grateful to my kids for being who they are. I couldn't have traveled so much and worked with others if my own children hadn't been in support of me. When you're gone a lot, working with other people's children and athletes, it's quite often at the expense of what you can give your own children. Tim and Tracey both handled it all beautifully and never seemed to mind all the time I spent helping others and traveling in support of so many divers.

But naturally, my amazing kids didn't raise themselves, especially when I was on the road so much for work and my diving endeavors. Joyce was incredibly supportive of all my efforts, and as we went along the way, all my friends within diving became friends to Joyce, too. The same has happened with Fran since she's been on the scene in the past 10 years. I am grateful to both of these dynamic, intelligent, beautiful, and strong women who have chosen to spend their lives with me.

And through it all, I'm lucky to be able to say I have few regrets. I've worked hard, loved fiercely, and did my best. I'm glad to be able to leave a mark in this world, however small. For this world is one of stunning, beautiful, breathtaking joy, and sheer delight. If only we have the gumption to try launching ourselves into flight.

About the Author

Thomas E. Gompf

Born in Dayton, Ohio, on March 17, 1939, Tom Gompf became a champion trampolinist, gymnast, and diver who earned the bronze medal at the 1964 Summer Olympic Games in Tokyo in the 10-meter platform event. His passion for diving propelled him to win numerous AAU and NCAA championships and the World Professional High Diving Championship in 1970 and 1971. From 1972 through 1981, he served as diving coach at the University of Miami where he coached more than two dozen All-American, national champion, and Olympic divers, including Melissa Briley and Greg Louganis.

In addition to coaching, Gompf is an ardent volunteer supporter of the Olympic movement and diving. In 1976 and 1984, Gompf served as the team manager for the U.S. Olympic Diving Team and from 1977 through 2000, he was a member of the U.S. Olympic Committee's Executive Board of Directors. From 1984 through 2004, he was a member of the FINA Technical Diving Committee, serving as chairman from 1988 through 2000. He also served as president of USA Diving from 1985 through 1990, and president of U.S. Aquatic Sports from 1999 through 2002.

For his lengthy service, Gompf has earned numerous awards. Most notably, in 2002, he was inducted into the International

Swimming Hall of Fame as an honor contributor. In 2010, he was awarded the USOC Foundation's George Steinbrenner Sports Leadership Award.

Considered the father of synchronized diving, Gompf led the charge to have the tandem discipline admitted as an Olympic event and championed adding the 1-meter springboard event to international competitions. He's currently leading a campaign to add high diving to the Olympic program.

An Air Force pilot who served in the Vietnam War from 1965 to 1967, Gompf flew commercial airliners for more than 30 years, and he is the father of two children and grandfather of seven. He currently serves as a consultant to Duraflex, as president of the Raymond C. Rude Foundation, and lives in Lakeland, Florida, with his wife, Fran.

A recent photo of the Gompf and Russell families. Top row (left to right): Chase, Trey, Holt, Mark, Tim, Sandy, Juliana, and Tom. Bottom row: Tracey, Fran, Faith, and Wil.

Elaine K. Howley

Elaine K. Howley is an award-winning freelance journalist and editor based in Boston, Massachusetts. A southern New Jersey native, Howley holds a bachelor's degree from Georgetown University and a master's degree in publishing and writing from Emerson College in Boston.

Specializing in sports, health, and history topics, Howley previously served as publications manager for U.S. Masters Swimming and managing editor of *SWIMMER* magazine. Her freelance work has appeared in *U.S. News & World Report,* AARP.org, *Atlas Obscura*, *espnW*, and *Outdoor Swimmer* magazine, based in the United Kingdom. She is a member in good standing of the American Society of Journalists and Authors and the Association of Health Care Journalists.

A lifelong swimmer, Howley is an avid marathon and ice swimmer who has completed the Triple Crown of Open Water Swimming (solo swims across the English Channel and Catalina Channel and a solo circumnavigation of Manhattan Island) and was inducted into the Vermont Open Water Swimming Hall of Fame in 2018. She was the first person to swim the 32.3-mile length of Lake Pend Oreille in Northern Idaho.